THE LAND CA. 1850

NOAH'S
GARDEN

BOOKS BY SARA STEIN

My Weeds: A Gardener's Botany

The Body Book

The Evolution Book

The Science Book

NOAH'S GARDEN

Restoring
the Ecology
of Our Own
Back Yards

S A R A   S T E I N

With illustrations by the author

Houghton Mifflin Company   *Boston   New York*   1993

For information about permission to reproduce selections from this
book, write to Permissions, Houghton Mifflin Company,
215 Park Avenue South, New York, New York 10003.

Library of Congress Cataloging-in-Publication Data

Stein, Sara Bonnett.
  Noah's garden : restoring the ecology of our own back yards.
    p.   cm.
  Includes index.
ISBN 0-395-65373-8
  1. Garden ecology.   2. Garden ecology — United States.   3. Backyard
gardens — United States.   4. Natural gardens, American.   5. Gardening to
attract wildlife — United States.   I. Title.
QH541.5.G37S74   1993
574.5'264 — dc20   92-45916
                                        CIP

Printed in the United States of America

BP   10   9   8   7   6   5   4   3   2   1

Unidentified drawings:
p.ii: Eastern chipmunk; p.vii: True katydid; p.276: White-tailed deer fawn;
p.261: Pair of small copper butterflies.

Book design by Anne Chalmers.

 Printed on recycled paper.

To Gerry Bleyer

Contents

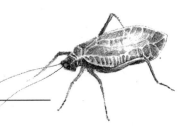

NOAH'S
GARDEN

I

Unbecoming a Gardener

I CAME INTO GARDENING backward, from the wild verges instead of through the garden gate. I knew *Aster novae-angliae*, plain New England aster, as a stout native that stood up for itself from New Mexico to Vermont. The phlox I was familiar with was a feral descendant of garden escapees that pushed up through heavy competition and never suffered mildew. Strawberries grew in meadows, blueberries in thickets, and to get the fruit one had only to be quicker than the birds. Outside florist shops, the roses I knew were those sweet single ones that spilled over roadbanks when country roads were dirt. During my childhood, a birch grove grew up all by itself from sprouted seed to full-grown tree in a burnt-over, onetime horse pasture beyond the summer privy.

This was apparently a wrong beginning. It led me to believe that plants take care of themselves, that gardening is merely putting them in place and leaving them alone. When my husband, Marty, and I began to tame our tangled piece of land some dozen years ago, our gardening library consisted of an inherited *House & Garden* book on landscape design published in 1945. Capability Brown sounded like a woman toting pistols; the Jekyll

I knew was the doctor side of Hyde. About the works of Russell Page, Fred McGourty, John Brookes, Rosemary Verey, Beth Chatto, Penelope Hobhouse — the modern library of gardening taste and horticultural savvy — I knew nothing.

I became an illiterate gardener.

Or did I become a gardener at all? And do I wish to address those ladies and gentlemen of the club who, by addressing one another with shared assumptions of taste and knowledge, assure themselves of membership? I write for gardeners, of course, but I want to suspend judgment on what qualifies a person to join that group and open the door to whoever stewards the land, whoever digs, whoever plants, whoever by even raking leaves tinkers with a system of which, sad to say, horticulture is shockingly ignorant. My purpose in letting in the hoi polloi is eventually to similarly fling wide the garden gate, to loosen the land's esthetic corset, let it grow more blowsy and fecund, allow it to bed promiscuously with beasts and creatures of all sorts. There is a moral imperative here and practical significance as well, but I'll get to that.

Let me tell you how I went from illiterate gardener to possibly not a gardener at all.

Of all the plants I planted in my unlettered days, few survive. Junipers succeeded, daylilies, some ferns. Asters fell from lack of staking and, undivided, soon dwindled away. Lilies rotted; phlox blackened; myrtle died of drought. Voles chewed the tulips while aphids sucked the lupines, and whatever lime or acid was needed by clematis and heather was not what they got, so they died too. The pretty alyssum called 'Basket of Gold' expired from sheer old age, a disease that to me did not seem to be implied by the term "perennial" on its label. And everywhere everything was overcome by weeds.

It was the mocking health of what I didn't wish to grow in the graveyard of our garden that finally sent me to the books. If buttercups shone among withering irises and daisies bloomed among dusty miller corpses, then there must be some fundamental difference between wild plants and garden flowers.

I attacked the question in two ways, botanically and horticulturally. Botanically, I wanted to know how plants grow; horticulturally, I wanted to know how gardeners grow them. One would think that the science of botany and the art of horticulture would necessarily merge, for surely what a gardener does is to give plants what they need to grow. What I discovered, however, were baffling divergences among the ways of plants and the ways of gardeners.

A fundamental disparity is that plants grow where they can, whereas gardeners grow plants where they will. The plants' "choice" implies no intent, merely the happenstance that their seeds fall or their rhizomes wander into circumstances in which they can survive. Gardening strives to defeat chance, or at least to rig the odds, and to do so is necessarily hard work. Thus I learned from gardening books to create good garden loam at the same time that I learned from botany texts that there is virtually no ground of any sort in which some plants can't grow well.

Horticulture told me to cultivate the soil to control the weeds; botany told me that the more the soil is disturbed, the more weeds grow. Gardening books said that grass needs fertilizing; botany books said that grasses produce the soil fertility that other plants depend on. I was advised to stake and tie stems that had evolved the strength to defy gravity 400 million years ago, to spray pesticides on species that over eons had formulated an infernal chemical arsenal of their own, to deadhead flowers that were doing their darnedest to go to seed, an activity that is at once their biological purpose and their natural wont.

By creating "good" soil, the gardener reduces the bed to a common denominator within the range of tolerance of plants that might behave quite differently in better or worse dirt. A wild New England aster growing on worn-out pasture is less lush than the cultivated *Aster novae-angliae* 'Harrington's Pink' growing in a garden bed, but poverty stiffens it against wind and rain without support by stakes. A mountain laurel becomes a fine specimen in a foundation planting, but it doesn't spread by layering into a thicket as it does in shallow, gritty, leaf-rotted woodland humus. Few garden varieties are as well adapted to the cruel exposure of an open bed as the weeds that outcompete them. Only a handful of perennials bred for the gardening trade have retained the chemical weaponry that kept their forebears healthy. Many are hybrids that reveal their mongrel pedigree when allowed to go to seed, as I found out through generations of drab lavender columbine whose parents had seemed to be true blue.

Botany offers no explicit cultural advice for garden plants; in fact, of cultivated species, textbooks dwell mostly on those rapid reproducers like beans and mustards that have become lab pets, the vegetable equivalent of white mice. Nevertheless, one's heightened awareness that plants have biological expectations quells one's response to glossy magazine come-ons. What might the featured gardener have gone through to raise on stoneless red clay lowlands Alpines that began in mountain scree? How can a nursery in sour New England tout delphiniums that prefer a sweet lime soil? What will this woodland garden, blooming with species that botany and horticulture alike call spring ephemerals, look like in July? Not worth a snapshot, let me tell you.

Between skepticism and experiment, the twin lodestones of the scientific mind, I learned at least to avoid anything that comes with a full paragraph of instructions for its care.

Nevertheless, there is no comparison between the photographs in textbooks and those in garden books. Biology deals in biomes: broad suites of vegetation constrained by climate and soil. All the dry grasslands of the world constitute a single biome. While photographs of biomes — desert, tundra, broadleaf forest — are beautiful, they are not homey. Even among the smaller habitats of a biome — a glade in a forest, the rotting tree that fell to form the glade — intimate scale is belied by the dark press of wild woods reaching to obliterate the clearing. There are no people in these photographs; not a footprint scuffs the soil at any scale. One feels left out.

Gardens invite one through the gate, down the path, beneath the arbor to the bench. Where grassland or forest dwarfs the human figure, a garden gives it comforting importance, enclosure without impingement, freedom within boundaries, small charms and charming vistas, shifts of shade and sun, flickering changes of hue and texture within a permanent structure. A garden is a safe place, made all the safer by the gardener's ability to keep wilderness at bay.

So I suffered from warring images: on the one hand the woodlands and meadows of my childhood, now brought into focus by my accumulating knowledge of the broadleaf forest biome of which they were a part, and on the other hand the reassuring transformation of these wild exemplars into grassy paths, glades, and garden rooms in which one knows that the way inevitably leads home again. The discomfort was still mild, like a tickle in the throat that may presage something worse to come. I persevered.

I redug and replanted flower beds. I purchased stakes. I hired a lawn care company. I subscribed to *Horticulture*. This last, seemingly sensible decision exposed the very roots of my duality, for just as I was becoming able to call myself a gardener, just when my peonies were finally flourishing and the iris garden looked quite like a picture in a book, Elsie Cox revealed me as a fraud.

When I receive my copy of the magazine, I turn immediately to Elsie Cox's Q & A column — not for the excellent information she imparts, though she is nothing if not encyclopedic — but as one might turn to Ann Landers or Miss Manners for voyeuristic and vicarious involvement in the complexities and misfortunes of other people's lives. To a woman whose pair of apricots failed to fertilize each other, Cox advised either to cut a branch from the earlier-blooming apricot while still in bud and retard its blooming in the refrigerator until the other tree was blossoming or, alternatively, to force a branch of the later-blooming one in a sunny window and, in either case, to place the now synchronized flowering branch in a vase beneath its mate and hope the bees would notice. To a gardener whose daffodils failed to bloom at all, the advice was to mark the clumps every four years, wait for dormancy, and dig, separate, and respace the bulbs. To the owner of a fig tree whose fruits were not maturing, Cox advised a twice-daily twitching of the fruiting twigs to aid in pollination. I believe that she is never wrong, but how do gardeners find the time to solve their plants' sexual predicaments in such artful and arduous detail?

Elsie Cox was not the only one to suggest that, compared with the truly devoted gardener, I was a plant abuser. Almost every issue of *Horticulture* brought a step-by-step article that seemed to chastise my insouciance. Do people really blanch endive in their basements? Is it possible that some gardeners divide forsythia? Books also gave earnest instructions that made me ache to read them. I began to see in the gardens so lavishly pictured a gang of hired laborers lurking behind the hedge.

Indeed, had I not been a gardening illiterate before becoming a gardener, I might have quit before I started. Arithmetic would have been against it. A hundred daffodils produce at least four hundred bulbs in four years, and they, respaced, four times four hundred four years later. At that rate, one would be respacing 6,400 bulbs by the twelfth year, the length of time our daffodils have been blooming undivided.

One gardening book described the installation of a 15-foot maple tree. What with digging the hole, amending the soil, soaking it in, applying a plank and plumb bob to match the rootball's depth exactly, ramping the tree down into the excavation, backfilling, stamping, diking, soaking, mulching, wrapping, staking, screening, and pruning, the job took one whole day. By that account, a grove of trees we planted should have taken two weeks of work. We'd have been crazy to attempt it.

It's all so effortful. The trick with strawberries, I read, is to prevent young plants from producing until their roots are strong. To do that, one pinches off their buds — for a month on June-bearing varieties, for three months on everbearing sorts — every day, on hands and knees. One would feel relieved, at least, to rise up occasionally to twitch the figs.

If one were not too busy with the primroses. Dear Elsie's faith in the vigor of her readers continues to amaze me. Regarding primroses eaten up by slugs, she advises: first, remove all slug hiding places — weeds, leaves, rocks, wood, even mulch. Then, apply around each primrose a circlet of sand, ashes, or limestone, whose grittiness slugs abhor. After each rainfall or watering, lay fresh circlets. Test the soil. Ashes and limestone may make it too alkaline for primroses. Instead, around each plant erect a sheet-copper cuff to "shock" the slimy slugs. Or sink beer-filled saucers throughout the garden, emptying and refilling these slug traps every morning. For night people, an alternative is slug hunts by flashlight with salt, kerosene, bleach, scissors, or a rock as possible weapons. Finally, one might use pellets of commercial slug bait, which, because they are "poisonous to small children, birds, and some animals," must be hidden beneath shingles, melon skins, or grapefruit halves.

Are primroses worth it? Isn't it easier to buy a fig than fertilize it? And what is more likely to entice a toddler than half a grapefruit secreting forbidden pellets in the garden?

My growing suspicion that I could never come up to gardening standards, my uneasiness about being caught with my slug holes showing, and my annoyance that primroses and their problems should cause such anxiety were soothed by the far end of my growing library, which ran from *Gardens of a Golden Afternoon* to *Plant-Animal Interactions*.

Ecology is a far cry from horticulture. Gardeners see aphids as enemies, moles as nuisances, and snakes as something the world would be well off without. Ecology sees all species connected in such a mesh of interdependence that one hardly dares step on an ant. The very habit of thinking of plants and animals as independent entities begins to seem wrongheaded. There's no such creature as a fig without its fig wasp, as I realize when, chewing more thoughtfully now, I eat the tiny pollinator the fruit has buried in

its flesh. Here was the real problem of that fig twitcher: she had lost her wasps.

Appropriately, it was the ecological concept called "edge effect" that finally pierced the boil of my uneasiness. Edge effect refers to the particular abundance of life and diversity of species that occur along the boundary of contrasting habitats. Rushy pond shores. Thicketed roadsides. Or — here was the knife — fields grown over but not yet grown up to merge with the woods around them.

When Marty and I bought our land, it was in just that stage of regrowth from pasture to forest that is among the most productive ecosystems on earth. It was covered with brambles, bushes, vines, and grasses that supported a large and varied animal population. Our footsteps stirred up flights of grouse, grasshoppers that rose on rattling wings, and panicky rabbits. Frogs of assorted size and voice croaked loudly by the pond. A woodchuck family lived below a large boulder; a fox had its den nearby.

This was the sort of land that real estate agents, embarrassed by its unkempt appearance, describe as "having potential." Here, where the goldenrod smelled rank in late summer, could be lawn; there, beneath tangled vines, a rockery; the young and gawky woodland verge would be much improved by removing the undergrowth.

We did all this and more. We cleared brush and pulled vines and hauled rocks and broke ground and dug beds until, after years of high hopes and hard work, we had an expanse of landscaped grounds and gardens that seemed to us like Eden.

Then it hit. I realized in an instant the full extent of what we had done: we had banished the animals from this paradise of ours.

America's clean, spare landscaping and gardening tradition has devastated rural ecology. The relentless spread of suburbia's neat

Opposite: The land, ca. 1950: abandoned field and pasture growing back to woodland

yards and gardens has caused local extinctions of such important predators as foxes, has dangerously reduced the habitat of many kinds of birds, and has threatened the total extinction of fragile species such as orchids that rely on a single pollinator, butterflies that require a specific host plant, songbirds that inhabit deep woods, and turtles whose routes to breeding sites are interrupted by roads or obliterated by drainage projects. Entire communities of plants and insects — the well-stocked pantry of our native countryside — have been wiped bare.

Looking back, I should have been alerted sooner. Grouse had been absent since we mowed their cover, and I had noted also the leavetaking of fox and woodchuck as their lairs were preempted for rock garden and daylily border. But the connection between such seemingly innocent acts and the faunal desertions they cause is not so obvious. We replaced loose stone with cemented brick — and lost the toad that had lived beneath the doorstep. We cut down dead tree snags, thus evicting the woodpeckers who had made homes and marketplaces there. We cleared wild roses, whose hips had fed the mockingbirds in winter. Had the pond belonged to us in those days, we would certainly have disposed of the tree trunks lying against the shore without realizing their implications for turtles, which need such ramps for basking

Bufo bufo,
the American toad

in the sun to maintain their bodies' store of vitamin D. As it was, it took us only a few summers of straightening up the place to degrade or destroy the habitat of most of the animals that had previously lived here.

More insidious and alarming was the absence of many creatures I could recall from childhood that at some unnoticed time during the intervening years had dwindled to rarity or disappeared, not only from this site, but from the very countryside. I recalled species I had once known that now were missing: orioles, purple martins, meadowlarks, bluebirds, box turtles, walking sticks, praying mantises, monarch butterflies, luna moths, red spotted salamanders, green grass snakes, little brown bats, weasels, and many more. That I could compile so long a list from memories going back no more than forty years was startling. What if I hadn't known the rural countryside before development transformed it? How does one miss what one has never known? What longing, then, would drive one to repair the damage?

These thoughts bothered me considerably. The move to the suburbs was not from rural to more residential areas but in the other direction, from the city to the country. I'm lucky to have spent my childhood summers among woods, streams, meadows, and marshes, but most suburbanites have never searched for frogs' eggs, caught fireflies in a jar, or peeked into a grassy nest of adorable baby mice. As the years pass, fewer and fewer people will long for the call of bullfrogs. Today's children, growing up on lawns and pavements, will not even have nostalgia to guide them, and soon the animals will be not only missing but forgotten.

Already our understanding of wildlife is based mostly on such presentations as National Geographic Specials; as a result, we are likely to have more sympathy for rhinoceroses in Africa than for toads on our own doorstep. One would almost think from watching television that Nature resides only in the wilderness, that to see it we must turn to that station, subscribe to *Natural History*, or take an ecotour. One also would think that to fulfill our moral obligation to this remote natural world we can act only at a distance — write to a congressman, join conservation groups, petition to preserve a threatened ecosystem. But all of us live within an ecosystem; like the Bluebird of Happiness, Nature is in our own back yard.

People don't think of the little land they tend as an ecosystem, but yards and gardens are a very particular and notably impoverished ecosystem that favors weediness in both plants and animals. In this respect, cultivated land resembles what ecologists call a seral community: it results from a local wound and acts as a bandage to cover the soil until the forest or prairie grows back. Yards are in an early stage of bandaging, a stage in which life is low in number of species, high in number of individuals, and typified by rampant reproduction. In the natural course of things, rapid reproductive rates are offset by the equally rapid disappearance of habitat, as when, for example, the rapid spread of weedy mugwort is checked by shade as trees move in around it. Yards, however, don't disappear, so they support an unnaturally persistent growth of dandelions and starlings.

This is an overstatement, of course. But look down the block, peer along the rows of yards, drive around the neighborhood. There are lawns (few species, many individuals), foundation plantings (count the kinds — yew, yew again, more yew, and a rhododendron), ground covers (pachysandra, maybe juniper). Everywhere is impatiens, named for its impatience to throw its numerous seeds, although where the climate is not tropical, aggressive fecundity doesn't work for it as it does for hardy annuals like crabgrass, carpetweed, and chickweed in troops uncountable among the grasses in the lawns. Count the kinds of street trees; ten fingers will do. Count the aphids on the roses; the digits of all the neighborhood's inhabitants are not enough. Look in vain for the ladybugs to eat them.

Still I am oversimplifying, but to make the point that simplicity is the problem. The impoverished nature of suburbia is not inherent in the land. The gardener (the homeowner, the steward of the lot) can hurry a piece along to a somewhat later seral stage typified by a greater variety of species within a more sophisticated, complicated web of relationships. Diversity of species is a form of safety in numbers — not numbers of individuals, but numbers of ways in which each individual's prodigious reproductive power is modulated by conflicts of interest among all the individuals with which it shares the land. The more species there are, the less likely it is that any one of them will get out of hand and — just as true — the less likely that any one of them will suffer unduly.

Total numbers are part of the picture too. Ecologists rate land by its carrying capacity — the number of individuals that a given habitat can support. By that measure, the interior of a forest is less productive than its edges because a greater number of herbivorous insects, browsing mammals, seed- and berry-eating birds — and predators of all of these — are supported by brushy growth along the sunny forest fringe than in the dark interior. Soil fertility and water supply are naturally part of the productivity equation, but the shockingly low carrying capacity of suburbia is due mostly to stingy planting.

There is not enough for the animals to eat.

The burst of comprehension that told me that, were I to be accepted among the gardening crowd, I would not have much to crow about, signaled the beginning of a large and lengthy experiment. Could we, within the bounds of human esthetics and the limitations of our knowledge, bring back some portion of the missing animals list? Right away I saw the sine qua non of gardeners: we are meddlers; we must tamper. I couldn't leave the land alone. But every kind of animal tampers by living, eating, breeding, and dying, and so do all the plants tamper with the animals whose services they court, whose ravages they revenge, whose appetites they feed, and on whose corpses they feed in turn. Our culture is perhaps just inexperienced at balancing the books.

The land we tamper with — almost six acres — is an excellent laboratory. The lowest portion is a ferny wetland thick with skunk cabbage and laced with shallow rivulets. A smallish pond, dug by a suburbanite in the 1940s, trickles into the wetland and is itself filled by runoff from the upland to the east, where our land rises toward the dawn. There are two woodland patches, both small: one to the far side of the pond, due south; the other, a strip on the opposite side of the property to the north. Between those shaded bounds is a hillside that begins against the rising sun with a high granite outcrop; as the slope descends first steeply, then gently, toward the sunset, it protrudes again here and there in knobs of various sizes. We therefore have as playground for our hubris dry heights, wet lowlands, and every grade between. Absent are extremes of climate: no desert, tropics, mountainside, or ocean shore. Rocks are ubiquitous. Sand is rare. The soil is uniformly acid (there are limestone areas down the road a piece). The soil is often surprising, sometimes deep and fertile, but as often hardpan almost to the surface and so abruptly discontinuous that one's shovel foot never adjusts to the resistance it might meet.

The earlier book I wrote about this place, *My Weeds*, describes the gardens we had developed up to that time and leaves them barely a season before our experiments began. In that text I expressed an inkling of dissatisfaction, a vague plan to favor species over hybrids, natives over exotics, in the hope that the land might thereby mature more gracefully with less care as we age. The pond then was a thing to covet: we bought it as I was writing the last chapter of the book. And for those who read the final sentence, yes, we planted a vegetable garden. But somehow the book sounds as though we and our gardens were settling down, mellowing out, finishing up.

We had done so much — so wrong. We had planted trees and shrubs whose sterile blooms produced no berries. It never occurred to us to plant hazelnuts in hedges. We didn't consider, when we cut down a stand of milkweed, how many butterflies it fed.

Such mistakes are general. Growers breed ornamentals without regard for their utility; nurseries neither know nor care which plants offer food as well as flowers; landscapers have no training in ecology; gardening writers think that only vegetables are edible. All of us, layperson and professional alike, fail to ask how creatures other than ourselves can share the goodness of the land. Yet if we don't, not only they but we will suffer.

I'm neither a romantic nor an altruist. I let grass grow for grouse, preserve dry-stone walls for toads, leave logs rotting in the woods for centipedes and such, less because it's the decent thing to do than because it's necessary. Gardeners who clear a wild plot, as we did, can easily notice why, for immediately the land needs feeding, watering, planting, cultivating, and pest control, whereas before it managed all these things itself.

We compost leaves and think we know something about making soil. It takes trillions of minute to microscopic organisms of thousands of species to decay to soil those leaves we think we compost. We haven't identified more than a tiny fraction of these organisms, much less understood their individual contributions or imagined the complex relationships among them by which the task is done. We sow seeds and think we know something about growing plants, yet the number of seeds we plant are a spoonful compared to the oceans of seeds planted by other animals that in their combined feasts and feces, travels, tramplings, burrowings, and stashings clothe the world in greenery. Consider having to pollinate by hand one's own garden flowers, as I must do with a certain gourd I grow because its night-flying moth is absent. The few kinds of pesticides gardeners keep on hand contain perhaps a dozen chemicals, whereas the varied species in a meadow use hundreds and house in addition a host of insect predators. We piddle around with hose and cloche, shade cloth and cold frame, while any little strip of woods or wetland conserves, filters, purifies, and recycles water; controls floods, checks erosion, builds soil, makes clouds, slows wind, and moderates air temperature.

We can't do without these environmental services. We don't know how to manage them ourselves.

Our intelligence, however prodigious we like to think it, is trivial compared to the accumulated wisdom of the hundred million species that make up Earth's biosphere. Since each microbe, animal, and plant possesses some minute portion of the know-how that makes the whole earth work, the loss of any species erases some portion of organic intelligence, and leaves the land more stupid. Moreover, an ecosystem's intelligence — its ability to run itself and to sustain its inhabitants — is more than a summation of the information each of its species represents. The intelligence of any system, whether a computer, a brain, or a meadow, arises from the complexity of connections among its separate elements. Removing an element unplugs many connections and therefore has a stupefying effect much greater than the mere subtraction of a part. By removing many parts and thus unplugging these connections, we have left our land too retarded to take care of itself, much less to be of any help to us.

This is not someone else's problem. We — you and I and everyone who has a yard of any size — own a big chunk of this country. Suburban development has wrought habitat destruction on a grand scale. As these tracts expand, they increasingly squeeze the remaining natural ecosystems, fragment them, sever corridors by which plants and animals might refill the voids we have created. To reverse this process — to reconnect as many plant and animal species as we can to rebuild intelligent suburban ecosystems — requires a new kind of garden, new techniques of gardening, and, I emphasize, a new kind of gardener.

The standards that have guided suburban landscaping have arisen, not from any concern for the environment, but from the dictates of gardening style. These have historically encouraged an esthetic based on class distinction and reducible to mere symbol. The great lawns from which our little ones descended proclaimed the extent of the landowner's holding. The grand hedges and topiary that spawned the shorn foundation plantings around our houses required crews of gardeners to maintain them. The Japanese cutleaf maple plunked in the middle of the yard is a relic of the exotics displayed by those who could afford to import rarities.

Can we look to our own rural past for an example? Ironically, part of the predicament we are in was caused by rapacious agri-cultural practices that denuded the land of its forests and prairies and left the soil dry, eroded, and infertile. Our suburbs are built on farmland that was so degraded it had to be abandoned. The "unspoiled" wooded lot one sees advertised is not unspoiled at all; it is second-growth woodland remarkable for a paucity of species and immature soil. Remnant meadowland is populated by field weeds, the alien residue of agriculture. Roses are *Rosa multiflora*, a pernicious thorn carelessly imported in this century as an orna-mental, as too were Japanese honeysuckle, Oriental bittersweet, purple loosestrife, and kudzu vine — all of which smother our native vegetation. These aliens not only suppress the total num-ber of species through competition but, because they did not evolve here, have fewer connections within the ecosystem than native flora. Lively as our own land was before we cleared it, it served up a skimpy portion of the banquet it might offer.

Certainly one can't restore the land completely to hemlock forest, sand barren, cedar swamp, prairie. The saving or restora-tion of vanishing ecosystems is not a backyard job.

Our task is therefore nothing less than to create a new land-scape. And, in a way, our failures have given us that opportunity. With the decline of family farming, land that is now suburban is for the first time in three centuries under no pressure to produce corn or cattle, so it can recover. If the high cost and heavy labor of stylish gardening have forced us to plant minimally, then we may welcome more carefree plantings of just those species that, because they have been considered too common for the garden, are the cheapest ones to buy. Even the peculiar bareness of suburbia invites experimenting with a lusher landscape.

Our first step was timid; we added fruiting shrubs to island beds and outcrops close to the house. As we grew bolder, we joined these small gardens to one another with additional plant-ings and brought them toward outlying woodland via thickets, groves, and hedgerows. We improved the woods, replanted the pond, and finally wove the whole together with native grass and wildflowers. The project is by no means finished, but the changes we have made so far are working: berries feed birds as surely as stone walls shelter chipmunks.

These changes are less apparent to the human eye than in the perception of other animals. The lot is still landscaped, the gardens are intact; but less is mowed, the choice of plants is different, and thickets have replaced some open beds. Although we have fewer flower borders, there are flowers everywhere all year except in the winter, when there are berries, holly red and inky black, and grasses, bronze and gold. Meadowlarks and bluebirds have returned. I haven't learned yet to identify all the butterflies. Tadpoles and fish fry are increasing among the vegetation in the pond, to the delight of the great blue heron and my granddaughter, who held a frog for the first time just the other day.

But is this new esthetic, this landscape of verge and thicket, storied grove and meadowed clearing, fitting for a yard? Yes, certainly. While our property is large, the plantings would fit anywhere — hedgerow instead of hedge (no trimming required); beds of prairie flowers (put away your hose, your pesticide sprayers); inkberries under oak trees (feed the birds for free): abundance.

When I was trying to become a gardener (only to realize that I was unbecoming), one book pricked my conscience in a different way. It is called *A Gentle Plea for Chaos*, by Mirabel Osler, an English gardener who plants trees in groves and lets the grass grow tall. She alone of the authors I read mourned the lack of an American gardening literature. What, she wondered, are our gardens like, how styled against our purple mountains' majesty, our amber waves of grain? I wanted to write to her, but I was at a loss. How to admit the barrenness of subdivisions? How to excuse the lawns that sanitize the fruited plain from sea to shining sea?

Yards and gardens patched with grass and stitched with hedges all across America constitute a vast, nearly continuous, and terribly impoverished ecosystem for which we ourselves, with our mowers, shears, and misguided choice of plants, are responsible.

We cannot in fairness rail against those who destroy the rain forest or threaten the spotted owl when we have made our own yards uninhabitable. Yet how quickly we could grow this land, spangle it with blazing stars, stripe it with red winterberries and white summersweet, let it wave again with grass!

Grow America!

Sounds like a bumper sticker.

Join the club.

2

The Lay of the Land

OUR SLOPED LAND lies below Great Hill, the highest point on
an undulating ridge that used to be the route of Indians traveling
between their wintering grounds inland and their summer encampments along the Connecticut shore. This ridge is echoed by
others parallel to it in the ribbed topography typical of glacier-
scraped New England. On the world vegetation map in my atlas,
New England occupies the top right corner of a green patch
labeled "Broadleaf Forest" that covers about a third of America's
forty-eight contiguous states. Turning to the map showing
population distribution and density, I see that the pink blotches
indicating high population coincide roughly with the broadleaf
forest. A stranger would surmise that most Americans live in the
woods.

In fact, almost the entire forest was cut down in the first two
centuries of European settlement. The following hundred years
saw the central plains — depicted in light green for tallgrass
prairie, gold for shortgrass prairie — equally destroyed by plow
and livestock. Since then, all the other ecosystems, represented

in shades from palest sand to deepest spruce, have been severely damaged. Most of us live on ravaged land.

I knew our own piece of land was in bad shape. The soil on most of the slope was pale, hard, dry, and sterile; only at the bottom where topsoil had accumulated against the old farm walls was there any depth of rich, moist brown. We'd been told, though, that the farmers on this side of Great Hill had supplied topsoil to landscape the grounds of the World's Fair in 1939, so I supposed our poverty was local.

Changes in the Land, a history of two hundred years of New England ecology by the historian William Cronon, made me reconsider. I now believe that if, indeed, the hillside was scraped of its remaining topsoil, it must have been the despairing act of a farmer about to abandon his already ruined fields. Starting in the 1620s, the European settlers systematically clear-cut the forest that had maintained the land in abundance and diversity for some ten thousand years. In less than two centuries, each individual's picking added up to a collective assault so powerful as to literally make the streams run dry. Leaching, erosion, compaction, and desiccation forced the abandonment of fields and pastures in New England and throughout the East beginning in the nineteenth century when, in the great westward migration, farmers plowed their way beyond the forest belt onto the rich American plains.

The story continued in this very different setting, but the plot didn't change. As Cronon describes in *Nature's Metropolis*, his ecological history of Chicago and its hinterland during the century following its settlement, the destruction of the northern conifer forest and prairie grassland was even more rapid and complete than the felling of New England. All across the continent, the farmers' leavings are now our suburbs.

I wondered, reading about New England, whether the American tall tale might have originated in the literal descriptions that the colonists sent home to England, where their claims were routinely disbelieved. Who would believe foot-long oysters that had to be cut into morsels to be swallowed? Settlers and travelers wrote of herring stranded knee-deep on the beach, flocks of passenger pigeons blackening the sky, fifty ducks at a shot, a dozen turkeys in a morning, a hundred deer per mile, acres of raspberries, huge wild strawberries, woods full of chestnuts, pine trees five feet thick towering two hundred feet into the sky, and that outrageous animal, the moose.

This was bounteous New England at the opening of the seventeenth century. One hundred years later, the moose were gone, wild turkeys were rare, and beavers survived only in isolated places. Deer had declined so alarmingly that restrictions were placed on hunting them. Populations of otter, fox, marten, mink, and muskrat were rapidly vanishing. Meanwhile, the European population had climbed to 93,000. One would think that since New England had supported between 70,000 and 100,000 Indians at the outset of the European settlement, this doubling of the population might explain what was happening to the wildlife. But in the first seventy-five years alone, the Indian population was reduced by epidemics of European diseases to just 12,000. The total number of people living off the land had not dramatically increased. The landscape, however, had been radically altered by the settlers, who saw the environment in commercial terms — as property, as commodity, as wealth to be mined for profit.

The Indians saw the environment in terms of usage: individuals or groups had rights to fish a certain pond, hunt or gather from a certain area. Similar rights could be extended to others, even bartered, but there was no concept that the land itself could be owned. Many place names in our area refer to Indian groups that once lived here, but the Indians themselves named places according to their use: Clam Bake Place, Rushes for Making Mats, Small Island Where We Get Pitch. The map of our town describes property boundaries; an Indian's mental image of the same area would have described its practical gifts.

In the north, the Indians followed their food through the seasons. In the spring, families and kinship groups met at rivers thronged with spawning fish; in the summer they gathered shell-fish and berries; in the fall they ate nuts and migratory birds, in the winter, deer and other game. In the more southern parts of New England, this mobile cropping system was augmented by a simple but effective form of agriculture. Clearings were made in the forest by girdling large trees or setting fires at their bases to kill them; the underbrush was burned as well. The ground was hoed into hills where corn and climbing beans were planted; the space in between was taken up with sprawling squash and pumpkins. Weeding was done once, early in the summer; otherwise, the ground was undisturbed. Such fields retained their fertility for as long as ten years thanks to enriching ashes, the nitrogen supplied by beans, and crop litter left to decay over the winter. When corn no longer flourished, new openings were burned for planting and the older clearings were left to grow back into forest.

Ecologists call the cycle of regrowth from natural or manmade disturbance to mature ecosystem a sere and the successive flushes of growth within the cycle seral stages. Each stage prepares the ground for the next stage. A sugar maple, for example, can't take root on dry, sterile ground but will succeed where the soil has been first built up by decaying accumulations of grass thatch, then loosened and made spongier by the roots of woody brush, then further enriched by the composting of leaves from pioneer trees. Like the abandoned field our place had been, the Indians' clearings regrew with grass and other perennial herbaceous plants, followed by such pioneer trees as junipers and birches and by grapevines, blackberry brambles, and thickets of berrying bushes. During these early seral stages, which continue for twenty years or more, the clearings attracted deer, rabbits, and game birds of all sorts. The Indians' fields therefore were productive for some thirty years, first for farming and then for hunting.

Even where they didn't intend to plant fields, the Indians used fire to clear large tracts of underbrush in woodlands of oak and hickory. These particular species, typical of upland woods where thirstier trees like beech and maple do less well, have evolved thick, corky bark that protects them from brief fires, provided the

ing but how to interfere without destroying the very ecosystem services that we and every other creature need.

"The city of New Haven," Cronon wrote in *Changes in the Land*,

> furnishes a good example both of the drying and the erosion which accompanied English agricultural practices. The earliest map of the town, dated 1641, shows a substantial stream running across the east corner of the original plat, and a smaller one which flowed from the south corner of the town green. By 1724, both streams had vanished from the original plat, although they continued to run to the southeast of it. By 1802, the small stream had disappeared entirely, and the flow of the larger one had so declined that it was labeled a "canal." Neither exists at all today.

So, as woods met ax, ecosystem services were terminated.

The services that forests supply are not different in kind from those supplied by earlier seral stages, such as meadow and thicket, or from those supplied in drier areas, where the final stage of succession is prairie, scrubland, or savanna. But forests are bulkier by far, their contributions are in important respects proportionally greater, and the loss of their crucial physical services dramatizes the loss when any ecosystem is obliterated.

One appreciates the services of a forest simply by walking there. The air is cool and fresh, the soil soft and moist, the streams clear, the wind stilled, the silence deep. Surprisingly, silence is the most recently understood of the woodland services. Noise abatement studies designed to discover how best to mute the roar of traffic along highways have found that woodland leaf litter muffles sound better than any manmade barrier — or than the trees themselves.

A remnant of mature forest still survives along the river into which the rivulets of our wetland eventually make their way. It starts abruptly. Stepping into it from the sunny busyness of its edge is like entering a dark museum from the noonday street.

The topmost tier of canopy trees traps the greater amount of light as it descends through their leafy crowns. The light that filters through is intercepted by shorter understory trees, some of which, like dogwood, are markedly horizontal in habit or, like redbud, have strikingly large leaves. Only ambient light is available at the forest floor, where ferns and carpeting mosses capture what remains. Because of this layered structure, forests milk the sun's energy with stunning efficiency for an annual net profit in biomass that is more than twice that produced by a hayfield.

Plants use light energy to build carbohydrates through the chemical process of photosynthesis. The raw material for photosynthesis is the carbon removed from the "greenhouse gas" carbon dioxide in the atmosphere; the waste product is oxygen. Because of its vast leaf surface, a forest supplies oxygen far more copiously than grassland does. Most of the carbon taken up by a forest is stored in the carbohydrate compounds of wood. By removing carbon and storing it, trees effectively prevent its recirculation as carbon dioxide. Woodland warehousing is long-term: canopy trees typically live for a hundred years or more, and the process of decay that ultimately releases their stored carbon may take another half a century. Although grass and flowers also store carbon, they live briefly and rot quickly. The amount of carbon dioxide removed from circulation by the vegetable kingdom is therefore roughly proportional to the volume of wood in trees.

What one can't see on a woodland walk is that a great deal of that wood is underground. Plunging below the forest floor, sometimes as deep as the trees are tall, a dense network of roots excavates the soil to a spongy consistency that holds up to 90 percent of rainfall, letting the accumulated water trickle only gradually toward low-lying wetlands. By comparison, as much as 90 percent of the rain falling on a lawn is immediately lost as runoff, and with it the soil's mineral fertility. The water held in a forest's extensive, spongy reservoir is over time absorbed by roots, ascends upward through trunks and branches into the interiors of leaves, evaporates through pores, accumulates as clouds of water vapor, condenses, rains down, and reenters the forest reservoirs. Groundwater also evaporates from grasslands, but a forest's capacity to store water modulates the water cycle, not only conserving water that would otherwise run out to sea, but spreading precipitation more evenly through the year.

The coolness of the woodland is not explained by shade alone. Its immense evaporative surface, unequaled by any other form of growth, cools the air in the same way that sweating cools the body. On a summer day, the air temperature in the shade outside the forest and within it may differ by twenty degrees or more. Shade, moisture, and the heat of decay moderate the soil's temperature throughout the year.

By retarding water flow both over the surface and through the soil during snow melt and heavy rain, forests control stream and river flooding. Their roots hold the soil against erosion, and this, together with the slowing of the water, keeps runoff clear and waterways free of excessive silting. Moderated flooding assures high water levels for long periods; water flowing slowly from the forest reservoir into drainage basins keeps streams and rivers running through dry spells. Indeed, this is one reason that the forest where we walk is still standing: the river that it guards supplies water to a nearby city, and without the forest the city would run dry.

Of America's original old-growth forests — not only the eastern broadleaf variety but also the conifer forests of the North and West — only 5 percent now remain intact. Topsoil on cultivated land nationwide is presently lost to wind and rain erosion at an average rate of 4.1 tons per acre per year (the rate in the hilly Northeast is higher, reaching more than 7 tons per year in some areas). During the earliest decades of European agriculture, contemporary observers already noted that the soil began to lose its fertility within the first two years after the forests were cleared. Others remarked on areas where erosion had bared the ground to underlying sand or clay.

Even in pasture similar to the grassy, unplowed clearings made by the Indians, leaching and erosion were accelerated by the eating habits of cattle that, unlike tip-nibbling browsers such as elk and deer, crop foliage right down to the crown. Dense herds of cattle compacted the soil, further reducing its ability to hold either the oxygen or water required for the healthy growth of plants. In addition, the farmers mowed their fields for hay no matter how thin the grass, thus baring them to erosion during the winter. No land was left entirely fallow to recover through the soil-building process of succession.

Erosion increased to such an extent that streambeds silted up five times faster than they had before the colonial settlement. Springtime's slow and gentle overflow had previously added a fertile film of silt along river floodplains; the briefer but violent floods that followed deforestation flushed that accumulation away and deposited in its place coarse subsoil and gravel that had been bared by upland erosion along the river's course. Silt-choked streams and ponds shallowed into marshes.

In 1809, a scientifically minded Vermonter reported in a history of his state that in the summer, soil in open pasture averaged about ten degrees hotter than soil in adjacent woods and that water set out in the open field evaporated one and a half times more quickly. Modern studies have confirmed that soil temperature and evaporation increase on cleared land and have verified that climate in general deteriorates over entire geographic areas where forests have been reduced to fields. Summer temperatures climb higher, winter temperatures drop lower, wind speeds increase by 20 to 40 percent, soil dries out, and the ground freezes to a greater depth in winter. As Cronon summarizes, "Cleared lands in New England were thus sunnier, windier, hotter, colder, and drier than they had been in their former state."

They were also skimpier. Our town was settled in the early 1740s. Photographs of farmland along this hilly ridge taken before the turn of the century show no trees except those few left to shade cattle along fence lines. Assuming that the land was farmed for two hundred years and that it eroded at an average annual rate

of 4 tons per acre, our cleared two acres of hillside might have lost as much as 1,600 tons of soil, the equivalent of eighty truckloads at twenty cubic yards per truck.

The World's Fair must have gotten a rotten deal.

Typically for our time, I heard of that sale without shock. I can sell tomatoes, firewood, pheasants, berries, soil, rocks — anything I can raise or extract from the land I call mine, including that abstract embodiment of it: its deed, its ownership. These concepts of land as commodity were developing in the early years of settlement. At first, property deeds described land by use — hay meadow, pasture, field, woodlot — much as the Indians did. Also like the Indians, most early settlers merely subsisted on their land. The difference was that the value of the land to the Indians was only in its sustenance — fur for warmth, bark for canoes, food for survival — whereas to Europeans both the land's products and the land itself were beginning to be perceived as having monetary value. European agricultural technology, especially the ox and plow, allowed intensive cropping, resulting in a surplus that could be turned to profit. Adding more land to one's original holding — and hiring labor to work it — increased profit. Thus by clearing, fencing, building, and expanding — literally, by improving one's lot — one stood to gain socially and financially in the increasingly mercantile world that would spawn modern capitalism.

The very concept of land ownership was inseparable from improvement. Town decisions regarding the amount of land to be parceled out per family depended on how quickly the family could convert it from wild to cultivated land. In some areas, landholders who failed to follow the biblical injunction "to fill the earth and subdue it" within a prescribed number of years might forfeit their property rights altogether. Among the reasons that Europeans felt few qualms about appropriating Indian territory

Opposite: The land, ca. 1850: farmland cleared except for shade trees and woodlots

was the widespread conviction that the Indians had property rights only to those clearings they maintained in crops. To Europeans, the forest by right belonged to those who brought it under the plow, an imperative not likely to preserve more than a modicum of shade trees.

Every sort of abundance, from beaver pelts to salt cod and chestnut planks, soon became commercial products distributed through Boston and other urban centers. The assault on the forest came to be fueled less by immediate need or moral precept than by the profits to be made from supplying meat, grain, produce, lumber, and other goods to both coastal cities and overseas markets. The use descriptions on deeds were replaced by the abstract metes and bounds we use today. Value was assigned to land in proportion to the value of the commodities that could be extracted from it, whether charcoal from its trees, meat from its grasses, or, ultimately, the body of its soil.

One day not long after we had moved here, we found a white quartz arrowhead buried under stone rubble on a granite outcrop a few steps from the house. Such a finding stirs the romantic imagination. When had he lived, this hunter? I place him prior to the European settlement — or at least not long after — because the rubble on the outcrop was from plowed fields and his arrow was beneath it. I try to picture what this land was like then. In light of Cronon's ecological history, and surveying the landscape from the outcrop where the Indian lost his arrow, I think I can see my way past suburbia, through farming, back to his time.

Up the hillside beyond our parcel toward the crest that once held barns and a farmhouse stands an imposing suburban home built over and around the original house, which is now our neighbor's kitchen. A wagon road, walled on either side and overgrown with brush, descends from the former farmyard and enters our land at what is now the pond. On an aerial photograph taken in 1926, the wagon way continues around the contour of the present pond, which was then a swamp.

Going further back in time requires mental bulldozing; I push three centuries of accumulated silt back up from the swamp to the surrounding slopes, molding them higher and steeper. The outcrop all but disappears beneath the soil. Acorns from the one white oak that now shades the rock grow up in my imagination, and looking down what has become a rolling incline, I see the stream below flowing deep and unimpeded through a narrow wooded valley.

So — and so quickly — has changed the lay of this land.

So, too, has its value. This abstraction on which I live, now described by points, lines, and angles on a piece of paper filed at the county courthouse, is assessed at a substantial figure.

Yet to that Indian it wouldn't be worth a gourd.

3

What Mrs. Dana Saw

THE TOWN OF Bedford — or the "village," as it calls itself — contains one of the most dangerous road intersections around. That the situation wasn't remedied for years, even after a prominent citizen was killed crossing the street there, is because Bedford takes such pride in being "historical." One remedy would have destroyed a portion of the original village green; the other, reluctantly adopted, intruded a traffic light. The town's rules regarding any alteration of the shops on Main Street facing the green are so stringent that about all that's left are real estate concerns. One shops for houses.

The town is an anachronism in another way: most of its roads are dirt. Real dirt. My own town, down a tarry road a piece, is not quite so precious, but its ordinances protect rock walls as well as trees, "to preserve the public health and welfare and rural character of the community which is reflected in the woodlands of the Town of Pound Ridge."

Of course I prefer preservation, historical or natural, to the rampant malls that cover so much of today's suburbia, but what exactly is the vaunted "rural character" of even these, our most lavishly protected and presumably least spoiled suburban landscapes?

Changes in the Land brings the ecological history of New England to the threshold of the nineteenth century, some sixty or seventy years before city dwellers, looking back with longing toward a poorly understood rural past, began to move into the pastoral settings of Scarsdale and Evanston. Late-nineteenth-century nostalgia is well captured in the writings of Mrs. William Starr Dana, a self-taught botanist who published the classic and best-selling *How to Know the Wild Flowers* in 1893 and, a year later, *According to Season*, a collection of her nature columns for a New York City newspaper. This latter book, recently republished, came my way some time after I had read Cronon, when I thought I had reached the last chapter of New England's transformation. But an epilog must be added. The farmland that Mrs. Dana eulogized on her weekend forays to the countryside may well have resembled the farmland of Mr. Cronon's narrative; it bore no resemblance to this land today.

"The pink azalea," Mrs. Dana wrote (and which I take to be pinxterbloom, *Rhododendron periclymenoides*), "grows in great tangles in the wet meadows," where in June "blue flags still lift their stately heads along the water-courses, and the blossoms of the blue-eyed grass are now so large and abundant that they seem to float like a flood of color on the tops of the long grasses." She reported lowlands where "one of our most radiant orchids, the grass-pink or Calopogon . . . is fairly illuminating this part of the meadow with its countless blossoms." Her walks took her along waysides "whitened with the large flowers of the lovely summer anemone," pond shores "blue with the long, close spikes of the pickerel-weed," thickets over which "the clematis has flung a veil of feathery white." In spring she found the morning air "alive with the happy tinkle" of bobolinks. In summer she waded "knee-deep among the myriad erect stems" of meadow lilies, of which, "with rhythmical sweep of his long scythe the mower lays low whole acres."

I became increasingly disturbed as she wound down the year

*Male bobolink
in nuptial plumage*

by rhapsodizing autumn, "when September lines the road-sides of New England with the purple of the aster, and flights its mantle of golden-rod over her hills, and fills her hollows with the pink drifts of the Joe-Pye-weed or with the intense red-purple of the iron-weed, and guards her brooks with tall ranks of yellow sun-flowers."

This is not the way it is now in the autumn of the year, when, if I were to rhapsodize the roadsides, I'd have to sing a song of ugly mugwort.

I've never seen a meadow lily or heard a bobolink. Where a hundred years ago Mrs. Dana might have found the former swamp here "bright with the great blue lobelia," I found a single specimen of *Lobelia siphilitica* growing lonely beside the pond. The vines draping thickets are now honeysuckle, not clematis. The blooms purpling damp hollows are loosestrife, not ironweed. The flowers whitening roadsides are the wild carrot called Queen Anne's lace, not anemones. These replacements of our native flowers are all alien species — and all weeds.

Cronon wrote that as long ago as 1672 a visiting Englishman listed twenty-two European field weeds — among them dandelion, chickweed, nightshade, and stinging nettle — that had become common in the Massachusetts Bay Colony. During the next two centuries the list expanded to hundreds, some arriving by accident in ship ballast and cattle feed, but many imported for medicinal purposes or as dye plants, livestock fodder, or garden ornamentals. Such plants, adapted over thousands of years to disturbed agricultural land, had an advantage over native species ill accustomed to stagnant water, sterile soil, compacted ground, mowing, plowing, heat, drought, and cattle. But native species that had played a successional role before colonial times also took advantage of the continual perturbations of European agriculture. The settlement of an area can be accurately dated, for example, by a sudden influx of ragweed pollen in lake sediments. Certain aggressively spreading species of native milkweed and goldenrod — especially *Asclepius syriaca* and *Solidago canadensis* — quickly acquired the status of weeds. By Mrs. Dana's time, the mower's scythe certainly laid low invasive indigenes as well as alien buttercups, thistles, daisies, and spurges along with the now all but vanished meadow lilies.

Mrs. Dana died midway through this century to the dirge of tractors and reapers and the death rattle of swamps being drained, meadows bulldozed, hills leveled, hollows filled, roads cut, sewers laid, foundations excavated, drives paved, and lawns planted to support the move to suburbia that her lush writings had in part inspired. We have wrought in our time a calamity of habitat destruction unprecedented even during the previous three centuries of agricultural abuse. In a last exquisite irony, the burgeoning interest in gardening that accompanied the move from city to suburb stimulated the nursery trade to import or to tout Norway maple, alder buckthorn, Japanese barberry, kudzu vine, Japanese honeysuckle, Oriental bittersweet, purple loosestrife, multiflora rose, and other "easy" ornamentals that are so invasive in damaged habitats as to preclude their natural recovery.

·   ·   ·

On superficial examination, at first our land seemed to exemplify recovery. The near shore of the pond, then beyond our borders, was mowed annually and so had remained in the early seral stage of perennial herbs and grasses. The center of the property, left undisturbed for perhaps fifteen years, was a community of pioneer trees and shrubs growing from a still-substantial turf of grass and wildflowers. The fringes had been abandoned at earlier but various times; the dates could be guessed by both the size and the species of trees that had since appeared. Laid out before us was an approximately fifty-year history of succession from abandoned field to woodland.

But, as I gradually learned, recovery was normal only in its general outline. The details were pathological.

When our neighbor stopped mowing along the pond shore, there arose, not the tall meadow-rue, swamp milkweed, Joe-Pye-weed, black-eyed Susan, New York ironweed, and other tap-rooted natives that, together with fibrous-rooted grasses, rebuild the soil in such areas, but an infestation of greedy, ground-eating, weed goldenrod and hundreds of multiflora roses. The eastern red çedars that had colonized the central field supported wrist-thick canes of these same gigantic roses, and among the evergreens and their young birch companions slithered tentacles of bittersweet reaching for purchase in their trunks and branches.

The sequel to that stage was revealed by the youngest woods, where black cherry, sassafras, and quaking aspen had sprung up only to be bent and broken under a mass of honeysuckle, bittersweet, and wild grape vines. That area could best be described as a baby forest smothered in its bed.

The oldest woods had eluded strangulation by virtue of its age: Japanese honeysuckle was not reported in New York until 1913, Oriental bittersweet not until 1952; presumably neither was established at this site when the now good-size elms and hickories were young. Alder buckthorn, however, has been grown in this country as an ornamental since colonial times, and this invasive alien had spread over the entire floor. If that woodland was trying to become the oak-hickory forest typical of this ridge, there was no sign in the understory thicket of the saplings necessary for its regeneration.

For years I noticed nothing more about the land's pathology than these obvious malignancies. A twist of mind was needed — set in motion by our buying the pond — to realize that what does not strike the eye is an even more critical indication of disease.

From a distance, the woods behind the pond presented a welcoming face of willow streamers and maple boughs as, in innocence and in shorts, I first ventured to explore it. Inside was fiercely different. In the oldest portion, where senescent willows bespoke an age of some forty years, I groped my way under and over tripping loops of arrowwood, through barberry prickles, buckthorn thickets, grape nooses, and jungles of poison ivy whose hairy stems crept like centipedes up the dying willows or grew head-high from their vast fallen corpses. Two thirds of the way around, solid stands of multiflora rose impenetrably intertwined with bittersweet forced me to crawl the remaining distance from rock to rock along the treacherous boundary wall.

I emerged bloodied but optimistic; the ground here was rich silt eroded off the hillside, logged no doubt for firewood, possibly grazed or hayed as well, but too wet certainly for plowing. Also, the sick strip abutted an area of seemingly healthy woodland already old enough on the 1926 map to cast a perceptible shadow. Although I really hadn't been able to see much through the wounding tangle, I was sure that its removal would reveal a youthful woodland struggling to emerge.

But as we cleared, the woods vanished. There was nothing holding up the rose canes and bittersweet vines except dead junipers and cherry snags. When these, too, were cut, that shore was bare. Even in the oldest portion, clearing the invasive brush and vines revealed how little else there was: of canopy trees, a poor stand of green ash, some young red maples, one sweet birch, and the dying crack willows; of understory species, none but the remaining arrowwood. The brush we had removed had been the woods.

Had we cut in error some sapling of hornbeam, some thicket of gray dogwood? I think not. I knew the weedy growth we cleared. The woods simply was impoverished of the trees and shrubs that, according to field guides, one would expect to find in this youngish pondside habitat.

It's quite an education to read a field guide. One places oneself mentally in, in my case, broadleaf forest about halfway between Maine and Maryland and sees what one can see. *Ilex opaca*, our fine American holly? Never saw it. *Rhododendron viscosum*, our fragrant swamp azalea? Not in these woods. Such pioneer species as American sycamore (*Platanus occidentalis*), winterberry (*Ilex verticillata*), and common witch hazel (*Hamamelis virginiana*) should have been early arrivals on the moist pond shore, but there were none. A boggy area was perfect for summersweet (*Clethra alnifolia*), a rise just right for rosebay rhododendron (*R. maximum*), deep clefts angling up the rock face of an imposing outcrop should have been thick with mountain laurel (*Kalmia latifolia*), but not a seedling of any of these was present. Where there might have been at least four species of dogwood — *Cornus florida*, *C. alternifolia*, *C. racemosa*, and *C. sericea* — as edge and understory in such a habitat, both niches were so filled by aggressive barberry and buckthorn that there was hardly an inch for shyer seedlings to get started.

The disappointment fueled my curiosity. I began to accumulate other reference books in order to learn what native species ought to be around. Sometimes I used the books to identify a sprig or blossom found on walks around the countryside; more often I wandered aimlessly through the pages of a world strangely new.

Surprise caught me up continually. Plants I knew well and assumed were native turned out to be exotics, and not only weedy species like the Japanese barberry and alder buckthorn we had cleared from the choked fringes of our land, but also lovely things like burning bush (*Euonymous alata*), cornelian cherry (*Cornus mas*), and all wild apple trees whose fruits are red, not green. What dismayed me was not just the number of species that had failed to appear on our particular plot but the number of species that in fifty years of acquaintance with this area I had neither seen nor heard of.

I knew our usual downy serviceberry (*Amelanchier arborea*), but that there is also a running serviceberry (*A. stolonifera*) only four feet tall astonished me. I had no idea there was such a thing as a native filbert, although in fact there are two: *Corylus americana* and *C. cornuta*. The first eastern redbud (*Cercis canadensis*) I saw was in a nursery. Of the twenty-nine viburnum species described in *Wyman's Gardening Encyclopedia*, eight are North Americans. Of these I knew just two, even though six are supposed to occur naturally in this area. One that I knew was arrowwood, *V. dentatum*, which I trip over all too often. The other — mapleleaf viburnum, *V. acerifolium* — I hadn't seen for thirty years. A third, called nannyberry (*V. lentago*), I eventually uncovered in a corner of our land in an advanced stage of suffocation under vines. But where were hobblebush (*V. alnifolium*), American cranberrybush (*V. trilobum*), withe-rod (*V. cassinoides*), black haw (*V. prunifolium*), and possum haw (*V. nudum*)? The nicknames of the unfamiliar plants I stumbled across only in books — staggerbush (*Lyonia mariana*), fetterbush (*Leucothoe racemosa*), hog-apple (*Crataegus crus-galli*), toothache tree (*Zanthoxylum americanum*) — suggested an eye-winking, elbow-jabbing intimacy with species that must once have been as common as traveling salesman jokes. Where were they? In guides and encyclopedias, but seldom here, in what once had been their native habitat.

Gradually I realized that the remnant meadows, thicketed roadsides, and extensive woods of this regrowing area are a mask of naturalness that, once one is trained to recognize the species, drops away to reveal an appalling blankness. Not only have Mrs. Dana's tapestries of orchids, irises, lilies, and gentians faded to obscurity, but the entire succession that ought to follow them is pitifully threadbare. Biodiversity remains only in scattered preserves; elsewhere, what has grown back over the fields of our forefathers is merely a fraction of the species that can, and once did, grow here. If I found an untouched lode of ancient humus, if, like the Little Prince, I assiduously kept back the invading baobabs, still no princess pine would come to grace my woods.

The reason struck me forcefully: our rage to clear, first for farms and now for yards, has made once common natives too rare in the wild to repopulate the land. No sycamores had pioneered the pond because the nearest parent tree lives miles beyond the wind's ability to blow its seeds to us. The nearest holly berries are well beyond the drop zone of our birds. Only Super Squirrel could bring us wild filberts, wherever they may be.

During the summer of 1991, one of our sons sent me the August 16 issue of the journal *Science*, which was devoted to land management policy. The many contributions to that issue made it abundantly clear that human civilization as we now know it, from grain fields to oil fields and from industrial to residential development, inevitably and inexorably reduces biological diversity. Throughout geological history, the "background" rate of extinction has been balanced by an equivalent rate of speciation: except during rare and drastic extinction episodes, Earth's number of species, though not its kinds, remained unchanged over billions of years. The recovery of biodiversity after major extinctions takes several million years. In the interval, the world is inhabited by a list of species more or less equivalent to ragweed and roaches.

Extinction is now approaching the rate prevalent during the catastrophe that killed the dinosaurs. For the first time in Earth's history, a major plant extinction is also under way.

Why this loss of biodiversity in both animal and plant life is potentially disastrous was stated most cogently in that issue of *Science* by Paul R. Ehrlich, an eminent population biologist at Stanford University, and E. O. Wilson, an equally prominent entomologist at Harvard University. In their article "Biodiversity Studies: Science and Policy," they described the impact of human activity on global net primary productivity, which roughly means all the food available on land. Humans now directly use or in other ways make unavailable to other animals some 40 percent of the world's terrestrial food supply. The ecosystem services in which our burgeoning population will soon have appropriated a majority interest include waste disposal, water purification, pest suppression, and plant pollination as well as atmospheric regulation, nutrient recycling, flood and drought control, and soil manufacture. The reliable functioning of ecosystems depends exquisitely on the diversity of species — plant, animal, and other — of which they are composed. As Ehrlich and Wilson wrote:

> The ecosystem services in which biodiversity plays the critical role are provided on such a grand scale and in a manner so intricate that there is usually no real possibility of substituting for them, even in cases where scientists have the requisite knowledge. In fact, one could conclude that virtually all human attempts at large-scale inorganic substitution for ecosystem services are ultimately unsuccessful, whether it be introductions of synthetic pesticides for natural pest control, inorganic fertilizer for natural soil maintenance, chlorination for natural water purification, dams for flood and drought control, or air-conditioning of overheated environments. Generally, the substitutes require a large energy subsidy, thereby adding to humanity's general impact on the environment, and are not completely satisfactory even in the short run.
>
> It is important to note that in supplying ecosystem services the species and genic diversity of natural systems is critical. One might assume that one grass or tree species can function as well as any other in helping control the hydrologic cycle in a watershed, or that one predator will be as good as another in controlling a potential pest. But, of course, organisms are generally highly adapted to specific physical and biotic environments — and organic substitutes, like inorganic ones, are likely to prove unsatisfactory.

In other words, we cannot go it alone. Nor may we pick and choose some few companions among the many to carry us into the future. If our species has preempted or co-opted Earth's own maintenance systems, those systems become our problem, to guard and tend at the peril of our own survival. As one who believes that in both biological and cultural evolution morality arises from necessity, this imperative struck me to the bone.

However, no contributor to that issue of *Science* had words of guidance for suburbia.

What is one to do on a quarter-acre lot?

The truth about those various colors by which an atlas theorizes the natural ecosystems of our land is that they are as lost to history as the flies and manure that once were the reality of Bedford's village green. We really occupy no color at all. There is no map tint for the peculiar — and peculiarly similar — patterns of flat lawns and bumpy shrubs, starlings and dandelions, that typify suburbia from one coast to the other. Everywhere the soil is poor, water scarce, growth weedy, succession sick, diversity a list of missing plants and animals. We are hemmed in by present realities: roads, neighbors, budgets, ordinances. We can't go back in time, either to the scythed meadows where wild lilies survived into the twentieth century, to the mosaic woodland that Indians sustained by fire, or to some primeval landscape as it might have been had humans never crossed the rims of melting glaciers. One can't advise Arizonans to plan their gardens around saguaro cacti that take forty years to reach chest height, insist to Kansans that prairie yards must annually be trampled by bison, sway Californians to the view that canyon fires are ecologically refreshing, or talk a Yankee into entertaining bears. The preservation or restoration of the wilderness is critical but not possible in one's own back yard.

One can, however, set aside a portion of this yard to plant, if not altogether naturally, then at least in a way not alien to the theoretical ecosystem in which one lives. The planting can be brought along through stages of succession or halted at a particular stage, and it can be encouraged to express apparent deficiencies in becoming ways that, since one is unaccustomed to the curly winter blades of switchgrass or the fuzzy yellow balls of a blossoming buttonbush, strike one as surprisingly exotic. So cleverly as to make one chuckle like a tickled baby, the suburban landscape can be teased to control its own pests, maintain its own soil, conserve its own water, support its own animal associates, and altogether mind its business with minimal interference from us.

But first one must make space.

The only way to do that is to take up less space oneself.

I read that the average lot size in suburban America has climbed to 10,000 square feet — roughly a quarter acre. Older lots tend to be smaller, but since house size has if anything grown faster than lot size, the pie of our land continues to be sliced pretty thin. On acreage subdivided into such portions, just the space required to maneuver excavating and roadbuilding equipment guarantees that little if anything will be left of the natural landscape; the cheapest way for a developer to leave the scene will be to throw grass seed in his wake. Into this intimidatingly blank surface the homeowner incises a bed that cringes along the foundation of the house and perhaps plants a weeping ornamental. The finished effect, in which the lawn serves as background for some baubles of exterior decoration, seems so normal to us that it is hard to view a piece of land in any other way.

It seemed so normal to us that even though we bought a glutton's portion — and there was no lawn at all — we immediately proceeded to "develop" it by clearing the brush and mowing. We started near the house. First, a back lawn, then lawn to either side, then a strip along the driveway, then loppings and mowings to roll the green rug over the land in all directions.

The first indication that we were doing something wrong was the disappearance of the pheasants. In those early days, we had planted behind the house a kitchen garden encircled by a hedge of currants whose brilliant berries were regularly enjoyed by a mother and father pheasant and all their little chicks. The distance from the hedge to the unmowed, tall grass cover was about twenty feet — a critical distance, it seems, for when we mowed a broader strip, the pheasants were cut off from their breakfast as though by an invisible fence. The more we extended the lawn, the less we saw of them, and finally we realized that there were none.

In this way we were introduced to a rather different concept of space than is implied by developers' and Realtors' use of "spacious." Spaciousness to us means not only roomy in area but visually open, expansive, uncluttered, uniform in texture, low in growth, without impediment to view. To others, "spacious" is closer to the biblical paradox, "My father's house has many mansions." The diversity and complexity of vegetation creates a spacious landscape for animals by offering each kind the opportunity to earn its living in its unique way. Remove the pheasant's cover or the butterfly's flower and you have erased its space. The less variety of habitat the landscape offers, the less space there is until, when all is mowed, even an expanse the size of a golf course becomes just a hole in the world.

Suburbia has more holes already than a slice of imported Swiss, and the routes along solid ground are becoming more and more difficult for animals to negotiate. They (we, too) customarily take paths both for the efficiency that comes with familiar routes and, like pheasants under brush or us along bright streets, for safety from predators. When mother woodchucks place their children in separate dens, they visit them daily along a set itinerary. Mice and shrews take tiny paths through grass. Deer forged the trails that the Indians used and that later were often widened into roads. Certainly the pheasant family, exposed to hawks by our ignorant mowing, appreciated the "space" we created across their path about as much as I'd appreciate the space created by the Triborough Bridge's collapsing.

With animals' fear of exposure and fondness for paths in mind, we began to envision basic changes in our landscape. If ordinary garden design begins with the blank space of a lawn which is then cut here and there to create beds of taller plantings, we can aim for the obverse: a tall growth of grass, shrubs, and groves cut by mowed or mulched paths that occasionally open into clearings.

Once one begins to think in terms of paths, one realizes that they already exist, although invisibly. One doesn't walk across a lawn every which way, only in the particular ways that get one from place to place. Some of the places are spaces in the human sense of the word — open areas for sitting, eating, playing. These are the clearings. Others might be spaces in the more usual animal sense of resources that are visited regularly: garbage pail, woodpile, vegetable garden, sandbox.

It's astonishing how little land a family really uses and how much can be left as *Lebensraum* for others. Who ever uses the front yard? Who strolls along the fence? When does anybody sit in the corner of the yard?

I could have offered — indeed, I originally intended to — an illustration of a hypothetical suburban lot planted the way I envision. I was saved the trouble of having to make that drawing from scratch by a letter from a reader, Michael McKeag, who had enjoyed *My Weeds*. Not knowing I was working on this book but realizing from the first one the direction of my own gardening, Michael sent a drawing of the landscape plan for his one-eighth-acre lot on a cul-de-sac in a tract house development in Oregon, along with a plant list and a map of the neighborhood.

Ring-necked pheasant. This beautiful import from Europe and Asia is a pest in some areas where it harasses native ground birds and compromises prairie restoration.

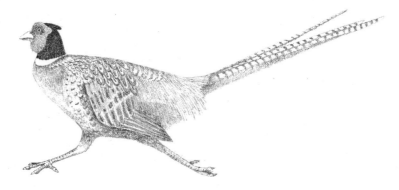

Michael McKeag's site plan for his lot in a tract development:

a. meadow: sedges, grasses, wildflowers

b. artificial pond

c. wetland for bog plants

d. hedgerow, mostly berrying species

e. corner woodland

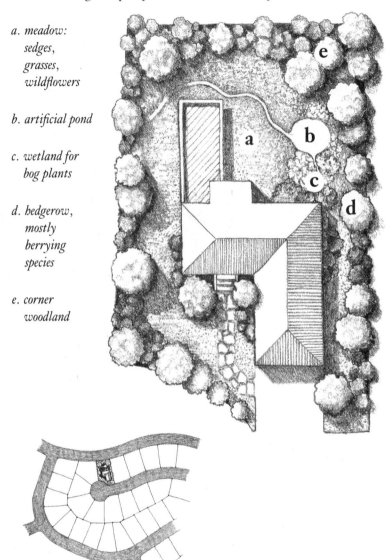

Let's fill a back corner with a grove of trees and underplant the trees with shade-loving shrubs, I had already written before Mike's letter — and there it was on his plan, the pocket woodland that almost anyone can tuck into a corner.

Let's edge the grove with berry bushes of varying heights and species, wrap this hedgerow along the back boundary, and spill it into the other corner, I had continued in that early draft. This, too, Michael's landscape architect, Gretchen Vadnais, had already done with serviceberries and currants, hawthorns and hazelnuts — good foods for songbirds and small mammals.

Let's bring the hedgerow forth into the lawn with native grasses and meadow wildflowers, I had added. Can there be such a thing as transcontinental ESP? Mike's plan showed not only grass and wildflower meadow but also one of sedges and rushes around a small pool, to one side of which was a tiny bog complete with ferns and skunk cabbage. The moist areas are fed by a stream — artificial but not less appreciated by wildlife than any bit of water — that flows below the deck from which the family surveys this mini-wilderness. The entire landscape takes up half the lot, a sixteenth of an acre, yet includes three types of ecosystem: woodland, wetland, and grassland.

Let's keep a mowed strip along the sidewalk so the neighbors won't complain, I had sagely advised, but Michael chose instead a low stone wall that, if laid up without cement, can harbor toads and ground squirrels. Footpaths don't show up at the scale of this plan, but they are there, going where the family wishes to go by the routes they wish to take.

In a later letter, Michael wrote of his hope that his yard might influence his neighbors and perhaps, through publishing the plan in this book, even homeowners on distant cul-de-sacs. I swear he had not read this chapter, which now continues in its original form.

Let's see what happens when the neighbors, curious at first — perhaps a little disapproving that someone has planted something other than lawn and yew — come to covet your woodland path, your fruit, your flowers, your birds and butterflies, and begin to follow your trendy example.

Take the rectangle of land; reproduce it twenty times; lay the reproductions out in rows; place the rows back to back. See the pattern that emerges? This pattern of small woodlots edged with thickets, connected by hedgerows, and dotted with flowering meadows is the mosaic ecosystem suburbia could piece together

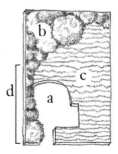

The mosaic ecosystem of future suburbia:
a. space for house and lawn or terrace
b. corner woodland
c. meadow
d. hedgerow

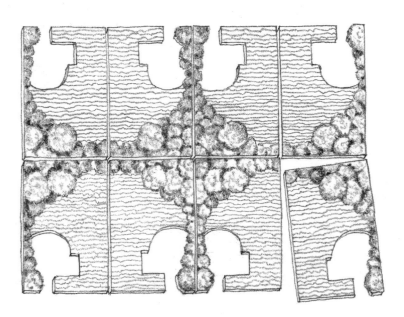

over much of America, and each neighbor who thinks your place is comely and follows your example adds another rectangle to the overall design.

Were the larger landscape of suburbia to be reshaped in this way, as much as half the acreage could be returned to its former inhabitants, and, by sticking to our narrow human paths, we could let those of other animals cross ours in safety. It took fifty years to erase what Mrs. Dana saw. Perhaps it will take another fifty years to create something again worth seeing. The ecological history of suburbia has yet to be written, and I'd like to see it unfold well and richly toward a future worthy of another Mrs. Dana to arise and rhapsodize.

4

Fruits in Their Season

IT IS NOW FALL, about midway between Halloween and Thanksgiving. The robins have assembled in flocks, their hundred eyes peeled for autumn fruits; the squirrels, intolerant of company all summer, have effected a truce of sorts on nut-strewn lawns.

And we?

In this the harvest season, in this fall fattening time, there appeared on lawns and doorsteps stuffed orange trash bags painted with jack-o'-lantern faces.

We've gone plumb crazy. Lost our gravity. Bounced clear out of time and season.

Before the frost was on the fakes, I ordered and heeled in for the winter an assortment of autumn-berrying plants to speak the meaning of fall plenty.

I used to think that the fruits and nuts now heaped enticingly in stores ripen at summer's end because that's how long it takes. Not true. Of the various trees, vines, and bushes that yield their crops in the fall, some have bloomed as early as April, some as late as August. By delaying or speeding ripening, all contrive to spill their cornucopias at once exactly when the demand is highest, when branches are lined with birds fueling for migration and dry leaves rustle with squirrels stocking up for winter. The meaning of this apparent conspiracy is that the plants' buried but uneaten nuts and spat out or defecated berry seeds will sprout next spring: for animals this is harvest time; for fall fruits and nuts it is the planting season.

Once this apple of truth hits one's head, it becomes clear that the planters and the planted have made a deal on which both rely equally; if one has lost one's berries, one is likely to lose one's robins, too.

In the true autumn spirit, I think we should therefore plant as well as feast. But to do so wisely requires choosing plants as different from the goblins and monsters now so popular at garden centers as real pumpkins are from painted trash bags. Untampered species, not showy oddities, keep robins winging into spring, sustain bumblebees through the summer, feed turkeys into fall, and bring chipmunks safely through the winter. The natural vegetation of our land that Mrs. Dana celebrated is what wheels all creatures through the year.

Gardeners are certainly aware of the march of seasons. Sequential blooming is the basis of flower border design; fruits are harvested in order, currants before blueberries, then blackberries, then grapes.* But we decide what to plant from our own point of view. A book may advise against a certain shrub because, although the berries are decorative, the display is too quickly eaten by the birds. Or a gardener may decide not to bother with August-blooming flowers because the family is off to the beach that month and would not appreciate the display. Such balloons need popping; flowers don't bloom or bushes berry for our admiration.

---

* Cultivated varieties of fruits may not ripen in this sequence; there are, for example, early varieties of blueberries as well as late ones and raspberries that produce both summer and fall crops.

From the March hellebore to the October aster, from the first strawberry to the last rose hip, each species times its bloom and fruit to the needs of those who pollinate its flowers and plant its seeds.

I'm not sure that gardeners understand the birds and the bees or the import of what they do in garden beds. Flowering plants are generally bisexual: they produce both the ovules from which their embryos will develop and the pollen grains that bear the sperm to fertilize them. Self-fertilization among plants is sometimes practiced for want of an alternative, but the resulting offspring, all alike and all burdened by a double dose of any faults their single parent might have, tend as a group not to fare as well as varied offspring enjoying the refreshing influx of novel genes from a second parent. Since plants can't move about in search of mates, most species rely on animals to pick up male pollen from the flowers of one plant and deliver it to the receptive stigmas in the flowers of another. For this service they pay a direct fee in the form of food rewards — nectar almost always, but often also a portion of their pollen. There is also overhead to pay: as in any business, indirect costs are incurred in advertising and conveniences offered to attract and keep customers. Bright pigments, for example, are an extra expense, as are the large nectar stores and extra-sturdy landing petals that bumblebees demand.

Similar deals are made to move seeds to suitable locations, or at least to disperse them away from the root zone and foliage shadow of the mother plant. A popular method is to induce an animal to eat a fruit whose seeds it will at some point distant in space and time either regurgitate because they are unpleasant or defecate because they are indigestible. Again, the plant pays for seed dispersal services in direct costs of food rewards and indirect ones of advertising and convenience.

The business analogy is appropriate. Each plant species vies with others for services, and each animal species vies with others for rewards. There are scoundrels in both kingdoms. Some plants falsely advertise, seducing a service without giving a reward; some animals are thieves, taking rewards without giving service.

Within the plant community, though, business is usually conducted by sharing resources. One flower may transact its pollinating business mostly with bumblebees, another specialize in moths. A plant may offer fruit to many kinds of seed disperser at a time of year when fruit is less a staple than a prized dessert or offer it to a more exclusive group low to the ground or high in the treetops. Or — in what one might call the holiday sale approach — many plants may offer their wares simultaneously when shoppers are particularly abundant.

As in any economy, self-interest weaves webs of interdependence. New Jersey tea, looking only to its own reproductive needs, does a brisk spring business supplying food to its tiny pollinating flies; hummingbirds, also seeing to their own affairs, feed the satisfied fly to their nestlings, which later in the summer join their parents in the sweetly rewarding task of pollinating lilies. These interdependencies are temporal. Bees and blueberries must make their pollen deals in May if robins and blueberries are to make their seed deals in July.

So one must wonder if one keeps the cupboard bare for four weeks during the season, What are the bees eating in August? How are the robins faring in that quiet month? If there are gaps in the sequence of food supply, are there not losses of pollinators and seed dispersers? And if the ranks of these crucial servants are thinned in the summer, what becomes of the plants that bloom or berry in the fall?

Like other gardeners, I had a bulging file of garden plans, but there is a Master Plan out there to which neither my drawings nor their actualities conformed. Like even the loveliest gardens illustrated in books, the original garden landscape that we produced was like a clock with just a fraction of its parts, a pretty ornament that didn't tick.

Several summers ago, visiting my son the plant molecular biologist, I ran across a slender book on biological clocks in the plant science library at Cornell. Everywhere in the library were external reminders of time and its passage: clocks, of course, and the posted hours of opening and closing, calendars of events, the day's paper, monthly journals, copyright dates, the librarian's outmoded rubber stamp. In the windowless but brightly lit and air-conditioned reading rooms there were no clues but ticks and print to time of day or year. In a corridor, a row of vending machines offered nuts, potato chips, granola bars, and apples all crazily out of season. Our human growth, ripening, and senescence are fundamentally controlled by biological clocks, and we, like other animals, are entrained by daily and seasonal light cycles, but nothing in my clockwork told me what I should be eating that July afternoon, nor could I distinguish among the available foods which were in peak nutritional condition, nor did anything within me tell me when or where or how I might harvest them were they not provided to me for a coin.

So there I sat in time limbo, munching an ancient fruit, reading about the exquisite clockworks of photosensitive cells, chemical sensors, thermometers, and rain gauges by which each species of plant and animal meteorologically coordinates its activities with the timing of other species to eat them, to employ them, or to escape their notice. Here was food for thought:

Oak looper eggs hatch exactly as the oak tree bursts its buds and complete their growth before the tree has time to choke them off with bitter tannin. The oak, however, escapes excessive damage by timing a second spurt of growth after the looper season. Birds arrive from their wintering grounds as the first insects hatch; they dine in turn on each species during its niche in time. Grapes wait out the insectivorous season until the birds, glutted on the protein they need during the breeding season, turn to carbohydrates to fatten for their fall flight.

Yet caterpillars know nothing of oak tree schedules, nor do berries know of bird departure times. These clocks run independently; each species times its seasonal strategy according to inherent, genetically set rhythms that have worked in the past and are merely coordinated by light and temperature. Throughout the past, oak trees that ripened acorns earlier in the summer lost their crop to insects or were never planted; the present oaks are therefore those whose acorns ripen after the insect season, in time for squirrels. There is a deep history behind seasonal stirrings, and each generation arises, like Rip Van Winkle from his nap, expecting to find the world still running on its schedule.

How does your garden tick?

There are yards here of nothing but cut grass and clipped conifers that are so static all year that were it not for a time-telling pumpkin bag, one wouldn't know that autumn had arrived.

The view from my attic window is now splashed with fruit: crowds of orange crabapples, tiers of crimson dogwood berries, drapes of Virginia creeper hung with sprays of blue. Opening the window, I hear the patter of falling acorns and thunks of hickory nuts. When the young plants I bought grow up a bit, there will be heaped on the platter mounds of white snowberry, bunches of purple coralberry, blue batches of viburnum, and crops of hazelnuts. Every longing glance outdoors — every pause to grope for the next word — finds a chipmunk hurrying along the garden wall and squirrels furiously digging in flower beds. Any day now, a flock of cedar waxwings will descend to strip the berries from the crabapples just below me. This fall commotion — these scurryings of squirrels and twitterings of birds among flights of painted leaves and twirling maple wings — takes me by surprise after the drowsy quietude of summer. Only the spring outbreaks of black flies and apple blossoms are so dramatic and so curiously clumped in time.

Except for black flies, "lively" doesn't describe the way the garden used to be — not in fall, not in spring, and certainly not in the lull between those raucous seasons. At the height of its cultural sophistication, when not only the pheasants but even the fireflies had deserted, the entire garden was visible from this window, a diagram of beds excised from lawn that swept boringly past the window's scope on either side. Directly ahead, a perimeter of classic garden flowers surrounded a rectangle of grass. To the right, the granite underlay of a rock garden showed through pinks and sedums. Beyond that bump, the larger outcrop that we call the mound humped like a smallish whale above the flat grass sea. Spots of color blinked on and off in these separate gardens, but there were long flowerless intervals, weeks of just plain green. There were a few trees, not many bushes. The stone boundary walls that stopped the lawn were clearly visible from my thought-provoking, plan-enhancing attic perch.

It's from this window that I first imagined bulging the formal rectangle out to one side with a group of wild blueberries — a small change, but shapely and in the right direction: into inedible lawn. From here, a stand-alone old crabapple that had escaped our saw looked lonely and out of touch with the stone wall from which chipmunks, had there not been so much open space between them and the tree, might have ventured out for apples.

Through avarice, we bought seven additional crabapples. Through accident, we bought ones with tiny fruits that birds as well as chipmunks can enjoy. Thus the three that keep the old one company; thus the four beneath my window. And thus the beginning of heaping berries against boundaries: bayberry, red and black chokeberry, alpine currant, viburnums of many sorts except those fruitless ones with sterile flowers, the snowberries and coralberries I heeled in this fall, and blueberries, of course.

Perhaps I should add more on how the gardens evolved from pheasantless to fruitful. What a hard thing to do, since it involves not just this chapter but the whole, yet-to-be-completed book! Also, I don't rightly remember. Did we plant the woodland garden of early spring ephemerals before or after I realized that honeybees are close to starving at that time of year, and that feeding early-hatching flies is critical to feeding early-arriving bluebirds? I'm pretty sure this year was the first time I observed the male bluebird, who arrives in some years as early as February, spending most of his time in the wooded wetland below the pond where carrion flies feeding on skunk cabbage nectar were the only plausible source of insect protein. Yet we had long since planted jack-in-the-pulpit, which serves a similar purpose some weeks later in the spring.

I was surprised to discover that the sour gum tree (*Nyssa sylva-*

tica) we planted to bridge a gap between the blueberries and some nearby red cedars was a berrying tree (at least if one is lucky enough to get a female of this dioecious species and if there is a male nearby). We chose it for its beauty, not its fruit. Since we call amelanchiers shadblows, not serviceberries, and planted them on the mound for ornament, not dessert, I was surprised that they fruit, too.

This summer, the fireflies returned in force. By noting where they twinkled in the greatest numbers, I discovered only then that long grass of a single species, such as the stands of switchgrass or dropseed that we planted in some areas in place of lawn, is not their habitat. And since firefly food is largely slugs and snails, those mollusks, too, must shun grass monocultures. So I can tell you neither that we planted flowery meadows where fireflies flicker in multitudes, nor islands of pure grass where they don't shine at all, with fireflies in mind. We were thinking grouse and pheasant.

What did I know, and when did I know it? Long ago, we planted in the herb garden outside the kitchen a weeping Siberian pea tree (about which Marty jokes that he put it in upside down in error) that is a far cry from anything I'd choose to plant now but that hummingbirds adore. The delight of watching a ruby-throated hummingbird dipping into yellow pea flowers as I sip my morning coffee led to my planting in the same garden a trumpet vine that hummingbirds feed from later in the summer, and to valuing plants elsewhere that I might otherwise have uprooted — common columbine on the mound, jewelweed at the pond shore, mullein in the meadow (this last a species wanted, not for its nectar, but for the leaf down with which hummingbirds line their tiny nests). We finally got around to installing New Jersey tea in newly broken ground to attract the small spring flies hummingbirds feed to their babies. But you have to understand that between pea tree and New Jersey tea, eleven years elapsed in which our raids on lawns and forays into gardens were as often fueled by plants we wanted as by plants that other animals might need.

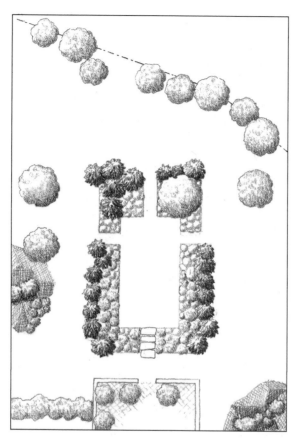

Originally, the rectangular perennial garden stood alone in a sea of lawn, isolated from the two rock gardens. The Mound, out of the picture at the upper right, was also an unincorporated island.

It's a fact that the barren diagram I used to contemplate from up here in the attic has been all but obliterated beneath a glut of vegetation that provides a continually changing menu from spring bloodroot to fall beechnut, but it's also a fact that we began to unlock the frozen mechanism of this place and allow the landscape to reel freely through the year long before my summer sojourn at Cornell. By that July three years ago, we had already let the lawn grow up with whatever wildflowers the soil harbored, had already indulged an interest in fruiting shrubs, had already planted a greater variety of trees, had begun to extend the

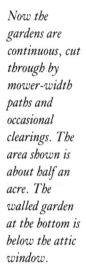

Now the gardens are continuous, cut through by mower-width paths and occasional clearings. The area shown is about half an acre. The walled garden at the bottom is below the attic window.

flowering season in damp woods and on dry banks beyond the confines of cultivated beds, and had bulged those beds and squeezed the remaining lawn between them to accommodate a still inarticulate urge to restore the land's abundance. But I don't want anyone to think that we knew what we were doing until much of it was done. The specific habitats we're now restoring — prairie meadows, brambles and thickets, pond shore and island, a reserve of native woodland species — date only from three years ago.

From the sheaves of notes and two cartons full of books that I took home from the library, I got a much clearer sense of how time passes out there in the garden below my window, how marvelously intricate the clockwork is, how various and strange the ticks and chimes gardeners are unaware of, and how many expectations we must meet. But one needn't be a clever watchmaker. One must merely supply an assortment of parts, then step out of the way as the timepiece assembles itself.

A Canada goose with injured wings was stranded here this fall. It has spent the summer here for years and is quite comfortable walking on the garden paths. But we call it the Gone Goose. Its time is almost over; it will starve to death when the grass turns brown. I see it outside the window, dragging across the lawn. Some days its flock comes by to graze during the daylight hours, leaving it behind at dusk. It won't be long before the family leaves for the winter. Quite a few apple leaves have yellowed and fallen already. The robins have finished off the dogwood berries and gone their way. A dead honeybee lies on the windowsill; it must have gotten trapped inside the house. A few crickets still creak, but slowly now, as though their mechanism had rusted. By Thanksgiving it will seem as though the clock had wound down and stopped.

But the pendulum has in fact reached the height of its swing, has stored more energy than at any other time of the year, and is poised to descend with all the gathered momentum of warm summer days downward through the cold to spring. Energy is stored in the goose that has been eating our grass all summer, in the honey the bees have stored up in their hive, in the fruit and in the sweet sap trees have stashed in their roots. We plant the grass, the flowers, the trees. We wind the clock.

Somewhere out there in the hollow of a tree is the dead honeybee's nest, the home of perhaps fifteen thousand of her sisters and holding sixty pounds of honey to sustain the family through the winter. We've provided bloodroot and bluebells to lift them up in April when they hit the bottom of the swing, and in May geraniums and apple blossoms, and fields of wildflowers that have brought them through the summer months to now, when they are at their peak of population. They're out there on this sunny afternoon harvesting our land's last blooming: wood asters that appropriate for their own noncompeting pollination this time of falling leaves.

So little is required to wind things up a bit: minutes to plant flowers, an hour to plant a tree. They tick on by themselves. Virginia bluebells are among those woodland ephemerals that arise before the trees above can grab their sunlight; their show is over so quickly here that it seems as though the clock is running *presto*. By June there's nothing left but their storage tubers underground. Months later, wood asters bloom exactly in the same place. Their flowering period is unusually long, perhaps because insects are scarce in the fall. I like to think, although I've never read it, that by inhabiting a marginal niche in time, both the earliest and the latest flowers also flummox biting caterpillars and beetles.

Black and ginger woolly bear caterpillars are finished fattening now, ready to ball themselves up for winter in the insulating leaf litter. Other moth and caterpillar larvae attach to the leaves in the fall, transform into pupae, and descend as cocoon or chrysalis with the falling foliage into winter insulation. Or the mother may lay her eggs on leaves, and the next generation overwinters in that form. Looking at the bags stuffed with leaves, one wonders how many overwintering lepidoptera are secreted there in the expectation of awakening to spring.

Everything the birds will need next year is, in one form or another, laid out on the table now, in fall: the insects that will hatch, the seeds that will germinate, the buds that will swell,

Woolly-bear caterpillar

even the dead straw and leaves that will nourish the earthworms through the winter so those departed robins will have food in the spring. To rake food off the table is to let the clock run down. This winter, doves and juncoes will scratch the beds for eggs and seeds, their version of meat and potatoes.

I can see the wood asters from here, over to the left past the oak where Marty built stone steps leading to the pond. Below the steps and extending to the water's edge is a planting that provides fruit all through the year: wild roses, raspberries, serviceberries, inkberries, strawberries, blueberries, and dogwood thrive in a setting part sunny meadow, part shady woodland edge.

Wild strawberries begin to ripen first, but teasingly. They bloom a few blossoms at a time, ripen one fruit then another, send runners looping overground, each in turn presenting here and there another tantalizing berry. Why so coy? And why are strawberries so especially delicious?

This strategy — like that of a stripteaser who prolongs the procedure — is typical of berries that ripen in the summer, when only local residents are shopping, when sated appetites are hard to pique, and when even the frugiverous robin prefers worms to fruit. What a predicament to be a luxury item, a mere sweet! All fruits have to withdraw toxins from their flesh if dispersers are to eat them, but the softer, sweeter, and juicier a ripe berry is, the shorter its shelf life. A defenseless ripe wild strawberry has just a day before it rots or is consumed by seed-destroying insects. So, each day, the plant offers to its dispersers only enough to keep them coming back for more. Foxes, possums, raccoons, chipmunks, mice, skunks, grouse, box turtles, and other omnivores learn to keep an eye on early fruits and shop for them regularly for dessert.

Plants that bear fruit in the summer generally dole their berries out as though by prior agreement, sharing the planting season so that each gets its turn and customers are fed from June through August. Each speaks to the locals who have time to learn where and when to find it. Raspberries, like strawberries, waft a fragrance. Blueberries and serviceberries speak in three colors.

Green fruits are toxic and not yet nourishing. A rosy blush signals impending ripeness (resident animals monitor blushing berries like children watch cookies browning in the oven). The blue ones say "Eat me" very clearly. We don't have to attend to these details. It's like buying groceries once and watching meals prepare themselves for years.

The summer snacks are finished now. The main course is on the table. And with what flamboyance it's been offered up! With what perfect timing!

Not only are insects scarce as the weather cools, but migrating birds, their young full-fledged and flying, need less of the proteinaceous foods fast growth requires than high-energy fuels to store as fat for fall's long journey. Points of view have changed. No longer can a bush tempt a robin hopping on the lawn by dangling a few ripe berries; the whole flock must now be halted at high speed, summoned from the sky. This is what grapes are up to when they curtain green roadsides in flashy yellow leaves; this is the ploy of the Virginia creeper, waving bright red banners from the oak tree in the garden. Vines typically color earlier than the trees they climb; they might not otherwise be noticed. One hardly sees these orange crabapples from below, sitting in the garden: from up here in the attic, their profusion of orange berries is breathtakingly arresting.

Sugary coyness is gone with the summer season. Birds want stick-to-the-ribs fruit stuffed with starch and fat — and by the platter, not the nibble. One can tell which berries are the most nourishing by noting which kinds the birds eat first as they fly through. Robins go for starchy dogwood berries first. Down in the pantry corner by the pond, less nutritious inkberries passed over by early migrants will remain available for months; they won't have to worry about slugs and rot in the winter. The least nutritious fruits hang on and on until, as a last resort, the over-wintering birds are forced to eat and plant them. That's our wild roses' stingy strategy, but the mockingbirds depend on it.

Day by day (page after page of writing!), the color of my third-floor view intensifies. The trees are breaking down the substance of their leaves, revealing pigments masked by summer's green, and storing nutrients in their roots, providing sugar (and sometimes alcoholic spirits, too!) to keep their numerous family of cells from freezing in the cold months ahead. Their buds are already set for the spring. Even now they have begun their winter countdown: monitoring day length and temperature, ticking the chemical clock. These apples out here figure spring should come after roughly a thousand hours of temperatures below 41 degrees F. Other trees use different calculations. The white oak, pattering its fattened acorns steadily through this breezy autumn afternoon, will bloom before the forest foliage impedes the wind its pollen rides.

This year is a mast year for the white oak tree. Mast, a German word, means roughly "forest food," the bulk of which is nuts. A mast year is one in which nuts are unusually plentiful, and the bonanza crop is the culmination of a prolonged game that oaks play with squirrels and chipmunks. Although oaks rely on these small hoarders to bury their acorns and, in failing to eat some, plant them, when there are many squirrels, all the cached acorns are eaten up by spring and no new oaks sprout. Oaks, however, control the squirrel population by producing acorns sparingly in most years. Then, when the squirrel population is low, comes a mast year when they produce a glut of nuts. Leftover acorns assure the continuance of oak trees and, when you come to think of it, the squirrels as well.

What if we raked up the nuts?

The wild roses we planted with the raspberries grow as a mixed bramble in a stand of switchgrass. The hip-high grass, its fine leaves delicately curled for winter, is pale tawny now, and from the haze of its delicate seed heads arch the naked rose and raspberry canes, the colors of their names. Grasses seem to me to take the long view, to get less excited than berries regarding their dispersers (the nickname "panic grass" for members of the Panicum genus refers to their seed heads' startled look rather than to haste), and certainly grass is less exhibitionistic. Sometimes the geese reach up to eat the grain (the Gone Goose is too far gone to do that). But birds are wasteful, shaking seeds loose and scattering them around. Ground-feeding birds — grouse and pheasants as well as doves and juncoes — peck around for leavings, and still enough grain remains for gleaning by ants and mice, the hoarders, buriers, and planters at this scale and level. Mice and ants will replant sunflowers in our fields and asters in our woods now that we let all the flowers go to seed.

As my view out the window has changed from one of bare lawn and raked, deadheaded beds to one of fruits, grains, nuts, and flowers freely seeding, so has my view of winter changed. Winter is at the very root of plenty, for it is that long period of cold which forces northern species to live quickly while they can — to bloom and fruit, hatch and eat, copulate and lay, breed and fatten, all in a summer's time. The meaty insects on which the birds feast here hatch with wonderful regularity and in incomparable abundance; they can do so because their food, too, leafs out in synchrony. Spring bursts in such a fit of productivity that the birds breeding here are able to raise twice the number of offspring reared by relatives in the tropics.

So let the goose rest down there in the bramble. Let it die. Winter is coming, the flock is getting fat! We're winding up, not winding down.

Thanksgiving will be here soon; Christmas will follow. I've made the apple jelly and harvested the squash in the same spirit

White-footed mouse

that squirrels have stashed their nuts and ants have dragged their grain. Our hearth is stacked with logs, our land is stocked with plants. I close my window against the frosty evening satisfied that ant, mouse, bee, bird, squirrel, bloom, and seed know well how to get from scary autumn to the next brief summer as long as we, bearing a shovel and a holly, can fill the gap-toothed faces of our land and make the seasons' smile complete.

Now, let me introduce you to my autumn cherry, *Prunus subhirtella* 'Autumnalis', best described as a missing tooth in the gears of time. I fell for it because it blooms in spring and again in fall. But the autumn blooming is of buds that were set during the summer and that in normal cherries would remain shut tight until the following spring. On this ill-timed variety, buds that bloom in fall aren't pollinated; others swell as though to bloom, only to be killed by frost; those that remain for spring are few. The bottom line is less than a handful of cherries for the birds. What a disappointment for all involved — including the sexually frustrated cherry tree.

Ill timing may not be all that ails the autumn cherry. Part of the innate scheme by which plants and animals expect their relationships to unfold at certain times of day or year are those signaling systems that verify or advertise the opportunity. Thus the pollinating skunk cabbage wafts a stinky signal to its flies, the ripe red strawberry arrests the eyes of passing mice, vines flag down early-flocking birds with red or yellow semaphores, and at nightfall the evening primrose opens petals as pale and brilliant as the moon to summon nocturnal moths. Sights, scents, even sounds — the thunk of nuts dropping in October — are the perceptual language that enables relationships among the plant and animal kingdoms.

I don't know who bred the autumn cherry or how it was done, but friends of mine who breed rhododendrons achieved a similar feat with azaleas. They started with a breeding stock of late-blooming azaleas, pollinated freely among them, harvested the resulting seeds, grew them up by thousands, waited, selected the trial plants that bloomed the latest, and continued to cross late bloomers with late bloomers until they got some that flowered weeks later than previous generations had. They then chose from the latest bloomers those of an esthetic quality that, to breeders and their customers, were worthy of a name. Unworthy individuals were culled; named individuals were reproduced in quantity by cloning.

This procedure is evolution in the fast track: it took a mere ten years. The breeders in this case were the selectors who, by giving a reproductive advantage to the individuals they preferred, guided the direction in which a lineage changed over time.

Other animals, too, have preferences. By choosing to drink from flowers that offer the greatest nectar rewards, bees increase the chance that those plants will be pollinated more often than stingier individuals, and so guide the lineage toward increased nectar production. Birds select for timely nutrition and easy harvesting, squirrels for compact packaging and keeping qualities, and every other animal for what, in its own esthetic scheme of things, bestows the equivalent of a name on those plants with which it develops a relationship. Dim recognition of this is occasionally incorporated into popular nomenclature — beebalm for *Monarda* species, bearberry for *Arctostaphylos uva-ursi*, butterfly weed for *Aesclepias tuberosa*.

In natural selection, many other forces are also at work. The plant pays a cost in energy to offer nectar, and there is a point at which the cost would be debilitating: the plant would be unable to grow sufficient foliage, manufacture sufficient chemicals to deter herbivory, or supply in its seeds enough nourishment for its embryos. Or a glut of nectar in each flower might lessen the number of flowers visited by the bees and so decrease the percentage of flowers pollinated. Climate, soil chemistry, attack by herbivores and parasites, competition from other plants, and many other subtle forces continually mold the characteristics of each lineage by favoring with a greater number of offspring those individuals best able to cope with the difficulties of living.

The simplest flower therefore holds in its genes a veritable encyclopedia of survival strategies written over a long history of encounters with its world and handed down through generations of flowers. Although the flower and its seeds arise from the same plant, selective pressures may differ radically during each stage of growth. Thus blueberries open their flowers all at once in a dramatic floral display for avid spring pollinators but serve fruit a little at a time to tempt summer-sated seed dispersers.

The plant, too, is a selector. It selects for reproductive advantage those herbivorous insects that can detoxify its poisons and so eat it with impunity, as cabbage worms can eat cabbages and increase wherever cabbages are grown. Or a plant may favor the bee whose proboscis is the most efficient length to reach its nectar store or the bird that visits it regularly through the fruiting season to eat its berries and plant its seeds. The selected in turn influence the course of each other's destiny: it is not farfetched to ask whether squirrels by planting oak seeds and birds by relieving oaks of loopers don't each help to make the other possible. One certainly can say that plant breeders tinker with rather a larger toy than they suspect when they express their preferences.

I bought a group of those late-blooming azaleas so patiently evolved through the efforts of my friends. There are questions about them that neither they nor I can answer. Are the pastel colors that are so lovely to my eyes equally attractive to their pollinators? Are the petals, seen with a bee's ultraviolet vision, marked with the nectar guides by which flowers direct insects to their reward? How much nectar does the plant produce, and at what concentration and composition of sugars, and at what time of day? What is the protein, starch, and vitamin content of the flower's pollen? How much pollen is there in each flower? Is the petal landing platform strong enough to support the harvester's weight? Is the blossom shaped for efficient harvesting? These are all factors that honeybees, an extensively studied pollinator, weigh when choosing among flowers to harvest and pollinate.

With any plant bred as an ornamental, there are many other questions one might ask. What about such traits as chemical defenses that, by their absence, might favor the reproductive

American bumblebee and honeybee. Honeybees were introduced here by settlers in the 17th century.

success of pests and diseases, or the plant's ability to form nutritional alliances with microorganisms in the soil, or the nature and quality of food rewards that might be offered to its seed dispersers? And what about the plant's behavior? I think, for example, of common violets.

These flowers are unusual because they bloom for so long — nearly three weeks apiece — and they move. They twist their petals; they lay them flat; they hang their heads; they lift them. Each position advertises the location of the flower's nectar reward to a different sort of insect arriving from below or above and provides the pollinator with the landing platform most convenient for it. In addition, the violet produces a secret flower that stays shut, digs into the ground, and fertilizes itself. Ripe seeds are propelled a modest distance from the mother plant — far enough to avoid competition, not so far that they land in unsuitable terrain. In case some better spot lies beyond ballistic range, violets induce ants to disperse their seeds by larding them with fat. Ants carry violet seeds to their nests, eat the fat as we would eat an olive, and discard the pit in the rubbish heap where, as it happens, they also dump their dung, their dead, and the rich remains of rotting meals.

How, in "improving" a violet, could a breeder monitor in all the experimental offspring the complexities of this behavioral repertoire? Plant breeders easily read the headlines of their subject's genetic encyclopedia — such blatant pronouncements as flower size and color — but can't see the fine print of subtle adaptations or the effects that alterations in the text might have on other creatures or on the whole environment. Nor can they be expected to; there is no plant in all the world that scientists can claim to have unraveled in all its multifarious connections.

Yet one is continually seduced: by fluffy peonies that can't be entered for their nectar; by plump crabapples too large for birds to swallow; by showy viburnums with sterile, fruitless blossoms; by scentless lilies that attract no moths; by red roses that look gray to bees — and by countless gorgeous misfits that, bred helpless to defend themselves against everyday environmental woes, at least save one the trouble of pulling them out by suicidally disposing of themselves.

One must battle one's own perceptions. To our human eyes, bigger fruits are better, exaggerated flowers more interesting than modest ones. I lose the battle often.

Too recently for comfort, I bought three butterfly bushes: the species, *Buddleia davidii*, whose flowers are small and pallid lavender, and two large-blossomed, well-bred selections, one a rich purple, the other a pleasing pink. Butterflies prefer the common sort. Maybe the nectar of those selected by breeders for their stunning blossoms is too thick for butterflies to suck easily through their extremely narrow straws, or maybe their smaller number of larger flowers are not as blatant an advertisement as the commoner's larger number of smaller ones, or maybe they are off-color or off-odor. Or maybe butterflies, like me, are annoyed by stalks so heavy with blossom that they can't stand up.

A few more lessons of this sort and I'm sure I'll learn once and for all to exercise good sense instead of foolish senses. If wild rose blossoms are pink, single, and bloom in June, if wild rose hips are red, small, and hang on the canes all winter, then planting large-hipped everblooming yellow doubles is bound to sabotage someone's expectations. Since a hybrid may look the part but carry hidden defects, I favor species. And since the genetic encyclopedia that plants carry was written in the historical context of their native land, I try to buy Americans.

I tell this to myself as much as to anyone. When the planting bug bites — when the supermarket puts chrysanthemums on sale, when a friend offers clumps of pachysandra, when tea roses are in bloom at garden centers, when books on English gardens catch the eye, when the latest style is an exotic grass, when Arbor Day reminds us of our environmental duties — think before scratching the planting itch.

I won't chop down my autumn cherry, but neither will I mourn it when it dies, nor will I replace it with a plant so stupid as to blossom out of season.

The reading interlude occasioned by the cartons of books I took home from the library at Cornell left me goggle-eyed and boggle-minded. I spent the following months studying awesomely complicated and almost incredible tales of how plants and animals run these entities we call ecosystems. Over the winter, I tried to translate this research into garden plans. I'll save you the time and trouble: it doesn't work.

Over the years I had developed a method of planning gardens. On a graph paper base on which I drew to scale the basic shape I wished to fill, I applied layer upon layer of tissue paper on which I drew splotches representing plants. One series of overlays might show a temporal sequence — which splotches bloomed in early spring, late spring, early summer, and so on. Another might show which areas in winter were evergreen, which deciduous, or what heights the plants would be after five years or ten. I could map the entire color scheme or stop the action at mid-May or late July to see which colors would be blooming where.

This whole scheme was, if not clever or original, at least a way to consume the obsessive restlessness gardeners feel during the drab months of winter. But to add overlays representing species pollinated by night moths or day butterflies, planted by summer generalists or fall specialists, providing leaf down for humming-bird nests or flies for hummingbird babies, is the fast route to opacity. You may read, as I have, happy lists of plants for hum-mingbirds or butterflies (and in case you haven't, I provide some in appendices), but don't take them as garden plans. Yes, eastern black swallowtail butterflies feed off *Buddleia davidii*, but eastern black swallowtail caterpillars feed off parsley, rue, and wild carrot. The larval stage of each species of metalmarks that also sip my Buddleia prefers a different food, and each of the plant species that supports caterpillars must in turn have pollinators and seed dispersers, and each of those servants must be supported by still other plants or insects day by day and week by week through the growing season. The Master Plan is too complicated for me or you — or, frankly, for the ecologists whose flashlights of observation tease me on — to write out, draw up, or even ever to comprehend fully.

But, paradoxically, the Plan may not be so hard to follow. The general outlines are before us in the woodlands, thickets, meadows, marshes, and other ecosystems still to be found, if not in our own back yards, then in nature centers, sanctuaries, and preserves. As to the bold brush strokes of the Plan, we can certainly draw up lists of plant species that grow in these habitats. As for the fine details, I think we needn't worry. This is a picture that, well started, will fill in itself.

All of us by planting anything at all have discovered, though possibly not appreciated, that our choice of plants determines the resulting community of animals. Plant a European weeping birch, and the bronze birch borer will surely follow; plant a tea rose and summon aphids; plant lawns for moles and tulip bulbs for voles; plant a vegetable patch, and see the cabbage worms, the squash beetles, the corn borers, the slugs, rots, rusts, and wilts flock into the garden.

Communities of animals attracted to natural plantings — pocket woodlands, berrying hedgerows, patches of native grass and wildflowers — also include the predators that keep the pests in check, and the plants themselves are armed with the defensive arsenals and avoidance behaviors so often lost in breeding cultivated types. Provided one plants a reasonable facsimile of a natural ecosystem — particularly with regard to a generous diversity of species adapted to the habitat — one can retire from that rank of gardeners and homeowners who, supposing that their services are the only ones that matter, work too hard, pay too much, and in return are cheated of the bounty that natural plantings offer.

I'm now three weeks into this chapter, up against its end. The cedar waxwings just arrived: 11/22, 1:46 PM, says the computer.

Cedar waxwing

5

*Who Gets to Stay
Aboard the Ark?*

A PICTURE OF Noah's ark hangs over the bed in one of our children's rooms. Noah, holding a wooden staff and accompanied by his wife (both blasphemously depicted as naked apes against the background of a town reminiscent of Jerusalem), are escorting the peaceable kingdom two by two up the ramp to safety beside the rising waters. Birds flock from the sky; mice and rats run along the ground; dogs walk with rabbits, and lions with sheep and pigs. But could one look past the door where an unidentifiable mammal, possibly a llama, is entering the hold, one would see disaster. The "balance of nature," to which all subscribe but which few support by the way they plant their grounds, is like a teeter-totter whose ups and downs are modulated by complexity of habitat. Without complexity, populations rise wildly or crash completely — that is, species become weeds or pests or they become extinct. Noah could have saved the animals only if he had rolled up the whole landscape and taken it aboard. Suburbia can save its animals by rolling a rich, new landscape over its denuded yards.

A question that has come up repeatedly is which animals I

intend to live among us. People who readily accept songbirds and butterflies and understand their need for natural habitat neverthe-less worry that bushy growth will provide breeding grounds for snakes and rodents. Thus a famous gardener cuts all her grass short to the very edges of her property to keep snakes away.

But here is the problem: that practice in one stroke wipes out not only the reptile predator but also the habitat of its mammal prey and the prey's soil excavation, seed dispersal, and insect control services, along with the owl that the famous gardener no doubt respects even as she banishes its dinner. One cannot play favorites if the land is to be shared.

Ah, I hear the din of outrage!

Have I tempted readers along this wild garden path only to let their lawns be torn by moles, their shrubbery consumed by white-tailed deer? I shall invite another sort of outrage by admit-ting that we have enclosed part of our land with electric fencing; it emits a once-per-second pulse of 5,000 volts that deer don't like a bit.

But let's put away prejudices for or against even Bambi long enough to consider what qualifies a creature as a pest.

A friend of mine, thumbing through the Yellow Pages for an exterminator to rid her home of rats in some kind manner, came upon just the thing: Humane Exterminators, Inc., a company specializing in live trapping and the release of animals into their natural habitat. However, the humane young man arrived with rat poison. There was no choice. The natural habitat of Norway rats is a human habitation.

To my mind, animals that are pests by nature are those that chew our sofas, bite into our cereal boxes, and leave their drop-pings on our floors. I'd count house mice and cockroaches as well as Norway rats among such pests, although one could make a case for puppies. We had rats ourselves once. They gnawed by night into the children's bedrooms and devoured their blankets. I call that overintimate. But such is the nature of creatures that have evolved with us within our homes.

In a rock dump on a ledge, we harbored for a while a perfectly nice wood rat family of the furry-tailed tribe also known as pack rats or trade rats. This eastern species' food is acorns, goldenrod rhizomes, catbrier tubers — not children's oatmeal, birdseed, dog chow. Its nest is sticks, not blankets. Its only incursion into human lives is its habit of exchanging a nest stick it is carrying for a more attractive object, such as a shiny key or coin. It never enters homes. (Too shy. Not interested.) If such a pleasant rat should ever rise to pesthood, the fault would not be in the beast but in its numbers.

The reproductive potential of most species is many times what is necessary to maintain their population. One wood rat couple can produce, in four litters of 4 pups per season, 16 offspring in its first year. If half of these are females, the family could theoretically number 160 in the second year, 1,280 in the third — and pack rats are sluggish reproducers compared to other rodents. Populations of even far less prolific species easily explode if not controlled by scarce resources and generous predation. Deer are an apt example.

Felix Salten wrote *Bambi* in 1928, a time when one could afford to be sentimental about what was then a vanishing species. By

*Eastern wood rat,
also known as a pack
or trade rat*

shortly into this century, white-tailed deer had been extirpated from New Jersey, Pennsylvania, lower New York, and much of Connecticut. Over their entire range, their population in 1900 was estimated to have fallen to under half a million. Although I cried to read about the death of Bambi's mother, deer hunting here had been banned for decades. In all my forays through field and forest, I never came upon an actual Bambi. Nor did my children, growing up only a few miles from my childhood home, ever see a deer outside a zoo. Therefore our first sight of a doe with twin spotted fawns browsing through a meadow here ten years ago was a thrill beyond description.

Beyond belief, now that I see them as house rats with hooves, emboldened by their numbers to eat the greenery from our very doorstep and lift their unblinking gaze to the tomatoes ripening on the kitchen windowsill. The deer population in the country as a whole has swollen to 25 million. In Westchester County, where we live, the herd is about twice the size the land can permanently support.

Some sources state that the deer population has now reached about the number that existed prior to the European settlement, but more likely it is already greater, and certainly will soon become so. Primeval forest doesn't support dense deer populations. The deeply shaded forest floor is too sparing of the forage and browse deer eat, and their number is further controlled by wolves, bears, bobcats, and mountain lions. Light woodland and woodland edges, clearings, riversides, and other openings rich in shrubs, berries, grass, and forbs support many more deer: the peak density remarked on by the New England settlers was due to the mosaic of clearings and second-growth woods created there by the Indians. In the North Woods, where the forest was not so heavily managed by the Native Americans, the deer population exploded as the logging industry got under way — and as large predators were exterminated.

The crash that followed throughout white-tailed country was caused to some extent by livestock competing for forage and by the radical clearing of the brush or woodland cover that deer seek in the daytime. Mostly, though, the deer went the way of Bambi's mother, shot by hunters.

Then, from 1940 to the early 1950s, conservationists gradually rebuilt the deer herds with remnant stock, from which our present deer are descended. By the 1960s, deer were spreading from the preservations where repopulation efforts had been focused onto abandoned farms grown back into sheltering woodland and the brushy growth that made our land so lively when we bought it. Each new residential clearing created more brushy edge against the woodland backdrop. Suburban plantings offered new variety and better nutrition: yew hedges, fruit twigs, azalea buds, daylily shoots, and fresh garden vegetables. For this particular species, suburban landscaping has greatly increased the land's carrying capacity.

The calories an animal can harvest in excess of its own expenditure is available for conversion into more animals. Deer convert nutritional profit into fawns with notable efficiency. Some 75 percent of does become pregnant in their first year. That birth may be single, but well-fed does subsequently bear twins and even triplets annually during their average ten-year life span. That's roughly twenty offspring per doe. If ten years ago we saw one doe with her doubled Bambis, it's no wonder that now city folk, looking up over our neighbor's unfenced land with eyes clouded by dusk and urban innocence, think they see a herd of cattle grazing on the hill.

Another neighbor, the one whose woods abut our narrow strip along the pond, was distressed to see a fence installed between us. She considers the woods a nature reserve where no twig should be cut, no animal excluded. That's the woodland I once thought was healthy. I see it clearer now. It *is* clearer: all the seedling trees have been bitten to the ground.

The deer of Westchester County are an infestation that has already consumed the woodland understory that would have yielded the coming generation of trees. Woodland edges can no longer support their exploding population. The deer here survive increasingly on what we grow, including those flamboyant plantings of berries, nuts, grains, and nectar flowers by which one hopes to feed so many others. The delicate nibbling of the doe and her fawns when they first appeared was a mere pruning of shrubs that grew all the bushier for an occasional trimming, but the Gang of Eight that she and her daughters eventually became wiped out our nursery of several hundred infant trees and shrubs in a single foray.

There have been other ominous repercussions. By destroying tender growth, deer destroy the foliage food of various caterpillars whose habitat is the woodland understory. With the death of caterpillars comes the demise as well of the parasitic wasps, viruses, bacteria, and fungi that prey on them. Then, every fourth year when peak populations of gypsy moth larvae defoliate the upper story of oak woodland, the pathogens that might suppress them are not available to do so.

The deer have had the opposite effect on the population of a pathogen called *Borrelia burgdorferi*, the spirochete that causes Lyme disease. The bacteria are carried by deer ticks, tiny things that are easily mistaken for specks of dirt. Although the juvenile ticks are most often found feeding on white-footed mice and other small animals, deer are the mature tick's preferred host and are the vehicle from which it distributes its eggs. Lyme disease was once a rare inflammatory illness, but with the rise in deer, the ticks they host, and the bacteria they thereby spread has come a serious epidemic. Westchester County, so close to New York City, has the densest population of deer in North America and also reports the most cases of Lyme disease. Forty-eight percent of patients have been infected in their own back yards.

But certainly I agree with my neighbor: it isn't nice, it isn't fair, and it isn't practical to fence deer out. There need only be fewer of them.

In a suburban mosaic, with small woodlots, bushy hedgerows, and meadowed clearings, a population density of perhaps fourteen deer per square mile (one deer on a little more than forty acres) could be supported — enough to enjoy but not to destroy the land. One might call this number, as was suggested in an article I read, the "cultural carrying capacity" of the land: a density tolerable to ourselves, healthy for the deer, and compatible with the ecosystem.

The same article, however, stated that to keep deer down to even their present number would require killing 40 percent of the stock each year, an unlikable and unlikely prospect.

Conservation laws and hunting customs that concern deer are very strange, anyway. In the absence of wolves and lions, humans are the only predator that could take responsibility for culling herds. But cats and canines kill the weak and the sick, while we by preference kill the very best. To our minds, the very best are male. Killing bucks, however, is an ineffective way to decrease deer herds. Whether there are ten bucks or one, all the does in the neighborhood will be impregnated. Quite naturally, a population that is mostly female produces more fawns than one in which half the deer are male, so the herd grows all the faster.

Like females of all species, does are accustomed to choosing the most impressive male of several contestants. Does choose mates as hunters choose trophies: the best buck is the one whose antlers are the most striking. Their size and number of points reveal a buck's nutritional status and age. Age, in turn, indicates the deer's survival skills. But a doe's choice results in genetic improvement to the stock, whereas our choice results in genetic deterioration. Dim-witted deer with intestinal parasites are not a worthy goal. If killing can do anything at all, it would be better left to professionals than hunters.

Professional culling is how kangaroo populations are controlled in Australia, where the national animal is as beloved as Bambi is to us. One idea posited for control in our woods and suburbs is to lure deer with corn and molasses to reservations, such as those on which they were released to multiply earlier in the century, and there thin their ranks intelligently. Our own Ward Pound Ridge Reservation is where children go to ski and sled, where families hike on the nature trails and picnic on potential killing fields. This won't do.

Nor, as the carrying capacity of the land is destroyed by over-cropping, would it be much fun to watch the deer die of starvation.

A high-tech solution now under development may soon become available: a birth control vaccine delivered to does in food or by dart injection. Attrition would be gradual, though bloodless. Professionals luring deer with syruped corn or salt licks would still be necessary. But I think the day will come.

I'll take down the fence. I'll share the land gladly. It's only a question of numbers.

The role of deer predator is an apt one for humans. We are biologically specialized for hunting game and can do it accurately and well. When it comes to the predation of small animals, we are not so well equipped. Our ears aren't attuned to grubs chewing on a root; our noses are too dull to sniff mice hiding in a hole. We're out of scale; we lack the necessary delicacy. When a mouse we have caught in a spring trap fails to die as planned, we don't even know how to dispatch it without bashing in its skull or flushing it, still kicking, down the toilet. I really hate those bug zappers that buzz and blink near swimming pools and patios, blunderbussing unnecessary holes in the nocturnal community of insects. They kill insects that navigate by celestial light or orient toward brightness, such as moths that guide their course by moonlight or search for pale blossoms blooming in the night. Mosquitoes out for blood are guided by the exhalations of their victims; they don't fly to light; they aren't electrocuted by zappers.

My advice is bats.

Also moles, lizards, snakes, toads, shrews, and spiders.

I know this sounds like the list of ingredients for something the three crones might cook up, but prejudices against these important predators are similar to those that misguide our choice of plants and should similarly be challenged by reason. Just as we have an eye for big apples, dating perhaps from our frugiverous and arboreal past, we, in common with other primates, harbor an atavistic horror of snakes. A monkey I once knew was panicked by a squiggly stick; an acquaintance became hysterical at the sight of an inchworm she mistook to be a serpent; a dear friend was nauseated at the mere mention of the S word. I suppose it doesn't help to mention that our species has grown rather large to fall prey to constrictors, that fatalities from venomous snake bites in the United States number less than one per year, and that snakes in general are shy, rare, and vanishing.

Reason does not easily prevail. A big-eyed bunny or a rotund ladybug brings out the crooning *ooh* and *aah* in us. Even though the first is a potential pest and the second a voracious predator, both look babyish. A crowned stag standing tall occasions silent awe, but a coyote's shifting gaze and skulking gait are at least contemptible.

Recall the fear elicited by the grasping hands, bared teeth, and looming posture of a witch, our mother-fearing prototype of fury. Think of bats. Think of the pouncing stance of spiders.

Don't a toad's warts look like something catching?

Unfortunately, the visual recognitions that humans use to make sense of their own world are hard-wired. Garth Williams, who illustrated E. B. White's classic *Charlotte's Web*, must have had a hard time with Charlotte. In the only two close-ups of the spider, she is shown first with two large eyes instead of eight beady ones, then in a most uncharacteristic spider pose, leaning her head on her hand in deep, heroic thought. Yet White and Williams imagined humanity into a predator without dishonoring her essential carnivory, and I think we should try to do the same.

If bats swoop toward one's head, it is one's mosquitoes they're after. One bat can eat six hundred mosquitoes in an hour; multiply that number by the hours from dusk to dawn and, for a nursery colony like the one we hope to entice into the loft in our garage, by ten to twenty hungry individuals.

Will bats nevertheless become entangled in one's hair? No; their seemingly erratic flight is extraordinarily nimble and precise, as anyone who has ever tried to escort one out the door with a broom or flyswatter will certainly attest.

Little brown bat

What about rabies?

I'll be very sober on this subject. Unless the infected person is promptly treated with a vaccine — an expensive series of injections — rabies is fatal. Usually the virus is communicated through a bite, but it can also enter through broken skin by handling a sick or dead animal. According to figures I obtained from the Centers for Disease Control in Atlanta, seven people died from rabies contracted in this country between 1981 and 1991. Five of those seven deaths were caused by handling rabid bats. The average human mortality from rabies contracted here from any mammal is therefore less than one per year; deaths caused by rabid bats are on the order of one every two years. The man I spoke with at CDC seemed rather fond of bats. He hoped I would emphasize that people should stay away from any animal that appears to be sick or behaves abnormally. The greatest danger of rabies in the Northeast at present comes from infected raccoons, which people approach to help because they look so cute. (It's not likely that raccoons got the disease from bats, for there is little communication between bats and terrestrial mammals in the United States. We don't have vampires here.)

I think we must amend our Dracular imagery. Picture a mother bat cuddling her single baby beneath her warm, enfolding wing, shifting it occasionally from one nipple to the other, nursing it through a sultry summer day on a quarter of her own weight in milk, the equivalent in human terms of fifteen quarts per day, made entirely from insects.

I wish I could (but I probably can't) make garter snakes entwined together for warmth during the winter sufficiently pathetic to earn your sympathy, or individualize the particular and long-lived black racer snake that used to sun itself daily on the elderberry bush behind the privy of my childhood and that seems to me now resurrected in the one that warms itself to action on the woodpile. Maybe I could get you to appreciate the toastiness of a basking ring-necked snake or even dare to experience the slender delicacy of its just-hatched infant twining among your fingers, no bigger than a noodle.

Or I might go, one by one, through all the predators I've mentioned to prove their value and extol their domesticity. I'm tempted to court your sympathy by reciting statistics: for short-tail shrews, twenty-five pounds of insects with a profit of thirty offspring in a one-year lifetime that, at the rate of twelve hundred heartbeats per minute, ends in what best can be described as burnout. Oh, valiant shrew!

But the total list of predators that control pest populations is very large, comprising — just for those that prey on insects, for instance, and just in North America — thirteen species of little brown bat of the genus *Myotis*, not to mention other bat genera, and seven species of moles, twenty-seven species of shrews, dozens of insectivorous snakes, almost all birds in breeding season, plus countless predatory lizards, toads, frogs, salamanders, fish, and insect-eating insects. Even foxes, which are fond of grasshoppers. All predators are admirable in their way, and each deserves more prose than I can give it.

Ring-necked snake

One still might argue that one can pick and choose among the various predators, but coverage would be compromised. No species eats the same diet, at the same time, in the same portion of the habitat as any other species. Owls and black racers both eat rodents, but owls hunt by sight, at night, and in the open, whereas racers hunt by scent, during the day, and often down into the rodent's very burrow. Foxes and coyotes eat mice, but also rabbits, and patrol a greater territory by far than do snakes or raptors. Foxes work singly, but two coyotes working as a team can take down a fawn. Should we prefer the swallow to the bat? Swallows capture flying insects through the day; bats snap up an altogether different crew that flies by night. Spiders trap night-flying insects among leaves and blades of grass. Shrews hunt insects that crawl along the ground. Moles are in a unique position to eat them underground.

Each animal plays a role for which there is no understudy, and

Least shrew

the whole witch's brew of toads, snakes, bats, shrews, and spiders is as necessary to a workable ecology as is the gracefully swooping swallow.

Let me amend that metaphor.

It suggests that an ecosystem is like a stage on which a cast of characters performs a play: for each character there is one role, for each role a singular effect upon the plot. Thus one might tolerate a mole on the stage of one's lawn for its role as a predator of turf-munching Japanese beetle grubs, but if one had no grubs, one could clear the stage and delete that subplot along with its protagonist. Rusting in our tool shed are mole traps that I thought would make a neat deletion until I learned that the very stage depends on its mole players in roles I hadn't imagined.

An excrescence of dirt hills erupted back beyond the herb garden one winter. They were presumably the work of the common eastern mole, *Scalopus aquaticus*. I think so because another of our common moles, the hairy-tailed, leaves modest heaps about six inches in diameter; these heaps were twice that size. (The name *aquaticus* was apparently suggested by the eastern mole's webbed front feet, but only the third mole found in this part of the country, the star-nosed, spends any time in the water. Our star-nosed moles live down by the pond, not in Moletown, out there on the high ground beyond the herb garden.) Over a period of weeks the town grew from three heaps to thirteen and covered an area the size of the average yard. But because I had started this book and had to demonstrate the courage of my convictions, I stayed my hand and studied up.

As it turned out, this was not a town at all but the result of one individual's ambitious excavations. Of American species, including three that inhabit the West Coast, only the star-nosed mole is known to form colonies. Others refuse to share their tunnels except for courting visits during the mating season.

Eastern moles burrow through the soil with a breaststroke powered by musculature mightier for their size than Arnold Schwarzenegger's. The record belongs to an individual that dug thirty-four yards of shallow tunnel in a day, a rate of up to five yards per hour. As it scoops dirt out of the way in front, the mole pushes its body forward while pressing the loosened soil upward with its back. This is the motion that forms those raised ridges in lawns that are a chronic nuisance to perfectionist groundskeepers, who stamp them out only to see them immediately reappear or meander off in new directions. Mole *hills*, on the other hand, are detritus thrown up from vertical tunnels; they appear only if the soil can't be compressed along the tunnel walls, as when the soil is saturated or frosty. We simply raked them out when the ground thawed in the spring.

By then my readings in mole literature had generously leavened my cultural carrying capacity. I became not only tolerant but positively proud of our moles' achievements. Each eastern mole inhabits a home area that, for this large species, may cover more than two acres. Home ranges overlap, tunnels may intersect and join, so there may be — indeed, I'm sure there is — a very extensive system under our land that has been dug by several eastern moles at least, and this upland system is no doubt joined to the lowland one communally owned and operated by the star-nosed tribe.

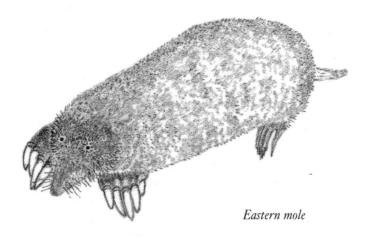

Eastern mole

Surface tunnels are the barest indication of what lies below. They are used as temporary foraging routes for the moles' chief food: earthworms and beetle grubs, sometimes slugs or snails, rarely a bite of root or bulb. A feeding tunnel may be foraged for a few days or a week, then abandoned and a new one dug. Feeding tunnels are connected by vertical shafts to a deep and permanent network of horizontal tunnels some eighteen inches below. Here moles move quickly between foraging areas, rest during the midday heat, warm up during the winter cold, and, in round rooms that hold a grassy nest, rear their annual spring litter. Generation after generation uses and elaborates this deeper system, adding to both its extent and its complexity.

Thus the stage is shaped and the plot advanced in unforeseen directions. The moles' tireless digging — day and night, in every season of the year — churns and aerates the soil, giving anchored roots the oxygen they need, providing the storm drains of an extensive flood control network much more effective than the measly pipe we buried when the house was built, and offering housing, too, for mice, voles, and shrews that would as soon profit from others' work as do their own. Who would have guessed engineering and cosmopolitan roles for moles?

If we ourselves previously played any part at all on the rooftops of Subterranea, it was as buffoons stumbling onstage with clap-traps and smoke bombs, oblivious of the deeper plot beneath our comical stampings.

The obvious solution to our mole "problem" was to replace the lawn with a meadow. I know moles live beneath our unmowed areas because their feeding tunnels cross our paths, but there could be many or few: tall grass hides evidence of their numbers.

I never was very good at numbers. I'm one of those people who shift decimal points around without noticing that anything has changed. This deficiency leaves chunks of ecology murky in my mind. If biomass is roughly equivalent to the calories it contains, and if an acre of meadow containing X kilocalories weighs Y tons, and if herbivores can harvest 10 percent of the vegetation and carnivores can harvest 10 percent of them, what poundage of predator does the meadow support?

You've got me. Don't ask me to weigh owls.

I do understand, though, the reasoning behind the formula for carrying capacity.

As much as plants are the ultimate source of all animal nutrition, they cannot be easy eating; if they were, animals would eat them up and that would be the end of both our kingdoms. It is in the interest of plants to starve, poison, elude, or in other ways to sabotage the reproductive potential of their eaters.

As vegetarians know, plants are poor in protein; for an animal to live exclusively on herbage requires that it eat in bulk. The bulk of vegetation a herbivore can harvest is limited by how much its belly can hold and how long it takes to find the food, consume it, and move it through its gut. Even the most efficient grazers and browsers pretty much have to live on their dinner plate, eating their way along like a caterpillar on a leaf or a rabbit in the lettuce, stuffing at one end and defecating at the other through most of their waking hours. Of the total harvest, much is spent in the animal's own life processes. What is left is the amount of nutrition that the animal can convert into more animals. By their nutritional stinginess, plants therefore limit the birth rate of their eaters.

Vegetarian potential is further compromised because plants protect themselves with toxic or repellent chemicals, such as the bite of mustard or the stink of citronella, and with physical defenses like prickles or fuzz. No plant is edible to everyone, and most are edible only to the select few species that have found a way around its defenses. Usually the animal can't afford more than a few of the chemical or mechanical devices it needs to enjoy a broad diet. Thus the cabbage worm, having invested in an enzyme to detoxify the acrid and evil-sounding isothyocyanate in members of the mustard family, is unlikely also to be able to disarm nightshades or milkweeds, and the deer, adept at nipping twigs, is loath to swallow holly prickles and can't gnaw bark.

Nor do plants ordinarily place themselves in a position to be easily found by those herbivores that seek them. In natural eco-systems, seeds are dispersed at sufficient random that individuals of each plant species grow in scattered patches among crowds of other species whose confusion of scents and textures provides welcome camouflage. Many plants are simply never found.

From these dining difficulties arises the stern arithmetic of calories and pounds. Because plants are hard to find and guarded by their own defenses, herbivores are unable to harvest more than a small percentage of them. Of the amount eaten, less still is digested. Of the amount digested, much is consumed by the animal's energy needs in the course of daily living. The result is that the total mass of rodents, insects, and other plant eaters in an ecosystem is typically a tenth of the mass of vegetation.

The vegetarian that nevertheless manages to make babies out of cabbage leaves thereby makes meals for predators. But here again, prey animals are protected by various defenses, are not altogether digestible, and are as hard to find as the plants they feed on. The poundage of predators in an ecosystem is typically one tenth that of the prey. Since predators must usually be larger than their prey to overpower them, their total mass is divided among many fewer individuals. Predators in any ecosystem are therefore generally as scarce as owls in suburbia.

But are there any owls at all?

Until his retirement some years ago, William the cat was a proficient hunter whose regular doorstep deliveries allowed us to keep a rough inventory of small mammals. According to this informal census, the unmowed ex-pasture that we bought supported the three species of moles, two of mice, two of shrews, and one each of vole and wood rat, all in sufficient number to feed William several meals a week — and also, I presume, feed the black racer that still lives in the woodpile and the owl that we used to hear in the night.

As we extended the lawn, the count went down and the owl went AWOL. From this I learned that shrinking the base of vegetation that supports the mass of animals not only decreases prey but may cut predators out of the system altogether. Then,

Meadow vole

regardless of the less weighty base, rodents can multiply to the limit of the remaining resources, and the famous gardener who mowed the grass to foil the snakes may come to regret the voles that eat her tulips.

According to *Walker's Mammals of the World,** the population density of the common meadow vole in old-field habitat fluctuates between a low of fifteen or so per acre to a peak of more than five hundred. The book doesn't say how rapid these fluctuations are. I can only judge from rabbits, which are abroad by day and large enough to notice. An eastern cottontail rabbit can produce a couple of dozen offspring in a season, and I think ours has twice in the last decade come close to that. The first time, a large hawk arrived on Christmas morning, stayed around 'til Easter, and ate the excess. The second time was last summer, when William came briefly out of retirement and, forming an unlikely team with Molly, the mini-bulldog, captured fifteen baby bunnies for his partner to dispatch. Thus, once predators have found them, bunny booms are reliably followed by bunny busts.

One can't stop voles or rabbits from breeding, so one can't avoid cycles of increase. What one wants, though, is to keep the upswing of each rise below pest level.

---

* Originally published as *Mammals of the World*, by Ernest P. Walker, but the greatly expanded fourth edition of 1983, published fourteen years after Walker's death, was retitled in his honor.

Here the formulaic model of ratios among herbage, herbivore, and predator is not helpful, for it is less quantity than quality of vegetation that controls the population fluctuations. In a simple landscape where prey is plentiful, evenly distributed, and easily found — grain fields, for example — predators will at first multiply rapidly on their profits, but when prey becomes scarce, the local predator population will crash to zero and the number of prey will rise wildly. The vole population on agricultural land can soar to more than *three thousand* per acre in the time it takes for predators to recover from a crash. Counterintuitive as it may seem, prey must be protected from overpredation if predators are to keep them from becoming pests. One must, in other words, give refuge. For this one needs a patchwork landscape of sufficient complexity that a suitable habitat is hard to find, but so is the prey that finds it.

In a patchwork landscape, herb and herbivore, prey and predator, play a continual game of hide and seek that keeps the seesaw gently teetering. Herbivores that find a patch to eat multiply and in turn are found by predators that, now also multiplying, spread out to search again. The surviving prey that find another hidden patch themselves remain hidden long enough to recover their numbers. Then they are found. And the game starts up again among the refugees.

Translated into voles, the game goes this way. A young vole setting off to find itself a living space comes upon a seed-rich meadow, where it rapidly multiplies. A hunting vixen eventually finds the meadow full of rodents and turns a profit in kits. Those prey that escape the vixen's appetite meanwhile search out other meadowed patches, and the young foxes spread out to search for them. By the time the refugees are found, they have replenished their number and a fox or so has died. Yet there remain enough of both that foxes still are fed and voles still are checked.

This small-scale cycle of boom, bust, and start all over again is the general dynamic of animal populations in natural ecosystems. The more varied the habitats and the more cryptic the pattern of their distribution, the steadier is the supply of prey and the more reliable its control.

By "natural ecosystem," however, ecologists mean something much more extensive than a yard measuring 50 by 100.

I wasn't able to discover in my favorite two-volume mammal source how large an area our eastern species of wood rat, *Neotoma floridana* (not of the genus *Rattus*, you'll notice), requires for its support, but my county agent found a population figure of two or three per acre, and a similar western pack rat species needs a home range of well over 500 square yards per individual. At such densities, one wouldn't expect to stumble on a wood rat often; we found our resident family when we cleared the rock dump in which the mother rat had found temporary refuge from the likes of Molly, who promptly ate her babies.

The refugee mother was then forced to seek another patch of habitat: a rock nook or cranny within foraging distance of her preferred diet. Possibly accommodations were available within the limits of our land, but possibly they weren't. What if our metes and bounds were actually to describe an ark containing the only suitable habitat in a suburban sea of lawn and asphalt?

Predators generally require very large areas. A fox can seldom support itself on less than 5 square miles. Coyotes average something like three tenths of an animal per square kilometer, which in my shaky arithmetic I take to be one coyote per 8.6 square miles, or a total of two and a half coyotes for a town covering 23 square miles, the size of Pound Ridge. Even the wild cat species from which William is descended hunts over a range of at least 125 acres.

Such large hunting grounds are necessary, not only because clumps of prey are widely separated, but because rodent fodder is also sought by hawks, owls, snakes, weasels, skunks, raccoons, and possums. Each of these also eats other items. Raccoons enjoy grapes and persimmons, corn and acorns, muskrats and rabbits, all large insects, and eggs of every sort. Both possums and rac-

William.
Cats are the primary predators of birds and small mammals in suburbia.

coons are nuisances with garbage; on the other hand, both are
prey to foxes. Owls raid the nests of insect-eating swallows.
There are snakes that eat frogs, snakes that eat slugs and beetles,
and even snakes that eat snakes. Our first view of the hawk that
arrived on Christmas morning was a close-up as it plummeted
toward William, then a tasty kitten. Everybody's got to eat something.

Textbooks, in fact, often illustrate the balance of nature dia-
grammatically as a web of eating relationships among animals and
plants. The metaphor has merit: one can imagine that any strand
loosened or tautened distorts the pattern, lessening tension on
some species, increasing it on others. The web is strong when
there are many strands and their ties accordingly complex; break
too many strands and it collapses.

The base of such a diagram is the vegetation to which all the
strands are tied through the animals that eat it. In my botany
textbook, the base is sketched as a bit of meadow; in reality, it is
the entire landscape — not only my part of it, but yours and
everyone's whose claim to ownership confers on us all the opportunity and responsibility to plant it richly. We are all connected.
A hawk may eat a snake that ate a mouse that ate a nut for
breakfast, but the beech nut may have come from your tree, the
mouse from my field, the snake from our shared wall, the hawk

from a hundred miles north, and all of them must be supported on a varied and extensive smorgasbord.

We don't have to — indeed, we neither can nor should — each provide all habitats, every sort of food. You plant nut trees and I'll plant spruce, you keep a berry thicket and I'll do the tall grass, or the bog, the woodlot, the crowds of fruiting shrubs and beds of wildflowers. But let us weave them together into something big enough to matter by connecting each patch with others at the corners and along the boundaries. This is the rich, new landscape; this is the new kind of gardener who asks not whether he should plant this ornament or another but which patch is missing from his community, how he can provide it, and how animals will move from his patch to the next.

This is the ark.

Look for Charlotte's orb web in the tall grass at dawn (her need to conserve protein is so great that she will shortly eat it and not spin a new web until nightfall). Play with it a bit; tug it here; snip it there. Picture the ark of our ecosystem as gossamer. Realize that its many strands will have to be flung wide over lots, tracts, neighborhoods, and towns if it is to hold us all and that we must try to construct this ecosystem without prejudice or fear, knowing that the passengers can be trusted to crop one another to neighborly proportions.

6

The Aphid on the Rose

I HAVE BEFORE ME two items that arrived in yesterday's mail.

One is an offering from a tree company to spray in May "all oak, maple and other appropriate trees and shrubs on landscaped area of property to help suppress gypsy moth and other leaf chewing caterpillars" and to spray in June and again in July "all oak, maple, spruce, pine and other appropriate trees and shrubs on landscaped area of property to help suppress mites, scale, aphids and adelgids."

The other is a catalog that offers, among other environmentally correct products, green lacewings, ladybug beetles, spined soldier bugs, praying mantises, parasitic nematodes, and three species of parasitic wasps of the genus *Trichogamma*.

The choice of how to spend my money is simple. Naturally, one wants to buy nature's solution. But something bothers me.

Can one buy nature? Why is it for sale? There is something about purchasing ladybugs by the can that makes me morally uneasy. It reminds me of where we Americans have come from: land that our fathers bought, land of commodities, where for every problem a solution is for sale.

For all our hopes of biological control, it is not for sale, and it is not for sale because it is not that simple.

In 1981, the year from which we date the formal launching of our gardening odyssey, gypsy moths devoured 13 million acres of deciduous woodland over twelve states. They ate our old oak. They ate our new wisterias. They crawled over our white stucco house in hairy hordes, repulsive and uncountable, distended to sausage size by 40 square inches of leaves apiece. We, like our neighbors, sprayed hysterically. There was talk of hiring airplanes to attack from the sky.

Gypsy moths have never since returned in such numbers, but it is not because of that summer's pesticide panic.

Like many of our most troublesome insect pests, gypsy moths were imported into this country without the poisons, predators, parasites, and diseases that controlled their population in their native land. This species was brought in from Europe in 1869 in an effort to produce, by crossing it with silkworms, a hardy, silk-spinning hybrid. Almost immediately, the moths escaped from the lab when a cage was knocked over; their progeny spread rapidly through oak woodland.

Biocontrol attempts began in 1910 in the Boston area with the release of a fungus called *Entomophaga maimaiga*, which more or less means "insect-eater of gypsy moths." It was known to infect a closely related species in Japan. However, our gypsy moth population continued to spread unchecked, and *E. maimaiga* was ultimately presumed to have become extinct.

From the 1940s on, synthetic insecticides were used, but to little effect and, after the publication of Rachel Carson's consciousness-raising *Silent Spring* in 1962, to loud outcry from the environmentally aroused. At last a biological control appeared in the form of the bacterium *Bacillus thuringiensis*, Bt for short. Bt is not persistent in the environment (its half-life is 36 hours). It is not toxic to mammals, birds, reptiles, amphibians, fish, earthworms, and many kinds of insects. Although Bt had been used by some farmers for pest control since the 1950s, its commercial debut among homeowners dates from about the time of the gypsy moth pandemic. It seemed that a consumer shift from "chemical" to "biological" might explain the pest's subsequent decline. It doesn't.

How can I say this strongly enough? There is no elixir. There is no panacea. There is no substance of any sort that ever has controlled any pest population all by itself.

What happened was this. The woodland didn't offer enough food to nourish the number of larvae hatching the spring after the pandemic. Oaks, whose foliage is preferred by gypsy moths, had been provoked to intense toxicity by the previous year's defoliation. For both these reasons, 1982's crop of larvae suffered malnutrition, stunted growth, and vulnerability to disease, so the population abruptly crashed. That was normal. It takes four years for gypsy moths to reach a population peak, and each peak is followed by a fall.

The higher the rise, the harder the fall, so the next peak, in 1985, was less spectacular than the one four years earlier. Meanwhile, public sentiment against massive spraying had moderated pesticide responses. There was therefore a larger reservoir of other caterpillar species and a consequently larger reservoir of caterpillar pathogens — among them a virus transmitted both through infection and genetically from one generation to the next, and *Entomophaga maimaiga*, the presumably extinct fungus. The summer of 1989 saw an infestation of gypsy moth caterpillars that grew to half-size, stopped moving, shriveled up, and died.

The resurrection of *Entomophaga maimaiga* had been a matter of time: it needed nearly eight decades to evolve adequate adaptations to this climate. Ecologists now believe that the slowness of other diseases to exercise control was a result of wanton spraying that, by killing a broad spectrum of host populations, narrowed the spectrum of controlling pathogens. Spraying was the problem, not the cure.

Bt is a spray made up of *Bacillus thuringiensis* spores, the encapsulated form in which bacteria survive in a dormant state when environmental conditions are hostile. The spores contain toxins that are "selectively" lethal to flies, beetles, moths, and butter-flies. In other words, Bt is not quite as selective as was thought by homeowners who, breathing a sigh of virtuous relief and believing they were targeting only the enemy, switched to this "natural" product to kill gypsy moths.

Although Bt is natural in that it has a biological origin, it's questionable whether spraying is a natural use of it. It is not an infectious organism, not a caterpillar disease. It is a soil organism, a decayer, that has no known relationships with insects. When the bacterium sporulates, the cell divides into two parts: a small capsule containing its genetic material and a minimal life-support system, and proteins extruded from the cell and attached to it as crystals. Spores and crystals, cajoled from the bacterium under arduous laboratory conditions, constitute the ingredients of sprays.

When an insect swallows these — and if its gut fluid has a pH of exactly 8.5 — the protein crystals dissolve and are fragmented by the insect's protein-digesting enzymes. By happenstance, one fraction of the protein binds to a receptor on gut cells and there forms a pore through which the gut leaks the insect to death.

Devilish.

But, one must ask, is the meeting of a soil spore with a gypsy moth caterpillar on an oak leaf natural? And is the death itself — a case of mistaken identity, a protein fragment grasped in good faith because it is similar to one that gut cells ordinarily welcome — a natural event? Researchers still have no notion of what Bt crystals are intended for in nature.

Bacteria come in thousands of strains whose protein products differ in kind, quantity, and proportion. By selecting among the strains in the same way that a plant breeder selects plants, bio-technologists have created Bt sprays that are not only more toxic than the original product but more effective against one sort of insect than another. Thus the "B safe, B sensible: Bt" spread in my biosafe catalog offers Bt/berliner kurstake for caterpillars, Bt/-san diego for potato beetles, Bt/israelensis for mosquito larvae, and Bt/H-14 for fungus gnats. Searches are presently under way for strains whose toxins dissolve at other pH values so that insects of differing gut acidity or alkalinity could be targeted. Some progress has been made in producing longer-lasting sprays. Selection, though, is a two-way street. The more lethal a toxin, the greater is the pressure on the organism it poisons to evolve resistance to it. In any large insect population, there are usually a few individuals resistant to a given poison. If the poison is only moderately effective, there are enough survivors of nonresistant types that resistance remains a rare trait in the population. But if the poison is lethal to all nonresistant types, then only resistant types survive. In that location, the breeding population becomes 100 percent resistant. The more widespread the spraying, the longer the spray persists in the environment, and the more it is used as the exclusive control, the fewer nonresistant individuals escape and the faster they are replaced by a resistant population. This is happening now with the diamondback moth, an agricultural pest. In some locations, a full half of the diamondback population is no longer affected by Bt.

Monsanto has announced plans to introduce within the next few years a transgenic cotton plant that will carry genes for Bt toxins either in its own cells or in those of its symbiotic bacteria. It will be followed by transgenic potatoes and other crops. At first thought this sounds, if not natural, at least a good imitation of nature, for don't plants ordinarily produce their own insecticides?

Yes, but not all the time in all tissues and all parts. Economy requires that plants manufacture costly products as needed: in response to injury, at the time of greatest vulnerability, or in that part most likely to be attacked. Since plants normally reproduce sexually, each individual differs somewhat as to timing and toxicity; individual insects also differ somewhat in their schedules and their talents. It is this genetic sloppiness of both pest and host that prevents either from becoming 100 percent effective against the other. Biotechnologists so far lack the finesse to mimic nature's wisely bumbled balance.

In the meantime, transgenic cotton and potatoes will be *too* effective: they will kill all nonresistant pests, leaving the resistant ones to multiply unchecked. The probable solution is that transgenic Bt crops will have to be planted alongside ordinary varieties to give refuge to nonresistant pest populations.

Sounds familiar, doesn't it? One mustn't kill all one's bugs. One must give refuge.

It is a quirk of the human mind to wish meaning into words that don't really say what one hopes they do. Thus when the tree company promises to "suppress gypsy moth and other leaf-chewing caterpillars," one wishes it means that only certain chewers — the unwelcome ones — will be suppressed.

All caterpillars chew leaves. All caterpillars grow up to be moths or butterflies. The words really mean that the spray will suppress, if one is lucky enough to have them on the premises, luna moths and sphinxes, metalmarks, fritillaries, cloudywings, and commas.

Luna moth,
now a rare species

One also tends to hope that what is unsaid is of no consequence. The tree company fails to mention that the active ingredients in synthetic insecticides are nerve poisons that do not distinguish among insects and spiders in the trees being sprayed, on the ground below, in the air around, and wherever the wind is drifting at the time.

How should one read the biosafe catalog?

Turn to sprays. A "dormant oil" — so called because it is sprayed on trees before the buds break in spring — is a biodegradable product containing no strong chemicals and recommended for killing scale, mites, thrips, mealybugs, whiteflies, and aphids as well as eggs of codling moths, oriental fruit moths, and cankerworms. But with no strong chemicals, how does it work? Dormant oil coats and smothers soft-bodied insects and the eggs of leaf-chewing caterpillars — and all other insect eggs whose hatching the insectivorous bluebird so eagerly awaits.

Natural plant products are environmentally safe — they decompose readily and therefore don't build up to toxic levels in soil or groundwater — but they, too, are nonspecific. Why wouldn't poisonous rotenone, a natural plant product, kill ladybug beetles as easily as Colorado potato beetles, or sabadilla dust wipe out "good" spined soldier bugs along with "bad" harlequin cabbage bugs? I looked up rotenone in the dictionary. "Of low toxicity to warm-blooded animals," it said. Good. We, mice, and birds have naught to fear. "A fish poison," it continued. Watch out, you cold-blooded snakes, frogs, toads, salamanders, and lizards!

Turn the page to traps. Can it really be that a yellow sticky trap lures pesky whiteflies, black flies, aphids, leafhoppers, moths, and gnats while "beneficial insects are not attracted"? Don't beneficial insects like the color yellow? Yellow, an entomologist explained to me, attracts those herbivorous insects that have learned in the course of evolution that yellowed plants are under stress and are therefore less able to defend themselves than healthy green ones. There's some legitimacy there. But black flies and gnats are like mosquitoes — out for blood, not color. I don't know of any adult moth that chews up leaves, and I can't see why a mother looking for a host plant in which to lay her eggs would prefer a dying one. Of the many moths and flies that may blunder into these traps, who is to say which is a pest and which a necessary pollinator?

The only specific traps are those for pests that, each lured by its own sex pheromone wafting through the air, fly passionately toward death. I tried the Japanese beetle version. Sure enough, it trapped beetles — but who were all those other guys that made straight for the grapevine?

The other guys were gals.

Some sophisticated trickery has gone into these traps, though. They're yellow. Their scent is compounded with floral fragrances as well as pheromones and so attract some females along with reckless males. The trap's design — an arrangement of vertical fins above the scented pit — takes advantage of a Japanese beetle's defensive maneuver, which is to tumble when touched: they hit, they drop, they're trapped. But even catalogs whose honesty is thin admit that the specific pheromone may bring Japanese beetles into one's garden from the whole neighborhood. The solution to that problem (I bet you've guessed it already) is to buy more traps.

(Marty just suggested another solution: put the trap on your neighbor's land.)

Surely, though, predators are the answer. What could be more natural, more ecologically correct?

Let's say I have cabbage worms on my broccoli and aphids on my rose and hope to control the two of them, respectively, with spined soldier bugs and ladybug beetles. I release three hundred bugs and a pint of beetles in the garden. Hurrah! It works! While the beetles munch on aphids, the bugs spear the caterpillars and, to the delight of all, suck them dry. Definitely, these good guys of the insect world are worth their price.

But what is this? Do I spy a soldier now dining on a ladybug? I might also point out among the carrots a ladybug chewing up black swallowtail butterfly eggs. Perhaps a praying mantis would have more discriminating taste. But no, it captures the mother

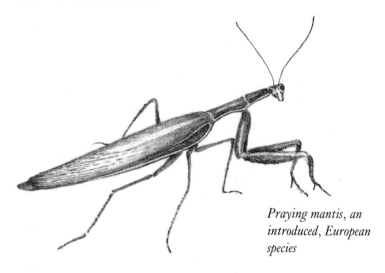

*Praying mantis, an
introduced, European
species*

butterfly herself. Never fear, though. This won't last long: once
the prey is eaten, the predators will die.

That's why, in spare suburbia, one has to buy praying mantises in the first place. That's why the catalog will offer them
again next year.

Every organism earns its living as best it can, and if we insist on
seeing in the resulting conflicts or convergences of interest friend
and foe, villain and victim, then we will continue to waste our
money on simple-minded nostrums that are both inelegant and
ineffective in systems that work only through complexity. This I
learned from aphids.

The waterside community where the star-nosed moles live is
now a wetland meadow where their winter heaps are no longer
visible. The planting includes, among many other species,
swamp milkweed. This milkweed occasioned my earliest wildflower delight, for just as the first buds opened there arrived a
monarch butterfly to drink and pollinate. There also arrived —
just as quickly and to every milkweed that we'd planted —
aphids as orange as the butterfly. They soon by their prolific

multiplication covered the succulent end of each flowering stem completely.

I was alarmed, as would be any reader of gardening books: aphids are the enemy.

But imagine me, in the grip of conversion, reading the radical literature of ecology. The aphid literature happens to be enormous for the crass reason that grants are given most generously for the study of the most damaging species, and aphids undeniably do damage. Here is a sample of the intellectually challenging and morally transcendent info I gathered.

Aphids are polymorphous, polyphagous, viviparous, parthenogenetic parasites of plants. Polymorphous means that different generations have different body shapes — in aphids so much so that summer colonies and their fall descendants have been mistaken for separate species. Polyphagous means that they eat more than one kind of plant. Viviparous means that they give birth to living young. Parthenogenetic means that they do so without fertilization.

Already one is in deeper than a mole.

Only the founding parent on an aphid's spring host plant has hatched from a fertilized egg in the ordinary insect way, and she is always female. Her own eggs develop into female embryos inside her and, like nested Matriushka, they contain still smaller embryos inside them. Daughters are born one by one, head first, as miniature adults pregnant with their mother's granddaughters.

These first several generations are wingless. Winged forms are born as the host plant can no longer support the growing colony. These winged aphids fly off to find a second plant species on which each will found a new colony — again born wingless and fatherless. (I judge by their time of arrival that the orange aphids on our milkweeds were this second crew.) As summer wanes, another generation of winged aphids journeys back to the original host plant species, there to give birth to males and females that will lay overwintering eggs.

Moves between host species are occasioned by incipient malnutrition. The nitrogen for protein manufacture is highest during a plant's active growth, lowest when leaves are fully mature, and rises briefly again during senescence, when leaf tissues are being broken down in preparation for dormancy. A usual pattern for aphids is to suck from a woody species while the shoots are growing, then to move on to a herbaceous species that continues to grow through midsummer, then back to the original woody host as it begins its autumn preparations. Telescoped generations and a two-host strategy allow a single founding mother to multiply to thousands.

Yet so poor is the nitrogen content of plants that aphids must process great amounts of sap to support their growth and reproduction. I didn't find an exact figure for aphids, but similar-size spittle bugs sometimes have to suck a thousand times their weight in sap per day. To avoid bursting, aphids exude excess sugar water in droplets at their rear, and this "honeydew" is enjoyed by the ants that shepherd aphid flocks. The ants milk their aphids of honeydew by caressing their behinds while guarding them from predatory insects. Shepherded aphids multiply more successfully than unprotected flocks.

Are ants therefore not parasite abettors?

But, since ants themselves are predators, they attack marauding caterpillars and leaf-chewing beetles, too. So are they not, in their carnivory, plant protectors?

Yet, were aphids not to tempt them up the stem with honeydew, would ants be on pest patrol?

The going gets rougher. In a similar accident of indiscriminate behavior, ants protect certain species of wasps that parasitize their charges. These minute wasps zip in fast and lay an egg inside each aphid. The larva eats its host's innards, then pupates into an adult wasp inside the empty aphid skin: a wolf in sheep's clothing, guarded by ant shepherds.

Things begin to seem decidedly untidy.

The relationship between milkweed and monarch butterfly is classic, the textbook model of mutualism. The caterpillar, immune to the leaves' poisoned sap, becomes poisonous to its predators. In return for that protection, the butterfly pollinates the flower. What, though, was the relationship between our orange aphids and the milkweed that they sucked? Maybe the milkweed was protecting its aphids with its nauseating poison, for neither ant nor any other predator arrived to milk or eat them. But I doubt that the milkweeds meant to be so kind to parasites. I doubt that milkweeds mean anything at all.

Here is the lesson that I learned.

Value judgments are out of place in nature, where the appearance of cooperation is as deceptive as the appearance of criminality, and ant shepherds eat their flocks when meat is scarce.

Of the approximately 1.4 million known species of organisms, 750,000 are insects. However, the total number of insect species, those named and those yet to be discovered, is estimated to be 30 million. Of very small or microscopic noninsect species that infect plants, parasitize insects, or in other ways mediate the relationships among them, authorities hardly dare venture a guess. Only 4,000 species of bacteria have so far been named. Nematode worms, fungi, and mites have barely been investigated; the species of each could number in the millions.

Therefore a catalog offering one bacterial toxin, one protozoan that infects grasshoppers, one fungus that preys on Japanese beetle grubs, one nematode that sickens beetle larvae, and seven parasitic or predatory insects isn't offering much. Yet reading the fine print suggests that even this simple offering is more complicated than one supposes.

The nematode worms arrive infected with a bacterium that does their killing for them. If nematodes are the problem rather than a solution, one can also buy food containing chitin to boost the population of soil microorganisms that infect the worms. (Why might one's soil be deficient in this nutritious chitin? Chitin is the stiffening ingredient in insect exoskeletons and fungi. Could it be one needs more molds and bugs?) The antinematode concoction is not advisable near fruit trees. Perhaps nematodes are needed by one's fruit.

Application, too, is complicated. With the strain of Bt that best controls European corn borers, one is advised to place a few granules by hand in each whorl of corn silk before the insects have moved inside the ear — which, my county agent advises, is just as the tassels emerge. He adds that it is an operation that must be repeated for every ear of corn every four to five days thereafter. Each of the six traps necessary to control apple maggots in an apple tree must be coated with sticky stuff (sold separately: apply with spatula or putty knife) and hung alongside a scented lure (also sold separately: keeps indefinitely if refrigerated). As an experienced and discriminating collector of such gardening arcana, my prize goes to the instructions for distributing a syrup that, if there are not enough pests to keep one's ladybugs and lacewings from starvation, one can feed to these admirable predators. Mix the stuff, the copy says, as thick as molasses. Put droplets on the foliage.

I turned my back on traditional gardening because of just such unreasonable demands, and I'm not about to goo up for biocontrol if that's really what it takes.

I think, though, that what it really takes is what I went for in the first place: planting plants.

Each "natural" pesticide derived from a plant is only a fraction of what a plant actually produces. Raw plant juices contain fungicides, bactericides, miticides, and vermicides; a mix of poisons effective against a broad spectrum of herbivores; and a miscellany of repellents, antiappetents, or even the plant's own synthetic version of insect pheromones, hormones, and neurotransmitters. This stuff doesn't come in cans. It comes in plants, attractively packaged, environmentally safe, self-dispensing, and in as many formulas as there are plant species.

For any pesticide, whether extracted from petroleum or plants, the timing of application is critical. Wait to spray gypsy moth caterpillars until they're sausage-size and you've waited too long. Usually, as with the tree company's offer or instructions on product labels, a spraying schedule is necessary — or, rather, as many different schedules as there are types of infestation. This timing, though, is about as numb to reality as was the ticking clock in the aseasonal library at Cornell.

One is not in direct communication with insects as are plants with the pests that eat them. That old white oak down there knows when it is bitten: injuries have chemical effects. And chemical results. A bitten oak, stirred to action by a factor in insect spittle, steps up its production of toxic tannins when it is attacked and withdraws nutrients from its leaves. Its defense is responsive to degree of injury: the greater the severity of the attack, the greater the ferocity of the defense. After a really rough battle with chewers, oaks adjust their timing for the long haul, as when they leaf out more poisonously in the spring following a gypsy moth attack.

Imagine a spray pack with a memory.

Maple trees play a sort of shell game: some leaves are good to eat, others are not. Their herbivores are forced to inch or flit from leaf to leaf — and expose themselves to predators. Alders alarm one another: an attacked individual gases the news through the grove, and the other alders arm themselves against the enemy. To us, the scent of an orange is an ad to eat it, but to herbivores that would attack the orange skin, the odor is like a skull and crossbones. If the glands that hold the orange oil are broken, the oil vaporizes into a deadly insecticidal gas. Insects read the lovely fragrances of citron, tea, chocolate, sage, bay, balsam, mint, cedar, eucalyptus, and sassafras as the opposite: warnings of worse to come if they should try to eat it.

Imagine a sprayer with foresight; a cautionary label readable to moths.

Every plant, however, has its herbivores — those few species that can tolerate its poison. To those species, the scent is appetizing and the taste is good. Black swallowtail larvae can eat rue, whose scent I find obnoxious and whose appalling bitterness lingers in the mouth and memory. They also can eat members of the parsley family such as water hemlock, whose nerve poison is among the deadliest known, and poison hemlock, famous for the

*Nine-spotted
ladybug beetle*

potion that killed Socrates. The Colorado potato beetle withstands nightshades, a plant family that manufactures a variety of
poisons from atropine to nicotine. The acrid sap that monarch
butterflies, milkweed bugs, and orange aphids enjoy is an alkaloid
used in former times to burn off warts.

It is also true that what an insect *can* eat is what it *must* eat.
Therefore planting an aphid's or a butterfly's host plants will
summon it from the sky. Gardeners may shudder to think of
advertising for aphids, but the necessity is inescapable and, in
natural plantings, the increase in sucking insects is hardly notice-
able. Unlike a bed of infested roses, where every plant crawls
with pests and every shoot wilts from their attack, in a natural
planting only a small percentage of individuals are infected, and
they cope so well that one notices nothing amiss. One can't, in
any case, advertise only for those insects one happens to admire.

The greater the number of plant species one grows, the greater
the number of herbivorous insect species one supports and the
more reliable the population of pathogens and predatory insects
that control them. Only the scale is different from the game of
fox and voles, for "habitat" in the case of a chewing or sucking
insect is its host plant — its goldenrod, milkweed, willow, or
birch.

So let us plant a meadow, a hedgerow, a sufficiency and variety
of food. Let there proliferate the soft eggs and squishy bodies that
are the lady beetle's meat.

Now, bring on the predators.

Green apple aphid
and child

The ladybugs one buys are adults, no longer growing and no longer eating much. Aphid control is exercised by ladybug larvae, which eat voraciously to support their rapid growth. In her wisdom, the female will not lay her eggs on a plant unless it is heavily infested with aphids, other soft-bodied insects, or their eggs: her larvae will have no other source of food until, as winged adults, they can seek another infested plant. Therefore one's roses (I suggest the wild types that cope with aphids well) had better be well stocked. And, if one is not to buy ladybugs repeatedly, one must have other infestations on other sorts of plants for this new generation to find when it is time for it, in turn, to lay the eggs of ladybugs to come.

The milkweeds didn't appear to suffer from the orange aphids. The same summer, another sort of creature severed thousands of leaves from a group of sugar maples. That ailment, too, passed without permanent effect. For two years previously, a red oak had been covered in spiny, two-inch, magenta galls — nursery chambers that plants are induced to make to feed and shelter larvae. No reason for alarm; no damage done; the oak is fine, thank you.

I've learned on the whole to become aroused to no more than curiosity by such episodes. I wondered to which alternate host plant the orange aphids headed after they were finished with the milkweeds. I tried to find this vividly colored species in my insect guide. It's not there — and not surprising that it isn't, given the hundred thousand or so insect species known to inhabit North America alone. I sent the galls to an entomologist for identification: oak hedgehog galls, each resulting from the precise injection of a growth hormone mimicking the oak tree's own by the minute wasp, *Acraspis erinacei*. I didn't find out for a long time who nipped the maples.

Finally I asked Camilla.

When I met her, Camilla Worden was an employee of a tree company, its specialist in integrated pest management, IPM. I saw her first in occupational disguise: a hard hat, face mask, and impermeable body suit, her extremities sealed in thick gloves and boots. She wore a spraypack on her back, a Santa Claus of sorts.

IPM is a service that has recently become available to homeowners, but its roots are in agriculture. The idea as it relates to farming is to use every feasible combination of traditional and modern technologies to control crop pests — weeds and diseases as well as insects — with the least possible harm to the environment.

Few doubt that pesticides as presently used are damaging the environment. American agriculture now uses annually some 700 million pounds of pesticides to control crop damage at a cost of $4.1 billion; an additional $1 billion is spent to counteract the adverse effects of pesticides on human and environmental health. Less appreciated is the fact that synthetic pesticides have not worked. In the 1940s, before modern insecticides were introduced, the crop loss from insect herbivory was 31 percent; it is now 37 percent, despite a thirty-three-fold increase in the quantity of pesticides used and a tenfold increase in their toxicity during the intervening half century. Resistance partly explains this one step forward, two steps back regression, but it is also due to the abandonment of farming methods that more closely imitated natural ecosystems.

In an effort to address the agricultural community with ecologically sound and economically viable alternatives, Cornell University recently published a work called *Handbook of Pest Management in Agriculture*. I didn't add it to my library; the "handbook," in three volumes, runs to 2,300 pages. Obviously the New York State College of Agriculture and Life Sciences at Cornell doesn't think integrated pest management is available in cans.

Briefly, IPM involves such techniques as spraying when pests are most vulnerable; rotating crops to prevent overwintering pests or pathogens from easily refinding their host plants from year to year; using mulches, interplantings, and "no plow" methods to curtail the growth of weeds between rows; incorporating "green manure" crops and crop residues into the soil to maintain fertility; choosing crops whose soil and moisture needs are appropriate to the area; using resistant varieties; designing smaller and more varied plantings to foil the spread of epidemics; luring insects from cash crops with traps and catch crops; interplanting crops that exude insect-repellent odors; releasing predators and pathogens to control herbivorous insects; releasing herbivorous insects and plant pathogens to control weeds; and maintaining hedgerows as refugia.

But this broad biological approach, the whole point of which is to use synthetic toxins as rarely and as sparingly as possible, was not what the tree company offered. Behind Camilla on the day we met stood a truck on which was mounted a sort of outsize soda fountain with flavors labeled Benlate, Manzate, Maverik, and Dursban as well as Bt and plain vanilla insecticidal soap. The stronger stuff explained Camilla's space age outfit — and why she ultimately quit the job she otherwise enjoyed.

Camilla arrived recently, undisguised, to help me prune the crabapples. IPM, as interpreted by her former employer, she explained over lunch, was a scheme to profit from what she calls the "green scene." Not that Camilla lacked the requisite expertise. Every other week, she inspected each client's property minutely, took soil samples, set traps to gauge when certain pests were ready to attack, and diagnosed ills by hand lens and identification keys before they got out of hand. But the recourse was always the same: spray.

And the spray, in a sense, was free; clients paid for the service, not the product. The more spray was used, the more customers felt they were getting their money's worth. The bottom line was that IPM, as commercially interpreted for the home landscape, used more, not fewer, chemicals than had been previously used by the homeowner. The result was an unblemished landscape, and customers were pleased.

Camilla now helps us to manage our pests. She identifies the mold, the mite, the weevil. Sometimes, as with the woolly adelgid that kills eastern hemlock within two years of its arrival, the choice is to spray the plant or lose it. I choose to spray hemlocks because they are otherwise headed for extinction, and sprayed specimens may live to see the day when the adelgid comes under biological control. I don't choose to spray European white birch against leaf miners; I replace them with native birches that control leaf miners by themselves. Sometimes the choice is between achieving excellent control with a highly toxic spray or good enough control with a milder product, such as insecticidal soap. I go for good enough.

But most often the best choice is to do nothing: to sit bemused under the maple tree as the leaves come twirling down so strangely in midsummer; to wonder what is up there in the tree, and why.

To finally learn from Camilla who nipped the maples.

It is the female petiole borer, a sawfly named *Caulocamtus acericausis*, incising each stem precisely one-half inch from the leaf blade to form a tiny tube in which to lay an egg.

The biocontrol catalog, printed on recyclable newsprint with vegetable-based ink, is primarily addressed to crop gardeners. Naturally; crops can't tolerate beetles, nor gardeners blemished crops.

I read about a wild potato plant that, when sucked by aphids, emits a synthetic aphid alarm pheromone that sends the pests to the ground in panic. Well-bred potatoes don't behave that way. If a cultivated cucumber occasionally pricks the finger, cramps the gut, or bitters taste receptors, that's a polite expression of what a wild cuke would do. We couldn't eat vegetables in the limited variety and large quantity we do unless we had bred their herbivore defenses out of them.

Disarming cultivated crops has made vegetables more palatable to insects than the wild originals are. We've made crops easier to eat in a physical as well as in a physiological sense. The root of a wild carrot — the roadside Queen Anne's lace — is not only strong to the taste but tough on the teeth. Then, too, we plant our fruits and vegetables in abnormally rich, moist soil to encourage mild flavor and juicy succulence. We also have seen to the excellence of their nutrition, the synchrony of their ripening, the prominence of their most delicious parts.

And we plant crops like proclamations. See the meal! Come and get it!

What we plant, and the way we plant it, encourages the rusts, smuts, spots, and wilts that afflict our gardens. Genetic impoverishment leaves these plants as vulnerable to diseases as they are to insects, and diseases, like beetles, spread unobstructed from plant to plant along tomato rows and across potato fields. Cultivation continually opens the soil to weed seeds, to evaporation, and to erosion. Removing the crop — not only the portions we eat, but the entire plant — robs the soil of nutrients.

How did we ever grow our gardens without the canned and bagged commodities that seem so necessary today? Yet how could we not have? It's hard to remember that fifty years ago, when half the population lived on and off the land, almost nothing that we depend on now was anywhere for sale.

Fifty years ago, my parents bought the acreage where I spent my childhood summers from Tony Causa, an old man from Sicily who continued to live on and farm the land until he died. Since that event took much longer than anyone could have guessed, my parents had many years in which to grumble at his methods. (Tony's chickens, to my mother's considerable distress, scratched for grubs and beetles among lettuces and spinach, manuring the soil as they pecked. One pays a pretty penny for free-range chickens these days, as she, a discriminating cook, might have done if only she had realized their gustatory value.)

Tony's was a movable garden. No, put that in the plural and deescalate the term: Tony cultivated garden patches — or patch gardens, as it were. We never knew where potatoes might appear, where splotches of tomatoes might be growing in any given year. Neither did their pests.

One might dignify this method by calling it crop rotation, but it was more like the skipping about that annuals are forced to do in nature as bare soil grows over in one spot and is bared anew in another. Last year's tomato patch, sprawled with dead vines, would regrow with grass; this year's new onion patch would sprout among splintered planks and shingles that served double duty as mulch and as paths between the rows.

Instead of buying the latest thing in vegetables, as my father yearned to do, Tony saved seeds from varieties that, because they had made it through summer after summer to the point of ripening seeds, had proved their resistance to insects and disease. His abundant and tasty-fruited pear and apple trees had been raised from the scions of escapees on other farms around. They, too, had proven their ability to cope.

The fruits were blemished; cosmetic perfection was not expected. Anyway, cosmetics were not Tony's strong point. His idea of gardening esthetics was a rough arbor made of red cedar posts on which he cultivated fox grapes whose fruit yielded his winter's wine. Perhaps the arbor was a mistake; its prominence in the otherwise confusing landscape attracted piles of copulating Japanese beetles whose death by kerosene was my particular and favorite summer job. For the rest, the meadow grew rampant until scything season, when hay was cut and stored for Roosevelt the horse. All the barriers to scything — stone walls, dumps, sumps, ditches, outcrops, edges where the grade changed suddenly or woods began — were marked by thickets and wild hedgerows.

This general messiness exasperated my parents.

This general messiness is where I found praying mantises — commonly and for free.

The scenes depicted in my catalog are, by contrast, fine lawns bounded by groomed shrubbery, long rows of perfect vegetables on weedless soil. That's what my family aspired to and, after Tony's death, what they achieved. But it's well to remember that the old man, to whom sprays were unknown, actually, if inarticulately and archaically, subsisted on the land.

Maybe I can't have my ecosystem, my esthetics, and my eggplants, too. Maybe I can't deny the sprayer's value or must learn to value even funny-looking fruits. I'm sure, though, that only when such emblems of cultivation are well knit within a richly embroidered landscape is it worthwhile to restock the land with bugs bought by the can. Biocontrol is inherent to landscapes that are natural: native, crowded, complex, and varied. It comes with the territory, so to speak.

By now, with meadows coming up and some thickets well established, our land may be ready to receive. I'll put in my order: lacewings, lady beetles, soldier bugs, mantids. With the order will come a bonus gift, one summer's supply for one tomato plant of a fertilizer containing nitrogen, phosphate, potassium, and trace elements in all-organic form as well as living microorganisms advertised to produce garden humus. I'm assured that once I try it, I'll be back for more.

But why?

Nothing will make me purchase the very soil.

7

Where the Gone Goose Went

THE GONE GOOSE DIED during Thanksgiving week. We didn't find the body. It simply disappeared as, sooner or later, all things that fall to the ground disappear. Perhaps in the wounded goose's case its disappearance was accelerated by a fox suddenly converting bird to mammal flesh and feces in the same way that the goose during its life had converted grass to bird meat and droppings (and goslings, too, of course), but why isn't the land heaped with corpses? Why isn't it buried in dead grass and manure? That all lives in whatever form eventually sink through the surface into the underworld should make us curious at least.

As a gardener I dutifully used to dig into the soil year after year dried manure, bonemeal, peat moss, and such without wondering what happened to it or how in the normal course of events cow pats, steer skulls, or dead sphagnum disintegrate and burrow downward without the industry of fertilizer factories and forking gardeners. That millions of acres of grassland in Australia could be caked to death under mummified dung for lack of a necessary beetle to initiate decay certainly came to me as a surprise, and that ants and earthworms cultivate more organic material into the ground by far than gardeners do was also startling, and that every time I turned a forkful of soil I was turning the earth's stomach upside down hit me with the shock deserved by mass murderers. This is how I came to leave the School of Neat and Clean.

I tried to reeducate Charlie, but he would have none of it. For many years he rented an apartment from my mother-in-law in the same house where Marty grew up in Queens, New York. Charlie boasted that the soil in the tiny plot he tended behind the row house grew currants as big as grapes, tomatoes the size of melons. This was a slight exaggeration — I believe he mistook gooseberries for currants — but the soil certainly was rich. And Charlie, living on a pittance, didn't begrudge impoverishing himself to make it so.

He stayed with us for a week one spring to help out. He couldn't be deterred from raking beds bare of winter litter. He was against stones as a matter of principle, no matter how small. He was for, in equal measure, cleanliness and dung.

This is the lecture I mentally prepared for Charlie but was helpless to deliver to that kindly and obstinate man.

Don't you realize, I raged internally, that plants eat stones? Where do you think minerals come from — those ions of such stuff as calcium and iron that roots absorb? From Earth's crust, of course, crumbled by frost, outgassed by volcanoes, dissolved by rain and groundwater, eroded by acid as tombstones are by the lichens that eat them. Can't you see that our northern soils are mineral-rich because glaciers ground our bedrock to a meal of stones and grit? That our wealth is not yet leached out as in the old stoneless soils to our south?

Leave the stones be, I say.

Here I imagine Charlie, never one to be taken for a fool, dropping a pebble into a glass of water, pointedly pretending to observe its dissolution.

Yes, Charlie. Rock dissolves very slowly. Not only that, but most of the minerals it releases promptly flow through bedrock's pores or along the surface and out to sea before plant roots can catch more than a tiny fraction of them. And true, too, that minerals aren't replaced anything like fast enough to support vegetation, vegetarians, or the entire food web that is life. Not even here, where the continent's granite body lies so close beneath our feet.

Still, dissolved stone is all plants eat.

This is as far as I got with my mental lecture. I would next have had to lead Charlie all the way back to the first lichens eating stone, maybe a billion years ago, and I knew he wouldn't follow me.

Lichens absorb minerals dissolving from the rocks they cling to and incorporate them into their cells as insoluble molecules — *organic* molecules, the stuff of grass and geese. Lichen — or any vegetation — thus becomes a mineral storehouse. Those that eat vegetation and those that eat vegetarians are also mineral storehouses. With exceeding slowness, but over the hundreds of millions of years since bare rock was first colonized, fantastic mineral wealth has been mined and banked in living tissue. Life itself, the tonnage of grass and forest and all the animals therein, is our mineral reservoir, and from it decayers recycle precious ions from old lives into new ones.

Decayers are soil organisms — most of them microscopic — that by digesting the fallen leaves and gone geese disassemble them step by step into their component minerals, which then become available once again to enter roots and ascend into life. The decayers' habitat is topsoil, which differs from the mix of crumbled rock and clay below in that it houses this teeming industry and the organic wherewithal to fuel it.

What you raked off the beds, Charlie, was my garden's recycling center.

What you stuck your fork into was its digestive system.

And, Charlie, if you hadn't raked and turned the soil, you wouldn't have had to feed the flowers, either.

My gardening primer warns, "Organic matter is not an addition you make just once and then forget about. It is always decomposing and being used by the plants; it must therefore always be replenished." That sounds sensible. But who was the gardener of Eden?

Such advice arises from post-paradise agricultural tribulations. When a piece of land is set aside to grow crops that will be harvested from it year after year, naturally the mineral wealth removed must be replaced. I have to do this with our vegetable garden, substituting in spring the manure Charlie favors for what we have taken the summer before and recycling back into the soil compost made over the year from weeds and crop residues. I don't like to do it, though: it isn't fun. And in more natural circumstances it isn't necessary.

Plants are capable of maintaining the fertility of their own soil and, indeed, of improving it. Imagine a bare bed of mineral subsoil with not a smidgen of mulch or fertilizer. Surely crabgrass will venture there. Crabgrass manages well on the spare mineral diet of such sterile soils. It efficiently absorbs the meager offering, incorporates it into its roots and leaves, goes to seed, and dies. Now what have we? The bed has a thin covering of dead grass at the surface and a skimpy network of dead roots below. Nickels and dimes, for sure, but the first organic deposit has been made.

As decayers mete out the interest on this deposit, dandelions, Queen Anne's lace, and foxtail grasses may find the soil good enough. Both of the wildflowers form tap roots that mine deeper minerals than the crabgrass could, and also serve as storage organs. The tops of the plants die in the fall, but, using the carbohydrates stored over the winter in their tap roots, the plants regrow the next spring. The foxtail grasses are annuals like crabgrass, and their fibrous roots mine poor soil with equal efficiency. But their top growth is luxurious: this second season's deposit has grown knee high.

And see the finches! Watch for mice! Foxtail's sumptuous heads of grain summon birds and small rodents that, by leaving high-nitrogen urine and rich droppings, further enrich the ground.

Probably by the third year the time is ripe for clover to arrive.

Clover, like all legumes and a few other plants, has a special association with a bacterium that converts nitrogen molecules to an ion usable by plants. This is no mean trick. The gas, N_2, is pairs of atoms bound to one another so tightly that no plant or animal can remove the single nitrogen atoms it needs to manufacture proteins. The clover bacterium's rare chemistry pries apart the gas, and each nitrogen atom attaches to oxygen atoms, forming the nitrate ion NO_3^-, which plant roots readily absorb.* All the nitrogen available in the soil and stored in plant and animal life has been "fixed" in this way, some by free-living bacteria, but most by species that infect legumes.

The association between the clover and its fixer is quite marvelous. As the seed sprouts, bacteria approach its root hairs. In response to their touch, the seedling grows to each a tiny tube through which the bacterium enters deeper into the root. The clover then grows round chambers where its bacteria, feeding on a carbohydrate specially prepared for them, rapidly multiply. In return for these favors, the plant receives a steady supply of nitrate during its life, and at its death the soil receives a large cache of nitrate from the root nodules the bacteria inhabited. A rich endowment has now been added to the growing mineral fund.

As organic material is deposited over the years, the subsoil near the surface becomes topsoil, first of a poor sort but growing ever richer — and thicker. Annual topdressings of dead plant material pile up; below, the roots of pioneer trees and shrubs now able to grow in this more fertile ground extend the zone of organic material downward. The more lavish and various the vegetation, the more opportunities there are for animals — more plants for caterpillars, more caterpillars for ants, more compost for earthworms, more earthworms for moles. Ants, worms, and burrow-

---

* An ion is an atom or molecule that has lost or gained an electron and therefore carries an electrical charge. The nitrate ion has gained an electron and is therefore abbreviated NO_3^- to indicate its single negative charge. A calcium ion, which has lost two electrons, is abbreviated Ca^{++}.

ing mammals are the mixers and diggers, the forks and spades, the cultivators of this self-enriching garden.

The elaborate network of tunnels and chambers dug by a colony of red ants may extend beneath an entire yard and well into the subsoil. Ants carry the excavated dirt, laboriously dug out grain by grain, to the surface, where raindrops and footsteps mix it with plant litter. Earthworms, which tunnel by swallowing soil as they push through it, back up to deposit their castings on the ground. Their tunnels often reach three yards deep, and decaying roots may tempt them even farther. No gardener turns a bed so deeply as these ant and earthworm cultivators, nor do we in our poor pokings tat so fine a lace of channels by which plants may receive a generosity of air and water.

Bring on the mice, moles, voles, and chipmunks! Let the woodchucks come!

It strains credulity, I know, that anyone should welcome woodchucks to the garden. They cost a lot of lettuce or the price of fencing the lettuce patch. But their excavation services are worth it. In New York State alone, woodchucks are estimated to bring to the surface 1.6 million tons of subsoil every year for conversion into topsoil. Let's do a little arithmetic. A local topsoil company sells its product — a mix of subsoil, sand, and leaf mulch — for $24 a cubic yard. One yard weighs one ton. The total for 1.6 million tons: more than $38 million.

Enough said.

But gardening books don't say it. We are led to believe that only our sweat, our mulch (our money!), can make a garden grow.

I had seen soil altogether wrongly. In my mind there was a sharp boundary, like a line drawn across a page, that separated underworld from upperworld, soil from litter. When I raked a bed clean, I defined the line exquisitely. When I dug compost in, I broke through it. But that image can't be right, for it suggests impermeability, a lack of natural movement through the boundary. If beyond one's clean garden beds detritus is continually raining down and plants are continually growing up, then there must be an active vertical transport system driving this recycling. It can't be otherwise; the interface between air and earth must be a blur of materials in motion.

A yard unraked is quickly littered, and with more dead leaves and limbs by far than with dead geese or fox scat. One reason is that the annual biomass of shed vegetation has an incomparably greater volume than that of all animal carcasses and wastes combined. The other reason is that flesh and feces are easily eaten and digested, whereas plant material is hard to eat and even harder to digest.

Toughness is due to two starches: lignin, the substance that hardens wood, and cellulose, which stiffens plant cell walls and gives vegetables their crunch. Lignin is best digested by wood-decaying fungi. Cellulose is digestible by various fungi, bacteria, and protozoans (other consumers of vegetation, including hay-fed cows and leaf-chewing caterpillars, lack the enzyme to disassemble cellulose). Most fungal and bacterial disassemblers are soil

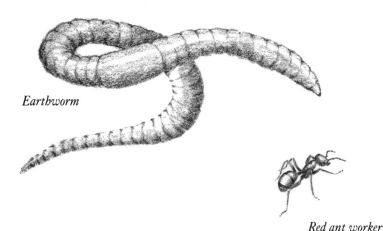

Earthworm

Red ant worker

*Woodchuck, also
known as a groundhog
or marmot*

dwellers that consume a rain of detritus that has already been chewed and partially digested by others. Their survival, the rate of mineral recycling, and the very maintenance of soil fertility depend on a host of these tiny chewers that, by passing litter through their own digestive system, prepare the meal for the microbes' final gleanings.

Gross evidence of maceration, though not the fine details of the chewers' own digestion, can be observed in an undisturbed cache of fallen leaves. On top are newly fallen leaves in their entirety. Below them are tattered ones from the year before, then crumbled bits, barely recognizable, and finally humus — that fragrant, soft, moist, friable, and chocolate-dark stuff that lies below leaf litter and that is characterized by fecal bits of such macerated but undigested items as twig lignin, insect cuticle, cone resin, leaf cellulose, and fruit wax all bound into delicate crumbs by the mucilaginous wastes of soil organisms that at that level take over the continuing digestion of the food bank.

Realizing how much activity is necessary to turn a bunch of leaves into a batch of humus, one would think the creatures doing it would be very much in evidence in the heap. But except for an occasional slug napping in the damp or a pill bug walking by, nobody seems to be at home. The throngs of chewers are too minute to notice.

Researchers sampling soil in a northwestern forest have identified some 3,400 species* of midget creepy-crawlies — many never before catalogued and most smaller than the size of the period at the end of this sentence — that are responsible there for humus deposition and thus for soil maintenance. They are arthropods — mites, microspiders, millipedes, centipedes, pseudoscorpions, springtails, tiny beetles — and each plays some herbivorous, predatory, or scavenging role in converting plant waste to soil wealth in a nearly microscopic version of the drama of fox and goose.

The process involves the movement of intact objects such as pine needles down through the guts of animals to their ultimate digestive dénouement in the underworld. A needle-chewing millipede leaves droppings for a turd-munching mite, which is eaten by a predatory insect, which in turn is scavenged, digested, and its fecal remains deposited as frass. Mouth to mouth, leaf to flesh, flesh to frass, each twig, cone, and needle is stripped to simplicity, pared to microscopy, disassembled step by step toward its eventual re-ascent in the tissues of a living plant.

A concept that had escaped me entirely when reading gardening advice was that soil moves as though on a conveyor belt. As new deposits of dead leaves accumulate above, the hypothetical

---

* The sampling to date suggests that more than twice that number will ultimately be found, or some 8,000 species of arthropods involved in recycling forest litter at that site. By comparison, the total number of species of reptiles, birds, and mammals on the same site is 143.

soil line I had naively pictured becomes buried beneath new layers of humus. Burrowers of various kinds and sizes transpose underworld to upperworld, and plants carrying minerals from the depth of roots to the height of branches also lift from the bottom and shed at the top. The motion is slow. Charles Darwin, a more patient observer than our Charlie, noted that over a period of thirty years, earthworms in a flint-strewn field buried all the stones by burrowing below and casting above, and worms are among the speedier mechanisms in this conveyor belt. Still, I think it unlikely that were I to place my house key on the soil I would find it again next year.

This churning motion that plant, worm, and woodchuck each does at a scale appropriate to its size is what gardeners emulate when they prepare a bed for planting. They may lightly fork fertilizer into the soil; they may lift and turn to incorporate organic matter more deeply; or they may shovel aside the good dirt on top in order to loosen and enrich the subsoil below before replacing the topsoil in the bed. This last method, called double digging, is the accepted apotheosis of bed preparation, but it wasn't good enough for Charlie. He dug out subsoil as well as topsoil, returned the topsoil to the bottom, and placed the lavishly enriched subsoil on top. When he was finished, the whole plot was topsy-turvy and the bed was two feet deep.

My primer calls this method deluxe double digging. I've tried it; plants like it.

But what a chore! And what subtleties might we be missing by disrupting microcosms on such a scale?

I began my own observations of what happens to a garden bed when it is simply let go in the small garden below the attic window where crabapples fruit and shed their leaves in the fall. Sure enough, the brick edging was quickly buried beneath worm castings.

This garden has been investing in apple leaves, flower leavings, and bird droppings for five years now. I weed the beds by hand from time to time and tuck the debris among the plants. I watch the little piles disappear. This is the richest, softest soil on the place. My toes sink when I step in it. I scoop up a handful: the soil falls like moist crumbs through my fingers. Arithmetic becomes meaningless at the scale of microscopic organisms that inhabit such a soil. Of those elephantine animalcules that are visible through low-power high school microscopes — oozing amoebas, darting parameciums — a teaspoon of good earth contains a million. In the same teaspoon are likely to be twenty times that many fungi and five *billion* bacteria. How many teaspoons are there in a handful? What infinity of creatures is being squeezed in one's hand when one follows the primer's instruction to evaluate the texture of the soil?

Each species of soil microorganism inhabits a certain level; thrives only within certain parameters of heat, moisture, and acidity; survives only in a certain ratio of atmospheric gases; prefers or is confined to certain foods; withstands enemies or preys on others with unique physical and chemical weaponry; lives a life as specific in its physiology and behavior as do animals that step on its realm, squeeze its habitat, or dig it up.

I don't know who lives where in that soft soil. I don't know what part each plays in digesting apple leaves. I don't know what antibiotics they make to thwart one another, or what their relationships are to the roots and worms they live among.

But I think it can't be wise to turn their ecosystem upside down.

Have I suggested too firm an image of a specialized industry, of a group of organisms dedicated to composting? The predatory fungus underfoot, whose deadly nooses tighten at a touch to garrote hapless roundworms, has no more interest in humus than does the fox trotting overground with a warm goose in its mouth. Yet they, too, are digesters. It is at once a dizzying and sobering exercise to imagine the world's stomach swelling to encompass all us eaters.

How went the goose from grass to root?

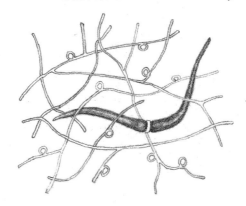

Each loop of this predatory fungus is made up of three cells that swell at a touch, strangling its nematode prey.

Of course, the goose was made of grass alone, for that is all it ever ate. Regarding the resulting gooseflesh, the fox perhaps had taken the first digestive step. If, indeed, the goose hit the ground the second time as scat, it might have been further macerated, digested, and defecated as smaller pieces still by maggots of bluebottle flies. And, when the fox dies, its carcass will most likely be pecked apart by crows, tunneled through by meat-eating fly maggots, and chewed from underneath by carrion beetles and their young. By penetrating the skin, biting through the meat, and partially liquefying it in the course of their own digestion, insect scavengers bring flesh into contact with the underlying soil and open the remains to decaying microorganisms.

Had the goose died as a gosling — a fate that befell one of its young that summer — burying beetles undermining the soil beneath the little corpse might have quickly sunk it underground. Working as mated pairs, these large and handsome animals may drag a mouse or bird several yards to where the soil is soft. When burial is complete, they remove the fur or feathers, knead the nude body into a ball, and lay their eggs in tunnels chewed through the flesh. Parents call hatched larvae to dinner with a rasping sound and feed them on regurgitated meat in the same way a fox feeds its kits.

But one never knows which way a goose will go. Some scrap scattered by a crow might be carted by an ant down into its nest to feed its young. Or, in the temporary guise of grub and maggot, the goose might become airborne in the belly of a cowbird, taking who knows how long to detour back to ground as dead flesh or dropping. Again, the nitrogen-rich cowbird plop could in a night drop three yards deep into the soil, clutched in the gut of an earthworm returning to the bottom of its burrow after supper.

Maybe the Gone Goose will return as salad from my garden.

The literature on mouth-to-mouth recycling is necessarily scatological: all animals suffer a degree of indigestion, and what is waste to one is food to others. At first the thought of caprophagy is repelling, but weighing the services of feces eaters against a landscape deep in dog doo, one is moved to benediction of the sanitation crew. The Australian range disaster occurred when cattle were imported without the dung beetles that customarily roll balls of cow manure into their underground chambers to feed their larvae. Left whole and baking in the sun, the cow pats dried to a crust that killed the grass and stayed undecayed sometimes for a decade. The problem was solved by introducing African

A pair of burying beetles securing their prize

dung beetles, which could cope with both wet pats and dry weather. Cow manure is especially nutritious because the cow's diet of grass, with its high cellulose content, is especially indigestible. In order to get any good from the grass, cows culture bacteria in one of their several stomachs. The bacteria digest grass, the cow digests their corpses and their wastes, and there's still food aplenty for dung beetles. One might consider cows and other grazers mobile collection and distribution vans or animated fertilizer spreaders. Certainly the former goose's kin, a tribe now numbering seven, leave generous green and grassy droppings containing nitrogenous wastes immediately useful to the lawn and much that interests earthworms. Wherever a goose has left a dropping, I find there some days later crumbs of earthworm castings, like streusel on a yeast cake, and the grass there grows greener.

There is an almost poetic and certainly voluminous literature on earthworms. Between fall and spring, *Lumbricus terrestris*, our common earthworms that clean up after geese, can transport underground 90 percent of the season's crop of fallen apple leaves in an orchard, a total of close to half a ton per acre. They do so elegantly, grasping each leaf by stem or tip and gently backing down into their burrows, where they dine at leisure.

This particular earthworm — one of 3,000 species that have been identified worldwide (about twice the number of rodent species, the most numerous mammals) — is a detrivore, or litter eater. Other species are geophages, or dirt eaters, that digest from soil what organics they come upon regardless of their source. Geophagous earthworms both eat and defecate their castings underground instead of at the surface, thus leaving in their wake networks of tunnels sought out by plant roots for their fluffiness, moisture, and casting-packed nutrition. *Eisenia fetida*, an English commoner naturalized in America, is notably competent at digesting feces. It grows especially well on a diet of dirt mixed with human sewage sludge, which is thereby converted to prized potting soil containing 3 percent available nitrogen, but perhaps sold only down under, from whence came the book I found on this engrossing subject.*

Soil enrichment is inherent in the way all earthworms burrow: by ingesting soil at the front and egesting undigested remnants at the rear. Between entrance and exit, gut bacteria dining on organics the worm can't digest may multiply twentyfold, and they continue to feed and multiply in the worm's castings. There may be a thousand times more decayer bacteria in worm castings than in the surrounding soil, five times more nitrogen, seven times more phosphorus, and eleven times more potassium.

These, please note, are the very minerals one buys in bags of chemical fertilizer.

They're cheap, too: earthworms can defecate annually two hundred tons of castings per acre.

It occurred to me that the dictionary sense of the word "decay" — the destruction of some wholesome and perfect substance into a base, disintegrated form — is emotionally overwrought. Surely a lightsome calcium ion, dancily depicted Ca^{++}, is more pure than spinach leaves. The more degraded — the more like dirt — a thing becomes, the lighter and purer is its substance.

I like to think I do my part by eating salad that may be goose and passing on the crude leftovers for bacteria to refine. Although we call what we do digestion and what they do decay, I'm not sure I see the distinction. We eaters of whatever size are all in this together, this business of replenishing the soil. Without plants to eat, we all would die; without us to eat them, so would the plants.

But I realize now that to help one's garden overmuch is to hinder it. I must have been living in another world when I wrote, only a few years ago and with considerable satisfaction, of the view from my window of our gardens "bare to their bones, neat and clean, nicely edged, weed-free." Now I see that there is

---

* Earthworms: their ecology and relationships with soils and land use. Lee, K. E. (Kenneth Ernest). Sydney; Orlando: Academic Press, 1985.

teeming life down there that, neatly and cleanly, I was starving. Why was I not replacing in their beds the limp bodies of weeds I had uprooted? What was I doing cutting flowers to the ground, raking them away, bagging grass clippings, blowing autumn leaves from underneath the hedge? I was robbing the life savings from my garden beds, exposing them to the elements to leach their lifeblood away.

I don't mean to say that we should hang up our shovels or trash our gardening books. Measure the ground's pH, by all means, but consider putting in plants that are adapted to that certain sweetness or sourness of soil. Recall, before laying down a mulch of pine bark, that each bush or tree is accustomed to a cover of its own dead leaves below it, and so are the decayers that refeed it. Keep a compost pile for kitchen wastes and cornstalks, but remember that fallen leaves, dead stems, and pulled weeds left in place supply a steadier source of humus than a once-in-a-springtime dole of rotted compost.

If such accommodations are unthinkable, then sure, fork in peat, spread mulch, give gifts of fertilizer. But realize that this deposit will gain interest only if the bed so started is thickly planted. The more webbed the soil is with roots, the more efficiently minerals will be harvested for storage. The more bulk of vegetation, the greater the storage capacity. The more kinds of plants there are, the more kinds of animals can live there, and the more competent the recycling business they can operate.

I mean to say that we should treasure the life in our garden both for the riches it holds and for the riches it sheds.

I mean to say that we should respect and trust our soil as an ecosystem which, if fairly treated, will thrive with minimal interference.

I mean to say that the gardener's role is neither to take nor to give: it is to plant.

8

In Respect of Grass

A LAWN DOCTOR TELEVISION AD proclaims, to admiring applause for a perfect expanse of green, that "great lawns like this one are made, not born." Quite true. What the ad fails to admit, however, is that the lawn so created is cut off from the life support systems on which the natural survival of grass depends, and it must therefore remain permanently in intensive care.

Lawn grasses are selected for their carpeting ability. Although each seed that germinates when the lawn is sown is an individual plant, the roots and stems soon form a feltlike mat from which the individual plants can no longer be untangled. The mat is seldom thicker than 4 inches; where developers have been stingy about replacing the topsoil they scraped away, the carpeting may be a mere 2 inches thick.

Naturally, so thin a skin dries quickly in the summer sun; unnaturally, we don't allow it to protect itself by tanning and taking its normal midsummer nap. To keep our grass green all summer, Lawn Doctor prescribed 1 inch of water a week, a total of 24 inches during the growing season, or more water than falls as rain from May through October anywhere in the United States.*

The manner of their growth puts lawn grasses in intense competition with one another. All the individual plants have the same mineral needs, all are crammed together as tight as they can be, and all share the same thin zone of soil at the surface, where the minerals are most easily leached away by those weekly waterings that also keep the plants from ever ceasing their greedy growth. Lawn Doctor scheduled five feedings: in early spring, balanced phosphorus and potassium with a wallop of nitrogen; a coated form of nitrogen later in the spring, like a hard candy for the lawn to suck more gradually; a light meal in the first hot weeks of summer; then a rich dessert of nitrogen again in early fall, with sprinkles of the two P's as well. The feeding season ended appropriately at Thanksgiving with a *digestif* of phosphorus and potassium to prepare the grass for the next glut of nitrogen come spring.

This generous menu resulted in splendid growth that required weekly mowing from early in the chilly spring through the muggy heat of August and on into frost. Lawn Doctor prescribed, but didn't provide, that service, but it warned that any failure to remove the heavy clippings would likely smother the lawn. To these ends, we purchased a tractor and cart with which to cut off and take away the green growth in which the grass had stored the nutriment Lawn Doctor had supplied. The company did provide herbicide treatments to kill the clover and, having thus purged the patient of this source of nitrogen, infused our naturally acid soil with lime to enhance the uptake of the petrochemicals that kept the grass growing as fast as we could mow it down and cart it off.

Continual amputation is a critical aspect of lawn care. Cutting

---

* The annual precipitation in the Northeast averages 43 inches, most of it during the cold months of the year. Rainfall drops off westward: to 37 inches in Pittsburgh, 33 in Chicago, 14 in Denver and Santa Barbara. Seattle, in the rainforest area of the Pacific Northwest, receives an average of 39 inches.

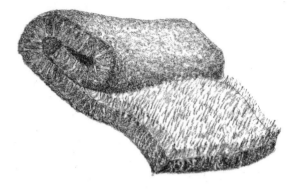

*Lawn turf,
rolled up*

grass regularly — preventing it from reaching up and flowering — forces it to sprout still more blades, more rhizomes, more roots, to become an ever more impenetrable mat until it is what its owner has worked so hard or paid so much to have: the perfect lawn, the perfect sealant through which nothing else can grow — and the perfect antithesis of an ecological system.

This is what Lawn Doctor did for us, and it was stunning.

That it looked so good was a credit to the doctor's art because only some portions of the lawn had been created in the proper way, on bare soil seeded with a mix of lawn grasses. Most of the expanse had been added by mowing whatever was already there, a procedure that will turn any sunny place into a lawn of sorts. Intensive care did wonders even for what had once been rough goldenrod and brambles.

From a distance, one couldn't tell the difference between where we had sowed and where we had mowed. Close up, the sowed areas were finer and more uniform in texture than the areas that had merely been cut, but even in the roughest spots turf grasses spread at the expense of bunch grasses. Our native little bluestem (*andropogon scoparius*), a grass that grows in clumps, all but disappeared, to be replaced by creeping bluegrass. Mowed stands of goldenrod were immediately wiped out; clover took a little longer. But by the end of this, our brief Estate Age, we were the proud possessors of an acre of grass where not even a honeybee could find a flower to sip.

The spring following the year the pheasant family disappeared, we pulled the plug on the lawn that swept over the hillside and down the drive. By May the patient had arisen from its bed. By June it was in bloom, sparkling with buttercups. We cut what paths we needed, and waited to see how things would progress.

Over the next several years, the meadow intrinsic to lawn showed up rather rapidly on the neglected greensward. Without mowing or watering, the grass went to seed, faded to buff, and peacefully fell dormant during the summer heat. Clovers penetrated — red clover, white clover, and the yellow hop clover — followed by several vetches. These are all legumes, and all provided the grass with the nitrogen it craved to feed what had previously been its petrochemical dependence.

The legumes, and many of the other wildflowers that appeared, are deep-rooted. They excavated the earth, crumbling it to a texture more capable of holding moisture and more congenial to earthworms and decayers. Mining the soil much deeper than the lawn grass roots, they transferred precious minerals up into leaves and stems that, dying in the fall, deposited on the surface of the soil the richness they had delved. The grasses, greening and browning in their season, in turn contributed their plentiful thatch to their wildflower companions.

So the system began.

As it progressed, the soil improved. Unlike a lawn that, for all the years it is in place, can still be rolled back to reveal intact whatever the builder originally spread beneath it, meadows create topsoil and deepen the bed in which they grow.

The meadow also revealed differences in texture, chemistry, and moisture in ground that had seemed uniform when carpeted by a regularly watered lawn. A mosaic developed: a stand of coarse grass as high as my shoulder in one spot, in another an airy patch of pencil-high fine blades topped by feathery bloom, and here and there grasses whose seeds were oatlike or wheatlike among the original lawn grasses. A brilliant butterfly weed came up in a dry spot where yarrow also grew. Sedges shared damp ground with the lovely little flower called blue-eyed grass, though not in the quantity Mrs. Dana had observed. Pinks, daisies, milkweeds, buttercups, wild madder, devil's paintbrush, butter-and-eggs, two-flowered Cynthia, black-eyed Susan — each expressed some preference, each offered some gift.

That gifts were being offered was evident in the general hum and flutter of insect life. The meadow was audible with bees and crickets; the mowed grass was silent. The meadow waved and nodded in the wind; crowds of leaf hoppers leapt to the brush of a hand. The lawn was deadly still.

It began to seem a gap, a blank of no interest even to common cabbage butterflies. Its blankness extended up into air empty of the dragonflies that jeweled the meadow and, in autumn, of the finches that dropped by dozens to harvest its plentiful seeds. The cat would disappear into the tall grass, his tail twitching in anticipation of fat meadow voles. He never stalked the lawn. Friends left with wildflowers: Who would ask for a bouquet of lawn? When the meadow turned to gold and bronze set off by purple asters and yellow goldenrod, the lawn remained the tiresome green that it had been since May Day and would remain 'til Christmas. Even under the winter snow, the difference was footnoted by the tracks of rabbits, mice, and birds that went about their business in the meadow but shunned the lawn.

Out of stinginess, laziness, guilt, and curiosity, we ultimately withdrew all treatment from the remaining lawn except for necessary mowing. This was not an unqualified success. While it is true that clover helps to feed the grass, it also spreads at the lawn's expense. Various other creeping flowers bloom at less than the three-inch height to which we now set the mower's blade, giving the lawn a patchy, particolored, multitextured look. The grass is anyway not as green as greensward ought to be, certainly not as green as the moss that has taken over in some places. We mow less often and leave the scanty clippings to shrivel in the sun. During August droughts we seldom mow at all. That's when the lawn turns brown.

So we have reached a compromise. When, after several years on its own, the lawn has obviously suffered a major relapse, we give it a brief course of treatment — though not as lavishly as Lawn Doctor did — with organics instead of petrochemicals and with little enthusiasm (Lawn Doctor now offers an all-organic option). Since enjoying the robustness of a meadow, I resent the neediness of lawns. They don't behave in the tradition of the Graminae, the great and multitudinous family of grasses.

I'd like to tell my lawn a thing or two about its heritage, smack this pampered child with the hard facts about its pioneering family. How can it demand coddling when the very character of grass is to thrive on hardship?

Grasses sweep over the bitter, windblown steppes of Central Asia, creep with ice-nipped roots over the tundra's permafrost, arise in hummocks from black and stagnant swamps, tuft rock crevices in the mountains above the timberline, and green the desert in the rain shadow of the Rockies. They survive the frying heat of African savannas, sink roots deep into dry sand dunes and salt-washed tidal marshes, lead the way in the wake of forest fires, crowd into the polluted Jersey Meadows, germinate in city sidewalk cracks, grow eagerly beneath the hoofs of thundering herds, and positively enjoy a good burn. With leaves cropped by grazers and seeds consumed by birds and rodents, they still lift their blades for more.

I'd like my grass to realize its historical mission: to explore bare soil, to sink new roots in the most forbidding places, to boldly go where no trees can follow.

The Graminae are a family of more than 620 genera and 10,000 species that constitute the dominant biome occupying inhospitable land worldwide.

The first grasses appear in the fossil record in the early Cenozoic Era, when there were no polar ice caps, continents were entirely forested, and redwoods grew in Alaska. This balmy climate was what the world had known for the previous billion years. The family evolved during the next 50 million years against a background of unprecedented geological upheavals that leavened the continents, created extensive drylands and deserts, dropped the average temperature at northern latitudes by fifty degrees F, and culminated in the final catastrophe of the Pleistocene Epoch when the Ice Age struck.

Dry grassland ecosystems date from at least midway through this period, 25 million years ago, when prairie grasses first appeared on the American Great Plains. The forests then were shrinking globally before the accelerating drought and cold. In California, magnolias became extinct. In Africa, apes evolved flat molars suitable for coarse grassland foods. In North America, horses left the forest to cross the plains on tiptoe, on hoofs, and in herds, exemplifying a pattern of physical and social adaptation to wide-open grassland that was followed in turn by the rest of the equid tribe and by bovines, caprids, camelids, and countless other large herbivores both extinct and extant.

Just short of 4 million years ago, two hominids left a trail of footprints at Laetoli, in the Rift Valley of East Africa, where there were also ostriches, rhinoceroses, pigs, hares, giraffes, elephants, and antelopes. The area was, and is, savanna.

The crossing of the threshold between hominid and human dates from about 3 million years ago, in the same grassland, at the beginning of the Pleistocene Epoch as the Ice Age opened. During that epoch, human populations multiplied to 5 million and occupied every continent except Antarctica. There was both vast deforestation and an equivalent spread of savanna, steppe, veldt, pampas, prairie, and tundra — grasslands all. Herds of horses 100,000 strong were common. There was a trend toward gigantism: mammoths, mastodons, giant ground sloths. The human brain tripled in size.

During the four thousand years following the last glacial retreat ten thousand years ago, agriculture was invented in the Middle East, North and South America, East Asia, Africa, and Papua New Guinea. Wheat, rice, barley, millet, rye, corn, sorghum, sugarcane, and bamboo are all grasses. Horses, camels, sheep, cows, caribou, water buffalo, and yaks are all grazers. Land that once supported 5 million now feeds 5 billion.

Lawn first appeared in the garden landscape five centuries ago. An upstart.

Unlike the overwhelming majority of flowering plants, grasses are pollinated by the wind. As a result, Victorian botany considered them a primitive family of flowering plants that had never devised the charms by which other flowers beguile their animal pollinators. But closer study showed that wind pollination has in all cases followed, not preceded, a history of animal pollination. Shucking the costly trappings by which grass ancestors had once lured insects reliably to their service was an economical but radical step, an option only for species that grow in crowds over unobstructed land where the wind blows free.

Whereas one may fail to see the forest for the trees, an appreciation of grass is complicated by the opposite view: one fails to see the plants for the prairie. In an effort to isolate in my mental imagery the individual from the aggregate — the timothy from the hayfield, the fescue from the lawn — I spent some afternoons examining various grasses.

The time of my excavations and dissections was late June. Ryegrass and bluegrass had already bloomed; timothy was about to; little bluestem had not even begun to extend its flowering stalks. The results of my investigations are drawn here and can be summarized thus:

1. Little bluestem early in the summer is darn hard to dissect because (a) it's as tender as lettuce, (b) the nodes to which each blade is attached and from which the stalk will lengthen are tiny and very close together, and (c) the whole nascent stalk is an arrangement of blade within blade within blade within blade, all clasped within the outermost, lowermost blade.

2. Timothy about to bloom is a tough customer. The nodes are as hard as knuckles; the sections of stalk in between are fully

LITTLE
BLUESTEM,
IMMATURE

*a. nascent
flowering stalk
with blades still
telescoped inside
one another*

*b. blades
removed to
show how
closely nodes are
spaced*

TIMOTHY,
MATURE

*a. node from
which blade
arises*

*b. section of
stalk between
nodes, partially
clasped by blade*

*c. tender
portion of stem
still growing*

d. dormant bud

extended and stiff as wire. (Remember that sweet and succulent little morsel of stem you nibbled as a child? That's the only portion still growing in late June.) I noted also dormant buds at the base of the plant from which the following year's stalks arise and by which clumping grasses increase in girth from year to year.

3. Ryegrass had, in addition to tall, tough flowering stalks like those of timothy, short, tender ones that resembled those of the immature little bluestem. These, a lawn manual told me, were tillers, sterile stalks that never grow up. Mowing, it said, encourages tillering; tillers spread the grass.

4. Bluegrass had, in addition to flowering stalks and tillers, off-

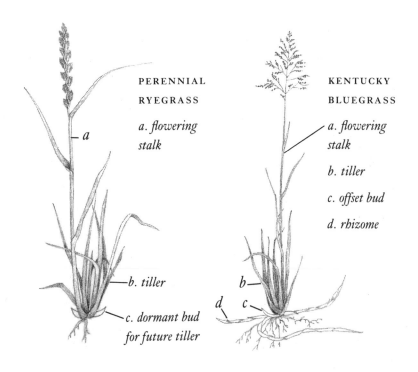

PERENNIAL
RYEGRASS

*a. flowering
stalk*

b. tiller

*c. dormant bud
for future tiller*

KENTUCKY
BLUEGRASS

*a. flowering
stalk*

b. tiller

c. offset bud

d. rhizome

set buds that were sprouting into rhizomes reaching sideways through the soil, creeping the grass along the ground.

Vigorous vegetative growth is, of course, the desired feature for a lawn grass, but it didn't seem to me that the lawn mower, invented only in 1830, could have caused it. And why had my lawn not thanked me for letting it grow free? Why, when I got the mower off its turf, did it allow daisies and timothy to penetrate it? It's fine that bluegrass *can* be mowed; why *must* it?

I became curious about the infantilism of lawns and this species' particular creepiness.

.   .   .

Not finding what I wanted — a book called *Everything You Ever Wanted to Know About Grass* — I searched through clues both ecological and historical.

Turning to *Plant-Animal Interactions*, I found tantalizing bits of information.

Grass maturation is defensive: blades are armed with shards of silica, seeds with needled awns; what nutriment is left after its conversion to toughening cellulose is drawn into the roots for the next season's rejuvenation. The mature timothy was not, in other words, the sort of mouthful a sensible grazer ought to seek, nor were its chin-high flowers convenient for a grazer.

On the other hand, and at a younger age, nibbles retard grass maturation. Moreover, both nibbles and drools of ungulate spittle stimulate juvenile growth: the sprouting of dormant buds, the proliferation of tillers. Any grass when grazed is able to so vegetate to some extent, depending on the intensity of grazing to which it has been subjected in the course of evolution. Could the answer, then, to why one grass is better than another at remaining a youthful rascal lie in the nature of their traditional grazers — in, for example, the contrasting behaviors of *Bos taurus*, the sedentary common cow, and *Bison bison*, our misnamed but migratory American "buffalo"?

Let bison graze the meadow. Loose them there on that day in June when I took my study samples. Watch them pass over the difficult timothy. See them lunge for the succulent little bluestem.

All the little bluestem's nodes that early in the season were still within one inch of the ground. A grazer could crop a foot or more from the rich, nutritious blades without harming the crucial growing parts. A few days' retardation, a modicum of tillers, would give the grass the insurance it needed to withstand the passing herd.

But what if the bison stuck around? What if we fenced them in or exchanged them for a herd of domesticated cattle? Then we would find, as in fact we already had found by mowing it to death, that little bluestem can't live by tillering alone.

But I had to hand it to my lawn grasses. What better way to endure the grazer's maw (the man's mower!) than to tiller through the summer without exposing nodes to injury? What better strategy than to grow sideways beneath the reach of teeth? I was pretty sure that lawn grasses evolved with Bos, not Bison.

Confirmation came from William Cronon. In *Changes in the Land*, he quotes one source as noting in 1633 that "in places where the cattle use to graze, the ground is much improved . . . growing more grassy and less weedy." Cronon goes on to explain:

> What in fact was happening was that a number of native grasses and field plants were slowly being destroyed and replaced by European species. Annual grasses were quickly killed off if grazed too closely, and the delicate crowns of some perennials fared little better. Not having evolved in a pastoral setting, they were ill prepared for their new use. That was why European grasses, which *had* adapted themselves to the harsh requirements of pastoralism, began to take over wherever cattle grazed. . . . Initially carried to the New World in shipboard fodder, and in the dung of the animals which ate them, these European species were soon being systematically cultivated by colonists. By the 1640s, a regular market in grass seed existed . . . and within one or two generations, the plants had become so common that they were regarded as native.

Like Kentucky bluegrass, for instance. Like ryegrass, fescue, and every other grass labeled for use in lawns. And like timothy, grown for winter fodder. And like all the grasses that turn tawny in the haying season, when little bluestem is so merrily dressed in green.

As the temperature climbed toward August, the little bluestem stalks shot up dramatically, like television antennas. Each stalk lengthens simultaneously at its many growing nodes. Grass blades that were originally inside each other rapidly emerge. The stalk reaches for the breeze, each section growing longer than the one below it until the flower head shoots out the top, leaving the wind-obstructing blades far behind it. The stalks bend to the wind and rebound, toss their heads, shake their anthers, twitch and shiver their pollen into the air with every stir of breeze.

All that was over for the other grasses. Already in July they were tawny, their husky grains shattered from their now empty stalks. But come the haying season, there stood the little bluestem, green as you please, basking in the hot sun, coming into bloom on the hillside above the lawn, which was already frying. There were some bright green patches on the lawn. They were crabgrass.

One doesn't notice in well-kept suburbia that there are spring- and summer-flowering grasses. Of course, other flowers, too, have different blooming schedules, but grasses don't need a niche in time by which to corner insect pollinators, nor do they need, like woodland species, to take advantage of the brief spring brightness before the leaves shade them out.

Grazing would explain varying schedules if grasses greened sequentially, each species in turn hazarding its blades only until the next species offered itself instead. But here were two altogether different seasons — lawn time and crabgrass time — that didn't overlap.

Bluegrass, Cronon remarks in *Nature's Metropolis*, was prime among the crew of European grasses that bested the native prairie species as cattle were introduced to the Chicago hinterland. Bluegrass was also the one that had crowded out little bluestem in the lawns we made by mowing.

I scrambled for my botany text and found what I was looking for in the chapter on photosynthesis. There are two broad categories of plants, commonly called cool-season and warm-season species, technically labeled C_3 or C_4, according to the number of carbon atoms in a critical compound involved in photosynthesis. The bluegrass cultivated in lawns and naturalized on my hillside is a cool-season species that uses C_3 photosynthesis.

Photosynthesis uses light energy to manufacture sugar from water and carbon dioxide. The more light there is, the faster photosynthesis goes. On a sunny July afternoon, therefore, the bluegrass in my lawn is photosynthesizing like mad and presumably manufacturing a great quantity of sugar with which to grow wonderfully tall and lush. Yet there it is, clearly shriveling.

Its problem is an enzyme meant to capture carbon dioxide for sugar manufacture that, at high rates of photosynthesis, becomes choked on oxygen instead. This chemical glitch sabotages the process, and the plant becomes starved of sugar. Worse, the starving grass expands its leaf pores in an attempt to let in more carbon dioxide but in so doing loses vital moisture through evaporation. C_3 photosynthesis is therefore inefficient, unhealthy, and even suicidal under hot, dry, bright conditions. In our climate, only liberal watering saves such a grass from crisping.

Little bluestem (crabgrass, too) is a warm-season, C_4 species. Warm-season plants evolved another sort of enzyme that more avidly captures carbon dioxide from the air spaces within the leaf and that refuses oxygen. Pulling carbon dioxide molecules from the air as quickly as they enter speeds the flow from outside the leaf, so a blade of little bluestem keeps itself generously supplied without opening its leaf pores to desiccation. This and other efficiencies allow a little bluestem in the noonday sun to produce three times as much sugar as a bluegrass and to continue to grow through summer's drought without fear of drying.

As it happens, those European grasses used for pasturage and lawn are all self-sabotaging cool-season species. Our native prairie grasses are warm-season species.

Some warm-season grasses are used for lawns across the southern tier of the United States in areas where no conscionable amount of watering would keep a cool-season grass alive. One is Bermudagrass. Originally from Africa, introduced as a pasture grass, it is listed as a weed in the government document *Common Weeds of the United States* and is also known as devilgrass. Another is kikuyu, also from Africa and also an aggressive spreader. One authority on lawn grasses recommends that kikuyu not be used anywhere in the continental United States. An article in *Horticul-*

ture propounding the use of drought-tolerant lawn grasses admitted that it was nearly impossible to control either devilgrass or kikuyu without using herbicides.

So much for warm-season species shaped by the intense herbivory of domesticated herds. Thank God that our deer and our antelope roamed.

I grew increasingly patriotic during the course of this research. My pride swelled with the prairie grasses' hot and hearty growth, with waves of dropseeds and cord grasses, bluestems and gramagrasses — natives, all natives, and all warm-season species. But why should warm-season members of the family Graminae be indigenous to North America, whereas cool-season pasture grasses came from Europe?

The puzzle was solved when I consulted an atlas. England, which in my mind's eye lay directly across the ocean from New England, lies in fact at about the latitude of Newfoundland. Central Europe is on a level with the North Woods of Maine and the province of Quebec in Canada. Not until one reaches the South of France is one out of the zone of coniferous or deciduous forests and into a zone where the light is bright enough and summers dry enough to favor warm-season species. Who would have thought resorts in the Midi were at the latitude of Lake Superior?

I could now tell my lawn straight out that it is in the wrong place, well south of its natural latitude, in a land where the summer is too bright, too hot, and too dry for it to thrive with less than heroic care. It wants its motherland's chilly fog, those dimming clouds and rains that surprisingly scud across the sky in seemingly fair weather. The whole of Lawn Doctor's prescription — water, nitrogen, mowing, removing clippings — would be obviated in an English pasture cropped by sheep or cows and nurtured by their excretions. Ruefully I had to acknowledge that the history of any species will reveal its essential validity, its place in the scheme of things.

Perhaps I owed my lawn an apology.

But by then it was August, when these grasses are most irritating. In the vegetable garden, the C_4 corn stood taller than my head. The crabgrass had triumphed in the lawn. The one feeds me; the other gets along without me very well. Why apologize to species that do neither?

Yet no one else was questioning their lawn's right to special attention and excessive space. Trucks from numerous lawn care companies plied from drive to drive along tarred roads nearly molten in the sun. And this in a town where no cows, one smallish herd of sheep, and some stables of riding horses are all that remain of the grazers that shaped the golf course bents, the residential fescues. Lawns can no longer claim pastoral validity. They have outgrown it monstrously. Though now I understand why they need such care, I question why we give it. We spend $25 billion a year coddling this carpet that on an August day lies sprawled over 30 million acres of America, stupefied in the sun.

How we love our lawn! How we take it with us wherever we go, plant and tend it even in the desert, can't get comfortable without it, must have it underfoot, are moved to display it proudly as the very emblem of our civilization!

And with what moral rectitude we mow.

Quite a few municipalities have laws against long grass. They will come and cut it down to lawn and fine you for the service. But these are actually weed laws; they are of agricultural origin, and so, I think, is the smugness that keeps them on the books.

It is little appreciated that agriculture came about in very much the way described in the Old Testament. The earliest evidences of domesticated grain and grazers come from the Jordan Valley and date from about ten thousand years ago, when prolonged drought forced a once leisurely society to plant and husband what they had formerly plucked and shot. The episode involved an actual expulsion: lakes dried up, fruit trees died, antelopes absconded, and the human population, faced with starvation, migrated to the one water source remaining. They survived by farming, a strategy that in the history of agriculture has repeatedly been born of famine. I read this in the *New York Times*, but I could have read it in the Bible.

One can't help seeing in this expulsion from numerous garden communities the biblical metaphor of Eden. Being human, one can imagine these people assuming blame for the land's apparent anger, accepting the punishment of hard labor, enjoying the relief of sweaty expiation and the full-bellied thanksgiving of the harvest. One's mind leaps easily across millennia to the scorn colonists heaped on the Indians for their easygoing life — the scorn still embodied in our weed laws.

Weed laws were meant to prevent the slovenly farmer from contaminating his neighbors' fields with noxious species, such as the docks, daisies, thistles, bindweeds, spurges, and other European weeds that visited our meadow and that, I came to realize, I should have recognized as the infestation they were. The origin of most aggressive and opportunistic forbs can be traced to the Ice Age when, during periods of thaw, the plants able to rapidly colonize bare, infertile ground were at a marked advantage. At the end of the Ice Age, that advantage was lost in America as forest and prairie gradually regained their former control. In Europe, though, agriculture nicely replicated the repeated disturbances to which these opportunists were accustomed: they continued their evolution into field weeds. By an irony that is revelatory to me, a select group of these forbs and their accompanying grasses became the lawn and the lawn weeds with which suburbia so conscientiously struggles.

Soil fertility has traditionally been replenished in exhausted fields by letting them lie fallow — not working them, not planting them, allowing them to grow with whatever seed lies buried in the soil. The meadow plants that over a period of years reworked the soil of a fallow field to something that wheat or rye might grow in were field weeds that, by the time the farmer allowed them to take over, had pretty much done so for themselves. Fallow land was put to pasture — left to cows or sheep and their nitrogenous manure in an ecology of benign neglect

until such time as the soil had recovered sufficiently to plow up
again for grain or hay.

Intensive grazing under this regime selected not only for lawn-
like grasses but also for low-growing or carpeting forbs, such as
those that give our remaining lawn its textured surface. This
look, apparently, is historically authentic. Lawns were named in
the fifteenth century after a nubby linen of interesting and irreg-
ular texture manufactured in the French town of Lâone. They
were planted with sod dug up from meadows and went also by
the name of "flowery medes." The grass was not mowed. The
flowers included dandelions, daisies, buttercups, and clover —
all early-blooming, cool-season European species and among the
first to put in an appearance in our lawn gone wild.

In our meadow, this low-growing and delicately flowered stage
was quickly followed by ranker growth. The same must have
been true of flowery medes, for a book about medieval gardens
mentions that such ornamental plantings had to be returfed every
three or four years with new sheep-shaped meadow. In the centuries that followed, as "laones" became much larger, sheep were
invited to the premises for that purpose.

What might such a meadow have looked like after the animals
had their fill?

Why, a modern lawn, of course.

It had been a grand tour: in time from the Cenozoic to now, in
space across the Atlantic and back again to my meadow along the
hill and down the drive. Yet rather than focusing criticism on my
demanding lawn while extolling the carefree meadow, I had
found the two to be more or less the same. They were intercon-
vertible: I could at any time cut the tall and grow the short, and
they would switch places and natures within four years at most.
True, the meadow was livelier than the lawn, but it was tarnished
by its history. I heard echoes of sanctioned procedures for bringing the land once more to the worthy purpose of growing grain
resound in the sanctified noisiness of Saturday in suburbia.

I decided to plant the real thing: a native American grassland.

9

To Plant a Prairie

A DISAGREEMENT HAS ARISEN between my gardening friends and me concerning grassland terminology: I call our planting prairie; they call it meadow. So, I suppose, would most people, gardeners or otherwise. But how am I to distinguish this grassland from the one that it replaced?

I agree that our hillside is a meadow in that it is a temporary ecosystem which, in the natural course of events, would grow back to the broadleaf forest the atlas says we live in. But the hillside doesn't know that. Its forbs and grasses originated on the central plains, trickled east wherever there was an opening through the trees, puddled in the spaces left by fires and windstorms, and won't realize until they're overshadowed that they're not in Kansas. They are native American grassland; they don't like to have their prairie heritage insulted by being called a meadow, a term derived from *medwe*, the Old English word for "pasture" and closely allied to *mawan*, "to mow."

Okay, I'll go along with the majority. But don't tell my western sunflowers and my prairie dropseed grasses that they're just a crop of hay.

One can't really plant a prairie anyway. One can plant a piece, a patch, a strip, a fragment. The indefinite article is not appropriate for the sea of grass that once rippled from the Rocky Mountains to the Ohio Valley, *the* prairie. One goes against the tide of history seeding even a little wave of grassland: our custom has been to rip it up and plow it under. Four million acres of tallgrass prairie remain. That's 1 percent of the 400,000 square miles there used to be. Most of the remnant is in Kansas, where the largest remaining portion of virgin prairie is scheduled for residential development.

Tallgrass prairie is one of the three major subtypes ecologists describe. The description is usually taken from west to east, following the tilt of the continent as it ramps down from the Rockies. There, where the air has been squeezed dry in its passage over high plateaus and peaks, drygrass or shortgrass prairie descends the mountain slopes and foothills, spreading eastward across the gentle incline of the Great Plains to Minnesota, Iowa, and Texas. Buffalo grass, *Buchloe dactyloides*, a fine-leafed, six-inch turf that spreads by stolons, is the dominant species. At its easternmost extent, shortgrass prairie bleeds into mixedgrass prairie, which, some hundreds of miles farther, begins to lengthen into tallgrass prairie. These transitions are gradual, a result of increasing moisture in an easterly direction and changes in the soil.

Not knowing the full extent and variety of this grassland, people referring to the prairie often mean tallgrass. The dominant tallgrass species are big bluestem and Indiangrass, but there are many others. In wind-shielded hollows where moisture lingers, big bluestem may grow ten feet tall, though eight feet is more usual.

Continuing eastward — and speaking theoretically in the color codes of atlases — tallgrass prairie becomes dotted here and there by trees, then, flowing in and out of the dappled shade of groves, washes against true forest just past Chicago. From there to the Atlantic coast, grassland occurs mainly as those transient puddles that, ignorant of the sea of grass that impelled the trickle eastward, the colonists dubbed meadows. (Our meadow of New York natives includes prairie dropseed grass and the wildflower prairie smoke. Both species are listed as endangered in this state, thanks to the munch-and-mow ecology of meadows.)

The paucity of named categories of grassland masks its actual variety. Within each broad category are smaller ones — streamside associations, limestone communities, sand companions; and smaller ones — groups that grow beneath an oak; and ones smaller still — the narrow niche holding the vanishing fringed gentian. Or is that gentian, pointed out to me by my father fifty years ago, found at all now? Some grassland ecosystems are ghosts: their restoration is more properly a resurrection.

Such was the case with a previously unrecognized and all but extinct subtype resurrected during the late 1980s by the Nature Conservancy on ninety acres in Northbrook, Illinois, and now known as bur oak savanna. The acreage was burned to rid it of European buckthorn and a miscellany of imported weeds, then seeded with tallgrass prairie species. These took hold in open spaces but died out under the bur oak groves that typically dot this landscape. There instead popped up a few odd species, unplanned, unexpected, and at first ignored. Nineteenth-century plant lists revealed, however, that the oddities had commonly grown in association with bur oaks and the more usual prairie types in this sandy glacial outwash once known as barrens. On the hunch of the science director, Steve Packard, seeds of these nearly vanished species were collected from undisturbed corners of cemeteries and remnants of railroad rights-of-way. Like a key turned in a lock, they opened the door to the rest of the oak savanna community. Species that had failed before began to thrive. Long-gone butterflies reappeared: Edward's hairstreak, Appalachian brown, and the great spangled fritillary. Cooper's hawk returned; so did eastern bluebirds.

Prairies don't come in a mix, like lawn seed; they can't be put in backward: orchids before grass, climax species before the pioneers. Subtle ingredients must be added bit by bit, one species summoning a fungus that makes an antibiotic that is needed by another species that then calls to its petals its vanished pollinator. At another restoration in the Chicago area, endangered orchids — the prairie white-fringed orchid (*Habenaria leucophaea*) and the small yellow lady's slipper (*Cypripedium calceolus* var. *parviflorum*) — appeared in their own good time. When the equally rare pale vetchling (*Lathyrus ochroleucus*) found conditions right for its regermination, it was followed by the silvery blue butterfly that feeds on it and that had not been seen thereabouts for decades.

How grand!

Yet how tiny the wild places here and there where seeds were gathered, where rare butterflies still lay their eggs, where fragments of the original prairie survived in forgotten corners!

With nurturing and know-how — and over I don't know how many patient years — one expert restorationist has been able to establish in his small front yard a bit of tallgrass prairie that contains more than 250 species. I suppose, since the seeds of oddities have survived in odd corners and so, too, have the rarities they feed, that his front yard may serve their resurrection. I imagine he has orchids. I wish I did, too.

But I don't kid myself about our meadow. It has fewer than two dozen species, the kinds anyone could grow: beginners' plants, a catalog might call them.

We have to begin somewhere.

Marty and I witnessed an idyllic sight one September. We were on the island off the coast of Maine where we vacation. Monarch butterflies were emerging by the hundreds, taking nectar in the meadowed areas that are still plentiful along ragged roadsides and beyond the margins of mowed yards. This was the season's last crop of monarchs; they were preparing to migrate to Mexico for the winter. They would come north again the following spring, breeding and dying for several generations along the way until, by July or so, the descendants of those we were seeing would return to their ancestral summer home. Theirs is a milkweed route: each northward-flying generation must find milkweeds on which to lay the brood that will advance the family through the

Monarch butterfly

next lap of that annual journey. How many remnant stands of milkweed, then, had nurtured the fall flutter of butterflies we witnessed?

That year, the house on the hill above our pond was sold. We returned home to find that the new owner had mowed to rough lawn the last of a stand of swamp milkweed along the boundary wall, just as we, as new owners, had mowed the portion of the stand that grew on our side of the wall.

Luckily we had, in the meantime, replaced the patch we'd cut.

I don't expect to see rare butterflies. I don't await the reappearance of Mrs. Dana's calopogon orchid, the grass pink that may have grown on this place in her time. Resurrection is less on my mind than preservation. If I can't please orchids, I'll welcome violets. If I can't provide for the silvery blue butterfly, those violets will summon the common blue. To these more modest ends, the number of people planting a piece of native grassland, not the size or sophistication of the individual plantings, is what will matter, for if we don't grow milkweeds in our gardens, we'll have to tell our grandchildren, "We used to see monarch butterflies long ago."

If it hadn't been for the pond, we might have planted a meadow on the order of a front yard. We could then have developed it like any garden: one bed at a time, from seeds raised in flats or plants grown by others, with the usual weeding and watering attentions, and over a leisurely period of time. But the pond was dredged that year. Our town doesn't allow trucking the muck away, so we ended up burying the entire hillside under 2,000 cubic yards of goop.

Goop in April. Cement in May.

What came out of the pond was raw clay, the color of granite, streaked with grit and just enough organics to smell like rotten bathing suits. It gullied in the rain. It cracked in the sun. Shovels couldn't dig this stuff unless kicked hard. The meadow of my imaginings — the graceful grasses, the slender wild onions, the pale asters nodding under the weight of bumblebees, and dark purple ironweeds stiff beneath the light footsteps of yellow butterflies — was to arise from an acre of lunar landscape during, as it turned out, a summer of killing drought.

The acre was not to be a flower mead. We had been that route before on a piece of ground at the foot of the driveway that resembled a vacant urban lot in its growth of burrs and chickory. We had approached that job as though the patch were to be a bed of flowers — indeed, the very picture on the label of a meadow in a can. We turned the weed-choked turf, shook out the clods, raked the soil, and sprinkled it with seeds. Eve could not have been more innocent.

A meadow in a can is a misnomer; the can we bought was real enough, but no meadow could have come of it. An essential ingredient was missing: grass. The mix was flavored with empty calories — slim-bodied, shallow-rooted annuals alien to meadow ecology but included to satisfy the same consumer impatience that demands instant soup. Annual poppies included in the brand we bought were California poppies, that state's official flower. Their reproductive habit is sensible for the Sierras: the seeds germinate in response to late winter rains and produce the next crop of seeds before the summer drought, leaving bare ground for the next generation the following year. I didn't understand the needs of annuals then. I have since looked up the annual ingredients listed on the can. Not a one but didn't come from some desert or alpine homeland where bare ground awaits each spring's new germination. Bare ground doesn't wait around here, where annuals and biennials are briefly successional. In the role of clothing bare ground until the perennials take over, ragweed, lamb's quarters, carpetweed, purslane, and crabgrass easily beat the poppies. Two biennials were also included in the mix: Queen Anne's lace, a weed of wastelands in these parts, and black-eyed Susan. Both did very well. They did well in the neglected lawn, too, where we hadn't planted them.

Perennial coneflowers and blazing stars appeared on the planted patch in the second year. So did quack grass, mugwort, horse nettle, Canada thistle, bindweed, catchweed, and burdock. By the third year, the annuals had disappeared, the perennials were disappearing, and everything else was rampant.

Our neighbor, Mr. Schnekenburger, kindly mows the messy roadsides along the short stretch of blacktop leading to his immaculate grounds. The first year, when blue cornflowers and orange poppies bloomed abundantly, he kept his blade lifted. The second year, he kept his gaze averted. The third year, he lowered both and mowed his usual strip. We finished off the rest.

After this lesson, we weren't about to casually sow meadow on an acre of the moon.

The January before dredging was to begin, we attended a wildflower symposium at the New York Botanical Garden to hear Neil Diboll, the owner of Prairie Nursery in Westfield, Wisconsin, discourse on prairie plantings. Neil's slide show started small: first, an exuberant window box clinging to a highrise apartment building, then a sidewalk border flowering in June (*click*), July (*click*), August (*click*), September. Both had been grown from transplants already two years old and set to bloom.

Another click brought the audience to a field more on the scale we planned. It was on Long Island, not far from here. Its height, ranging from knee to shoulder but mostly waist high, reminded me of meadows long ago. Unlike the smaller, ready-to-bloom gardens started from transplants, this meadow had been sowed as seed and was presented as a sequence covering its first three years. Just the opposite of a canned meadow mix, a prairie planting looks horrid in its first year, disreputable the next, and splendid at the age of three.

Splendor was what we had in mind.

But, we realized as Neil's talk progressed, planting a field-size meadow is more like farming than gardening. Neil became the equivalent of our county agent.

His first advice was to toss the plant list I had compiled based on pretty pictures in favor of one he drew up based on which species could cope with pond "spoil," as it is aptly called in the dredging trade. The list varied according to the degree of moisture on the hillside: Meadow A on high ground, hot and dry; Meadow B sloping toward the pond, moderately moist; Meadow C along the shore, saturated to damp. These were to be seeded. For an island that was to be built of excess clay, Neil suggested grass transplants to prevent erosion.

The planting strategy for a prairie is the opposite of that for a lawn. One plants a lawn in early spring or fall in the expectation that the grasses' rapid cool-season growth will beat the weeds to mowing height. One doesn't try to beat the weeds in a prairie planting. One encourages them, even nurtures them, gives them free rein to romp right through weeping April and into merry May. Then one kills them, then one plants the prairie. Or, if weeds keep coming, one kills repeatedly, nurturing and murdering crop after crop of weeds until, as Neil put it, one commands the ground.*

We made a plan. The pond spoil was to be in place by March, tilled in April, allowed to grow up in weeds in May, herbicided twice, then lightly raked for sowing in early June. But when we

---

* The New England Wild Flower Society advises that those who don't wish to use herbicide to get rid of field weeds for sizable meadow plantings must till repeatedly at two-week intervals starting in the spring and continuing to the fall, and possibly to a second summer, too. The Society opted for herbicide when preparing to plant its meadow, and so did we. Use only one whose active ingredient is glyphosate, which neither poisons the soil nor persists in it and is least toxic to animals.

were supposed to be tilling, the spoil was still in the pond; when we were supposed to be herbiciding, we were tilling, and when we were supposed to be planting prairie, we were killing weeds. When the grass plants arrived for installation on the island, we spent a weekend removing the plugs of its particularly impenetrable clay to replace with topsoil for the grasses' good beginning. By the time we were ready to take on the hillside, it was the beginning of July, a month past the optimal time for sowing, weeks since the last rain, and well over 100 degrees Fahrenheit out there on the baked clay.

A memorable weekend that, when we raked and sowed an acre.

The seeds of prairie species are bizarre: thimbleweed, which looks en masse like a mouse nest; Culver's root, which appears to be just dust; fluffy little bluestem seed that even in small quantities fills a sizable sack and wants very much to blow away. No lawngrass spreader can handle these wild seeds.

One mixes the seeds with damp builder's sand in a bucket to separate them from one another so that sowing is even and sparse. One then broadcasts the mix in wide strokes through slightly open fingers the same way one sows a lawn but, in my case, apprehensively, mindful of the price. The perennial ryegrass I'm used to sowing costs about $2 a pound; prairie dropseed sells for $15 an *ounce*. How to ascertain that it's distributed at the rate of one seed per square foot, a proper distance for this lovely but costly grass? Only later did it occur to me that I had, as usual, let the numbers scare me from calculation. The ounce of prairie dropseed contained 14,000 seeds that covered an area 100 by 140 feet — a cost of about a penny a yard. To sow the same area in ryegrass would have required 75 pounds of seed at a cost of $150 — ten times as much, a dime a yard. I could have afforded to waste some dropseed. (And, *mirabile dictu*, the two-year-old transplants on the island produced four ounces of seeds for free that first summer.)

More enervating than a weekend's raking and a few hours of worried sowing was the wait that followed. I examined the hillside daily, minutely, impatiently. But the germination time of prairie species is slow: three weeks, five weeks, even longer; some species may not sprout until the following season. The sprouting is not dramatic, nothing like the flush of green when a lawn springs up. I rejoiced with prairie blazing star (*Liatris pycnostachya*), the first flower to sprout a pair of cotyledons, only to watch it sit that way for weeks. Finally, sulkily, it added one true leaf. Stiff goldenrod (*Solidago rigida*) came up hairy, a proper prairie trait for capturing dew and dripping it down to its roots, but how much dew can two tiny leaves collect? Switchgrass (*Panicum virgatum*), which we planted as a solid stand, is advertised to grow hip high, but it grew just hand high that summer. Fall found no species taller than six inches.

It was on one August day during this waiting season that I went out and bought the three butterfly bushes, plunked them into the herb garden, and watched the butterflies come. Instant gardening; immediate gratification. On the hillside in the background the blazing stars still stood knee high to a grasshopper, not a butterfly was in sight, and the color green was apparent only at the nearsighted distance of the crawler I had become. But underground, the prairie was growing valiantly and rapidly through the clay.

The length of prairie roots can be stupendous. Germinating seeds may grow a root two inches long before venturing a leaf. A one-year-old prairie dropseed plant may show a tuft of blades no more than finger high when its fibrous mass of roots has already grown a foot or more. By its first birthday, prairie dock (*Silphium terebinthinaceum*) has produced a single modest leaf, but may have dug its taprooted shaft *seven feet* into the ground.

This sci-fi information, read at the kitchen table while admiring the new butterfly bushes, sent me crawling out again to see what a sliver of switchgrass might be up to. At one month old, it was already shooting out rhizomes around the crown, preparing to take on the dozen raspberries that Neil had agreed might be a sufficiently brambly companion for this aggressive grass. Or worth a try at least.

This planting was a trial in both senses of the word: the clay, the drought, the craziness of rowing cartons of grass plants to the island with tools and topsoil in the smallest rowboat made, and watering the island weekly from a bucket. We weren't certain the island plug system would work. We couldn't believe that seeds as tiny as those of Culver's root could cope with a concrete hill.

The fact is this: in the worst possible ground, during the worst weather imaginable, the meadow grew.

The lawn, reseeded to replace its buried predecessor, died.

In the second summer, the grass roots on the island grew well beyond their clay potholes and that planting needed no further attention. Nothing required watering any longer (the meadow

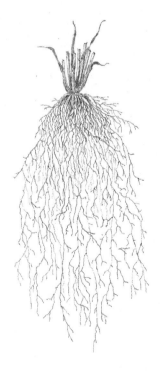

Fibrous roots of a
prairie grass

didn't then, and never will, need fertilizers or pesticides). Elsewhere, weed patrol was necessary.

An area of little bluestem in dry Meadow A grew up with Queen Anne's lace, wild indigo, daisy fleabane, and oxeye daisy — an arrangement so dainty and delightful that a garden photographer memorialized it the week before we cut off the flowerheads to prevent their reseeding and to give the young grass the full blaze of sunlight that warm-season species need. We used a weed whacker for that job. A few plants of invasive purple loosestrife appeared in moist Meadow C beside the pond. We pulled them out by hand. In Meadow B, the middle area that was neither high and dry nor sodden, there were reprisals of yellow nutsedge and uprisings of ailanthus (the tree of heaven that I'd as soon see in

THE ANATOMY OF WATER CONSERVATION

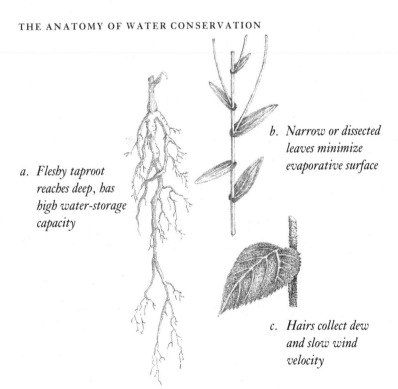

b. Narrow or dissected leaves minimize evaporative surface

a. Fleshy taproot reaches deep, has high water-storage capacity

c. Hairs collect dew and slow wind velocity

hell). These we herbicided. We also divided clumps of grass and
redistributed them to fill in the bare spots where weeds had been
or where seeds had failed to germinate during a somewhat spotty
irrigating regime the previous summer.

All three areas grew very rapidly in this second year. The
switchgrass and little bluestem bloomed; so did smooth penstemon, wild bergamot, prairie blazing star, and pale purple coneflower, along with blue vervain, a welcome addition that we
hadn't planted. At sundown, *Rudbeckia subtomentosa,* a more subtle
version of the black-eyed Susans that inhabited our former
meadow, captured sunlight from the west with such felicity that
I imagined they were saving it up to inject into the eastern sky at
sunrise. It's only in the third year, though, that many species
crouched against the ground venture up to bloom and prairie
plantings rise to meet proud parents' expectations. On the whole,
the meadow that second year was embarrassingly pubescent —
gawky, splotchy, ill groomed, and in need of supervision.

What price magnificence!

What moment shall I choose to paint the picture? Shall I paint
the bleak of winter when in the low light of the day's dying the
feathered stalks of the little bluestem glow pink above the snow?
Or shall I offer the first buds of the swamp milkweed opening to
the monarch butterfly, miraculously arrived to celebrate the moment with a drink? Or August, when the switchgrass droops
beneath its load of ripening seeds? Or earlier, when ruby-
throated hummingbirds snap gold and emerald flies from the
white blossoms of the New Jersey tea, or later, when they dip
into the wild bergamot? Or should I first present the panorama
on a windy summer day in flowing greens and bobbing yellows
and spatterings of purples, pinks, and whites? Maybe I could try
a time-lapse in which the colors spark, spread, fade, deepen,
bleed, run, and leap through the patterns of the seasons with
breathtaking vivacity. Or, looking now toward summers yet to
come, I could visualize a frame in which one year the surprising
orange butterfly weed jumps halfway down the hill, and then

again when blazing stars contract into a shocking intensity of color, and then another year as the penstemons go awandering. Wild plantings never settle down the way cultivated flower borders do. These natives thrive or are thwarted by the whims of weather, move here or there by seed or rhizome, clump up or trail away or catapult to unexpected spots according to factors and vectors too complex and numerous for gardeners to control. It seems to me that only the grass stays put, anchoring these flowery Ariels that otherwise might actually take flight, capturing their colors in a net of green, subduing them with the weight of a dignity borne from ancient days.

Between the high rock outcrop and the mowed path that leads over and down the back of the hill to the woodpile is a small strip of former lawn not included in our meadow plans, yet it became authentic American grassland before any planted portion did.

Neil had discovered in this strip the straw remains of little bluestem stalks among the bluegrass, ryegrass, and other lawn escapees. This was where butterfly weed and yarrow also grew. He suggested that we conduct an experiment when the sugar maple leaves were just beginning to unfold. At that time, in early May, European grasses are well above the ground, whereas warm-season species, flowers as well as grasses, have not yet emerged. On the chosen day, when the ground was damp and the wind calm, we were to mow a firebreak along the rock outcrop (the path would serve as a firebreak along the lower edge of the strip) and burn the thatch starting at the top, using rakes to coax the flames downhill against the prevailing breeze and also against fire's natural inclination to climb upward.

I was less anxious about the prospect than was Marty, a city boy; we had often burned pasture in the country when I was a child. Compared to my exciting recollections, though, this fire was a dud, barely licking, needing more encouragement than a baby's first steps and leaving what could hardly be called scorched earth. The grasses we had tried to burn were in fact still green when the last reluctant flame had flickered out.

The next weekend they were yellow; then most of them were dead. Another week, and little bluestem had poked blades above the ground. By the time we planted the rest of the meadow at the beginning of July, we had a miniature preview of what lush bluestem grassland looks like early in the summer.

Hunters and herders have burned grasslands to rejuvenate them and destroy the encroaching brush since Neolithic times at least, and casual observers of the prairie crossing the Great West by train in the nineteenth century reported grass fires lit by lightning with almost tedious frequency. Yet until ecologists began to experiment with fire on the first attempted prairie restoration, at the University of Wisconsin at Madison in the 1940s, ecologists hadn't fully appreciated its role. The persistence of the prairie for at least ten thousand years in post–Ice Age North America had depended on regular burning.

The site of this first restoration was abandoned old-field farmland, pretty much like that where we tried to plant a meadow from a can, and although the scientists sowed the land with genuine prairie seed, the results were similar: the natives were soon overwhelmed by alien weeds. Fire discouraged these unwanted forbs and grasses, killed the top growth of the brush, and left behind a blackened surface warmed by the sun, bathed in light, and rich in minerals released by the burnt thatch from which, like a phoenix, the prairie then arose.

In the ensuing decades, ecologists have documented through many an arsonous experiment that where fire is an unavoidable natural phenomenon in ecosystems, it is also a necessary one. Left unchecked, natural fires renew tallgrass prairie twice a decade on the average. Scheduled burning every four years has promoted the greatest diversity of native species on some experimental plots; elsewhere, though, annual burning controls weed growth better. Our experimental scheme is to burn one third of the meadowed area every year so that each section is burned every third year. Our estimated cost in labor is about two hours per annum, most of which is spent in preparations such as laying out hoses and wetting down flammable junipers and thin-barked fruit trees. This conservative schedule assures that overwintering insects and their eggs will survive in unburned portions and that there will always be areas of tall growth for nesting birds.

Prairie plantings larger than a hand-weedable flower bed can also be maintained by annual mowing and the judicious use of herbicides. Neil has had success with a regime of May Day mowing followed by a good hard raking so that the clippings don't shade out resprouting plants and germinating seeds. The New England Wild Flower Society, which maintains a quarter-acre meadow at its Garden in the Woods in Massachusetts, uses a sickle bar mower but suggests that a weed whacker might be more congenial in backyard habitats. One contributor to the society's helpful pamphlet *Meadows and Meadow Gardening* suggests various herbicides that can be used to control broad-leaved weeds, weed grasses, and woody species.* I can't claim innocence of herbicides (I defy anyone to get rid of horse nettle in any other way), but spraying is a heavy chore physically and morally. I'm not much more fond of mowing.

For years we owned a sickle bar that could cut through brush a half-inch thick — but it could cut as easily through toes and fingers and once chopped a snake to bits. That wasn't fun. I don't enjoy weed whackers, either: too hard to hold at any given height; too tricky to use near trees with tender bark; too hard to start. They're all too hard to start, these gas-driven cutters. Give me my loppers, my sickle.

Give me a match.

When I called the town office to ask how to get a permit to burn, I was told there was no such thing. No open burning was allowed of anything, anywhere, under any circumstances. I asked for the actual wording of this ordinance. There was no ordinance.

I called the New York State Department of Environmental

---

* *Meadows and Meadow Gardening* can be obtained from the New England Wild Flower Society, Garden in the Woods, Hemenway Road, Framingham, Massachusetts 01701. The article I refer to is "Meadow Management," by Barbara Emerson.

Conservation, Bureau of Source Control (source of what? another mystery). They said the "regs" were no open burning within village or city limits, nor in any municipality with more than 20,000 people. We are outside the village limits of a town of 4,500. But who granted the permit New York State was sure we must have? The Source didn't know.

I called my volunteer fire department. Instantly, I hit a vein of nostalgia about the days when firemen used to help farmers burn their fields but uncertainty about where permits come from. Perhaps the health department.

Yes, the Westchester County Health Department, Bureau of Environmental Quality, grants burn permits, but it was out to lunch. One must be as persistent as a horsenettle to light a match outdoors.

Eventually, our small-town lawyer ("It's not what you know; it's who you know") referred me to a helpful member of our county's legal department, who explained the basics to me.

Burning is never allowed during a drought because of the danger of flames getting out of hand. During stagnant air conditions, the soot particles in smoke contribute heavily to smog, and open burning may be forbidden for that reason. Under any circumstances, burning releases the greenhouse gases carbon monoxide and carbon dioxide into the atmosphere, thus the official reluctance to allow grass fires.

I agree that the perfume of burning autumn leaves and the thrill of bonfires in the winter are pleasures too light to outweigh medical and environmental caution, and leaves are better used for compost, brush better chipped for mulch or stacked tidily to decay in place. But everything considered, I'm not sure that grass fires and the ecosystems they maintain don't outweigh the environmental onus of the lawns prairie plantings usually replace.

On our meadow's side of the scale is a single item: a once-every-three-years burn. On the lawn side hang air-polluting mowers, blowers, edgers, thatchers, whackers, and aerators fueled by gasoline; the petrochemicals that make up lawn fertilizers, insecticides, and herbicides; the fuel-hungry industrial pro-

cesses by which these products, the bags and bottles that contain
them, and the spreaders and sprayers that distribute them are
manufactured. And trucking, too, of course. To that side of the
scale must also be added water, both the incredible volume that
keeps lawns green and the onus of water pollution caused by
chemical runoff.

Could an hour of triennial smoke possibly be so heavy?
Other items remain incalculable. How to measure the societal
benefits of increased weekend leisure? How to weigh the environmental benefits of habitat enrichment? I can't translate into numbers our ease within the grassland that we planted or its ecological
potential, but common sense placed on the scale seems to me to
sink the lawn out of sight beneath the rising phoenix that, plumes
shining, trails but a tendril of smoke as the price of its magnificence.

There did turn out, though, to be an ordinance: Code of the
Town of Pound Ridge, Chapter 57 Fires, Control of, Article III,
Section 57–10 (no wonder it was hard to find!), which can be
overridden by a New York State Department of Environmental
Conservation Permit for Restricted Burning (issued pursuant to
6NYCRR 191, 215 and Environmental Conservation Law).

We got the permit.

We burn.

My mind goes back to the Indian who lost his arrowhead on the
rock beneath the oak, that ghost of three centuries ago who,
traversing this hillside, trod on soil deeper and richer than what
remains. Maybe soil pulled from the pond and spread uphill
redressed the loss somewhat, but there are yards to go and fertility to build.

This is a grassland job.

For all the environmental services that forests incomparably
provide, no forest can manufacture soil as deep as that of grassland in any length of time. The nutrient cycle is too slow — trees
store nutrients too long; their decay releases nutrients too slowly
— for organic soil to build to the thickness of a prairie. Grass

gives the earth the fullness of its body every year and replenishes root and stem in rapid cycles, transforming gray clay to brown humus, mineral crustiness to silky tilth, with a speed and to a depth unknown even in the old-growth forests still remaining in the West.

One reads this. Tries to picture it. Hopes to find new richness revealed in one's own sorry spoil.

Curious to see if magic were happening yet, I dug down one day three years after grass had first germinated in the clay. I found an earthworm. But my eager human rhythm was out of step with grassland time, and my vision was insufficiently near-sighted. I couldn't see that much was happening. Let my grand-children dig the hillside at my age, though, and they'll see a topping of good earth.

What else will they see, will they point out to their grandchil-dren? Will they see the walking stick that I knew in childhood but that hasn't yet returned? Will they be startled by the noisy flight of red-legged grasshoppers whose legs kick hard enough to hurt and who spit brown drops like chewed tobacco? I see mead-owlarks, but there aren't any bobolinks yet. I look in vain for the green grass snakes of my childhood.

One can't plant the prairie. One can plant only shreds of it that in time may weave themselves together more completely. Among the additions we hope to make to our meadow is a sunflower, *Helianthus giganteus*, that will bloom in the shade of a hickory tree toward the bottom of the hill. No nursery that I know of lists it. The only source for seed hereabouts is a stand of this native sunflower that someone planted long ago to dramatize a mailbox. That's not prairie, but it's a piece of it.

10

Frogs:
In Memoriam

AN AQUATIC PLANTS CATALOG in my mail order collection offers tadpoles with the promise, "Grow up into frogs!" As if I didn't know. As if I hadn't grown up with a swamp next door, a lake down the road, a stream, spring, and frog pond within yards of the house. But this nursery must know its business. It must have reason to believe that its customers are pollywog naive. It must suspect, as I do, that there aren't many frog ponds anymore.

Ours was a mere dent, an oval maybe twelve feet wide by a little longer, on a long slope that drained runoff into a neighboring swamp. There was neither inlet nor outlet. Possibly it was the remains of a stock pond dug by two bachelors, Civil War veterans who built the cottage, barns, and rubble walls. Or perhaps it was a spring like the deep, cold, mossy one in the dark woods over the wall where we kept a dipper hung from a nail on an overhanging tree from whose great roots the clear water seemed to rise.

The frog pond, shallow and sunny, was the home of three species — pickerel frog, northern leopard frog, and bullfrog — and so many of them that any time it came into my head to catch a frog, I could. This miniature habitat was surrounded by a dense growth of rush and sedge. Water striders and whirligig beetles dimpled the surface. Below their strange domain — the tissue of tension by which they are supported — grew dragonfly nymphs that, breaking through into the air, emerged as adults with stiff glassy wings to shimmer above the shore. The water level lowered somewhat in the heat of summer, baring mudbanks where butterflies came to drink and bask. Small clouds of dancing flies would appear, the minute individuals hovering, dipping, darting, rising, while the cloud itself hung motionless in the air. There were red-bellied daddy longlegs whose sickly sweet smell deters other predators and whose skinny legs, in a second line of defense, break off at the slightest tug, and a pair of handsome black and yellow argiopes whose two-orbed web was marked by a zigzag band woven by the male on his side of their joined masterpiece.

What did I do at the frog pond? Searched for polka-dotted jelly, watched the round black eggs take tadpole shape inside transparent spheres, watched the pollywogs squirm free, watched their legs grow, watched their tails shrink, watched day after day this transformation into frog.

I saw the hatching of spiders, the capture of flies. I saw the

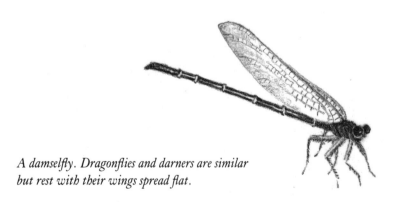

A damselfly. Dragonflies and darners are similar but rest with their wings spread flat.

flirtation of butterflies, that slow winking of wings that is their sexual display. I saw dragonflies coupling in flight or alighting on a rush to complete their copulation with bright red or iridescent blue abdomens bent to the task for minutes on end. I saw the pond, one summer, bulldozed to oblivion.

Too bad the frog pond lay in what was to become front lawn. Too bad it was filled in, drained out through tiles that conducted its once teeming water directly to the swamp. Too bad the swamp, too, was eventually drained for tract housing on quarter-acre lots. Too bad for the children who moved there that they could no longer, any time it entered their head to catch a frog, find one. Too bad there has grown up a generation that must be told what tadpoles grow up to be.

Since the loss of wetlands is so much in the news, I wouldn't discuss it were it not that the full extent of the loss has been obscured by its very largeness. The plight of great rivers, great swamps, great lakes, hits the newspapers. But let's look at something smaller than the Colorado. Let's look at seeps, rivulets, sumps, hollows, bogs, ditches, frog ponds. Let's examine the face of the continent through a magnifying glass, noticing less the large protuberances and declivities than the fine texture of its

Black and yellow
argiope spider

skin, its pores and little wrinkles. Let's get down to the minutiae of puddles. Let's look at our own back yards and ask where butterflies can drink.

It won't take long. There's nothing much to see. No bumpy dirt drive where water puddles after a rain. No ditch along the driveway, either. No hollow trees. Whoever lives now on the land that held the spring wouldn't be able to find it even if the dipper still hung to point the way. The spring has long since disappeared along with the sinking water table. Think where the rain goes now; look for suburbia's water underground, in pipes. This country is obsessed with drainage.

How much water does it take to quench a butterfly's thirst? Give a dove a bath? Provide a laying place for toads? No more than a puddle.

Consider the kinds of puddles. There are shallow ones, entered by wading, where songbirds splash. There are mud ones in the sun where butterflies perform their triple-duty ablutions, sipping, sunning, and flirting simultaneously. There are deep ones with submerged vegetation that last for weeks in the spring; these are where male toads congregate to trill musically and lengthily until the willing females hop to their embrace, where eggs are laid in strings on sticks or stems, where tadpoles transform into terrestrials. The quantity of water is less demanding than habitat requirements, which explains why jays, swallowtails, and peepers aren't cavorting in suburbia's many swimming pools. (I once saw toads lustily copulating and laying in puddles on a flat roof without benefit of vegetation. Don't ask me how they got there. Up the waterspout? The tadpoles, however, perished.)

What I am trying to get across is that the concept of wetlands could benefit from miniaturization. Then, looking around our yards, we might at least see some moist potential. Perhaps there's a woodpile. The rotting bottom logs are a wetland habitat for pill bugs, millipedes, and salamanders. Examine the foundation. Green algae growing in the dank indicate a habitat that might be kept moist enough for toads if planted with a leafy growth of ferns. Jewelweed signals moist conditions; the orange blossoms of this succulent annual are a favorite drinking stop for thirsty hummingbirds. Watch where the rain goes. Swales, gutters, waterspouts, and curtain drains could be directed into bogs or basins instead of lost to culverts. A friend, showing me her back yard, asked how I liked the birdbath. I looked for the classic kind, perched on a pedestal, but hers was of a more ancient pattern: a broad stump sawed to ground level, rotted and hollowed in the middle, filled by a garden hose.

To my neighbors down the road a piece who have been unable to sell their real estate because a substantial puddle occupies the front lawn two thirds of the year, here is my advice: in lieu of crushed bluestone and perforated PVC, plant a bottomland of shiny inkberry pierced by yellow birch; a stand of swamp azaleas (most fragrant of them all); Turk's-cap lilies, bottle gentians, and turtleheads set among lacy meadowrue; or a grove of witch hazel; or pussy willows.

Or dig a frog pond.

If whatever moisture now lingers in the dimples of our increasingly sere continent is newly precious, then the preservation of open water — pools, flows, falls, trickles, bubbles, leaps of fish, divings of ducks, mayhems of muskrats, stillness of herons — is a responsibility as heavy as the fall of Niagara. We have a pond. No neighbors share it, although that is an accurate statement only in the sense of plat and deed. In fact, it receives the runoff of some thirty acres, delivers that water through stream and marsh and half a dozen other ponds to the Mianus River, to the reservoir the river sustains, and thence to the population of Stamford, Connecticut, a city of 108,000. That's just the human count. No one's wetland is really his to do with as he will.

We began some years ago to notice a decline of frogs. Living by a pond, one gets used to the nightly calling, the distinctive tone, timbre, and rhythm that identify each species and that, when all are croaking at once, create a comical effect, like children with improvised instruments. When we moved here there had been many bullfrogs in the chorus, but by the summer we let the lawn grow wild, the big bass section had been reduced to a single voice. Soon other sections, too, were thinned.

There were several possible explanations. The big boom in gypsy moths had caused us and the whole neighborhood to spray our trees in panic. That might have done it. We had cleared the brush from one shore of the pond and mowed it down to lawn. Could that have exposed the frogs to more than the usual predation? On the other hand, the pond itself had changed. During our first years here, the water had been clear; now, by late June it was covered with pea green duckweed and algal slime, a sign of aging called eutrophication.

A pond is not forever, but ours was too young to die. A series of photographs in my biology text shows the succession by which a pond about the size of this one shrinks and shallows as plants trap silt and build new soil. The process is inevitable and even rapid: the time from pond to swamp to meadow is about the same as the time from meadow to brush to forest, about 150 years.

Aerial photographs taken of the neighborhood before World War II show the farm road whose ruts are still visible when they catch the snow in winter, but no pond. The road, however, followed the present shoreline exactly, and, like a ghost, the full shape of the pond was revealed in a patch of vegetation that differed in texture from the surrounding pastureland. The pres-

Bullfrog

ent pond, redug to the shape of what probably had been a farm pond scooped from swamp in the previous century, materialized on a 1951 map, making it at most a half century old, mature but not elderly.

What we were seeing, then, was not normal eutrophication but premature senility, in which excess phosphates and nitrogen feed unnaturally heavy blooms of algae. The algae, annually dying and sinking to the bottom, support unnaturally heavy populations of bacterial decayers, and the decayers, in their massive digestion of gross vegetable bulk, consume the water's oxygen. The result is not only the suffocation of animals that need high oxygen levels but the spiraling strangulation of the pond by plants glutting on rich mud.

The prognosis was that ours did not have long to live, and its sickness almost certainly had been caused by the runoff of fertilizer from our lawn.

How did our commitment to redig the pond take hold? Through futile inquiries into algicides (illegal) and equally futile attempts to gather the gunk in nets (exhausting, endless). Through years of greening water growing viscous, smelling bad, dumping duckweed on downstream neighbors. Through no frogs returning. Through a sudden mental image: a cross-cut through the land, so much to be lifted from the hollow, so much to be piled on the hill. Through the vanished woods. Through images of prairie. Through the abrupt coming together of it all: wetland, woodland, grassland, edge.

Pond "clean-outs" aren't uncommon operations here, where ponds are many and aging. On the whole, though, the operation is destructive. The esthetic ideal seems to be a pond entirely edged in stone coping; barring that, mowed right to the water line all around. Streams are improved in a similar style: cleared, cemented in with rock, and mowed to a ribbon through the lawn. These are not habitat restorations; they make no allowance for inhabitants.

Wetland rejuvenation requires a good deal of thought and

planning. Each species that shares the water has specific needs. Big fish, such as the largemouth bass that lives beneath the bridge, can't overwinter at depths of less than eight feet. Algal germination is better suppressed at the darker depth of ten. Bluegills, called sunfish or sunnies here, spawn in shallow water well heated by the sun. Fish fry (tadpoles too) need water weeds along the shore where they can hide from predators. Ducks and geese have difficulty with steep banks. Turtles must have gently sloping rocks or logs on which to bask. Cattails grow at one depth, water lilies at another, but if neither is to take over, those depths must descend abruptly into deeper water. The heron appreciates high perches from which to sight its prey. The flight paths of wood ducks must be considered if one hopes to house them. For each species there must be suitable food as well as shelter.

The plan we devised included all of these provisions (the island, much enjoyed by all of the above, was serendipity, suggested by the dredger, who saw no possibility of otherwise disposing of so much clay). The woodland shore is overhung with arching viburnums and low-limbed maples. We didn't disturb it when dredging; the shore harbored a muskrat couple in a burrow entered below the water line in the roots of a rotting snag where, during the following spring, they raised three babies. We left the

Painted turtle

large logs that leaned against the shore for turtle basking; turtles also bask now on the sloping rocks that form the ends of the little island. The island, planted in prairie grass and a single cornelian cherry, has become a popular bird bathing spot. The great blue heron fishes there. Some handsome boulders that I coveted for pondside seating we reluctantly replaced on the pond bottom from whence they had been dredged; the dredger, a sometime fisherman, preempted them as hangouts for the fish. The shore-line boulder beside which our resident goose couple traditionally nested was also left in place, although this occasioned a crisis when the female laid two eggs that would have drowned below the water line when the pond was refilled (we removed the eggs, the geese removed themselves, and the pair came back three weeks later with their goslings). We graded the sunny shore gently for bluegills; it had always been their favored nesting spot. The slightest lowering of the water level reveals a mud flat loved by butterflies, and it is but a wing's flap to a delicatessen of blossoms, upland or pondside. We mow a short strip of this shore to the edge for boat launching and foot dabbling. Else-where around the perimeter the pond is lined with food plants: berries, seeds, leaves, stalks, tubers. Geese eat (and fertilize) the lawn.

Bluegill, otherwise known as sunfish, "sunny" for short

It strikes me that no other description in this book could mention so many animals in one small habitat, and I haven't mentioned minnows, bats, a jillion insects, raccoons and possums, water snakes, garter snakes, kingfishers, mallards, killdeer, and every sort of bird that lives who-knows-where but comes to drink, and all the transient fliers, too, that congregate by the pond during migration as travelers congregate at McDonald's, as shoppers congregate at malls. The pond is an emporium, a spa, a skyway rest stop. No other feature summons more wildlife than a spot of water.

But the question will arise: Did dredging not kill the fish, the turtles, the few frogs remaining? We lost one medium-size snapping turtle and three bluegills. Otherwise, no. The lone bullfrog croaked (in the proper sense of the word) the next May.

Another question: Why, when aquatic vegetation eventually turns ponds back to meadow, did we plant such things as cattails? Answer: What is a muskrat to eat?

And, finally: How much did this cost?

One third the price of a smallish swimming pool.

.   .   .

Muskrat

Coming up the drive, the machine looked like Godzilla, its long, bucketed neck poised to bite the treetops. The monster, a thirty-year-old Bucyrus Erie dragline, had a plump cab counter-weighted behind with a solid steel bumper heavy enough to balance the forty-foot boom and bucket out front. The total weight of the machine was twenty-four tons. As it crawled through the meadow (yet to be prairie) and down the hillside on giant caterpillar treads, it dwarfed the landscape and the puppet man inside — Ralph Nau, the dredger — who pulled and pushed the levers that made Godzilla go. But in its natural wetland habitat, the machine diminished in size. Its maw, though bigger than a bathtub, in fact guzzled mud one yard at a time.

I've always found it both riveting and painful to watch great lumbering machines. Their work is powerful but slow, and one's muscles strain to speed them, to lighten their effort, to give them grace, to urge the smoothness and ease with which children at the beach shape sand to their design. Yet a giant looking down on the dredging operation would be reminded exactly of the little ponds, dams, and channels that children so joyfully construct at the water's edge. When the water had been lowered somewhat by pumping it downstream through hoses, Ralph dug a deep refuge for the fish and turtles and let them swim to it through channels as the water lowered farther. He dammed this area to keep it filled while he continued pumping, constructed deeper drainage routes, built shoreside holding pools in which to sort organic ooze from sterile bottom clay, and heaped up a ramp over which he trundled his machine into the middle of the pond. From there, one mouthful at a time, the dragline swung slurps of mud and bites of clay from the pond's bottom to the holding bowls ashore. It was playful, really, although the scale was large and the movement ponderously slow.

A month after the old Bucyrus Erie had first tilted down into the pond, it lumbered ashore again, chewing its ramp away behind it, and turned uphill to disgorge the spoil from the holding bowls in heaps over the hillside, lick it smooth with slow sweeps of its steel maw, and pour over that heavy cake of clay a thin icing of organic ooze. Another two weeks, and the dragline had worked itself up to the top, back down along the drive, and finally, tamely, it heaved aboard its trailer and was gone.

On the last day of April, Ralph hauled in his hose, shut down his pump, and let the water rise to fill the pond.

The day the pond reached level, when the water first spilled over the outlet fall to fan through the wet woods below, the UPS man knocked at the door. *Typha, Nymphaea, Peltandra, Pontederia, Sagittaria;* in my aquatic memory, I had it all by heart except the delivery date. It struck me late and hard that I had no idea how to plant a water lily.

In hip boots? The year before Marty had waded out into the mud in thigh-high fisherman's boots to remove fallen willow boughs from the clogged inlet and — sucked in and slowly sinking — had barely made it back to shore. By boat? That seemed risky, too.

I called the nursery for horticultural advice. The woman I spoke with said there was no trick at all; one simply lowers the pots into eight inches of water.

What pots?

According to this expert, one never plants aquatics directly in the mud. One pots them, places the pots in shallow water for the summer, moves them to deep water in the fall, pulls the pots in the spring, puts them back into shallow water, and so on, for as many as five years, until the plants are well enough established to go permanently to ground.

How was one to find the sunken pots come spring? "That," she replied, "is why we don't recommend earth-bottomed ponds."

How can a nursery that specializes in aquatics be so archly biased against the natural wetlands in which their specialty originated? On the other hand, if ornamental pools are becoming as popular as the number of nurseries offering them implies, then purveyors of aquatics are performing an important service. Artificial waterworks might be the only way to replace the springs and trickles that no longer wet the land.

Michael McKeag, of tract development lot 43, has managed an artificial stream, pond, *and* bog to complement his sedge meadow, which he has edged with berry bushes and backed by woods. He wrote to me, "Today was a historic moment for our little backyard wilderness. [We] powered up the pump and our 60' private stream filled its bed and now babbles endlessly as it circulates in its own hydrologic cycle. . . . A backyard without a stream now seems to me as lifeless as a living room without a hearth."

With the stream flowing (and the pool also complete), Michael and his son were about to excavate the bog. Curious about how such things are done, I bought Ortho's publication *Garden Pools & Fountains*, which offers clear do-it-yourself instructions and many designs for streams, falls, and bogs as well as pools and fountains. The work is similar to such chores as excavating new garden beds, laying stone paths, or installing simple irrigation systems. The smallest and most modest design shown in the book is a fountain that spills into a shallow saucer lined with smooth stones. Others are nearly the size of our childhood frog pond, and some are as ambitious as Michael's backyard system.

But the "wildlife" in the illustrations was not what I have in mind for America's back yards. Our ambition shouldn't be to accommodate exotic goldfish and tropical water lilies. We should serve the dispossessed: the sipping butterflies, the bathing birds, the laying toads, the overwintering minnows and common newts. I'd want a tamped earth beach for butterflies; a nonslip pebbled bath for birds (graded gently from the shore to four inches deep, as the Audubon Society suggests). Instead of the overhanging coping styled for formal pools and not negotiable by amphibians, I'd provide inclined or stepped-down edges for newts' and toads' convenience; and, for fish, I'd dig some portion three feet deep at least so they wouldn't suffocate for lack of oxygen under the ice in winter. I'd put wild celery (*Vallisneria americana*) in the water along the edges to protect their fry, soft rushes and sedges where dragonflies could perch and frogs could hide, and maybe cardinal flowers to attract hummingbirds as well. And a bush or little tree; there has to be a place for birds to perch while waiting to bathe.

Then I'd hie me to a bait shop and buy some local minnows and hope the newts would make it overland on their own as terrestrial red efts. And yes, I'd order some catalog tadpoles and watch them grow up into frogs.

Rana catesbeiana, as it happens: bullfrogs.

Nothing can keep Marty away from muck. It's not the dirt that draws him but the water in it: he must make it flow.

Every summer evening he strolls around this place, but never up the hillside, never toward the sunset where the mountain laurels grow. Always, every evening, he prowls down around the pond. If he disappears during the weekend, I know where he is: by the pond, hacking channels, fishing branches, netting weeds, or — most eloquently — sluicing water along smooth rock works

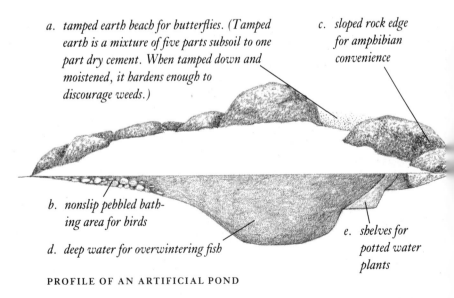

a. *tamped earth beach for butterflies. (Tamped earth is a mixture of five parts subsoil to one part dry cement. When tamped down and moistened, it hardens enough to discourage weeds.)*

c. *sloped rock edge for amphibian convenience*

b. *nonslip pebbled bathing area for birds*

d. *deep water for overwintering fish*

e. *shelves for potted water plants*

PROFILE OF AN ARTIFICIAL POND

of his own devising to ease its satisfying flow. It wouldn't surprise me if psycho-archaeologists were eventually to surmise that irrigated agriculture sprang from men's urinary interests, as ancient as the cave boy's urge to pee on the campfire.

Visiting children gravitate to the pond. Perhaps its elemental vigor suits their gargantuan appetite for authenticity — the bass leaping for its prey, the heron swallowing the bass — and adventure (the boat, the island, the only souvenir that surfaced in the dredgings: a Borden's milk bottle with the admonition, "Elsie says BUY WAR BONDS Everybody — Every Payday 10%" Remember?).

Memory is what drives me. The memory of stagnant waters, for in truth the inlet usually dries up in July and doesn't flow again until September. And something deeper than memory but also written on the brain: a love of wetness and fecundity, the smell of mud.

Never mind what misadventures we enjoyed as we planted water lilies, cattails, arrowheads, et al., using ropes, bags, tubs, stones, boards, oars, and other improvisations. Nothing grows like a water plant. We shoved into the mud duck potatoes (wapatoes, arrowheads, tubers of many species of the genus *Sagittaria*) no bigger than baby turnips and somewhat resembling them, and three weeks later leaves had reached up to our knees. That much time again and the plants had flowered, with sprays of white

Bullfrog
tadpole

blossoms set gracefully like tropical orchids on tall stems. We received from UPS a plastic bag of grimy cattail rootstocks, their tops shorn to gooey stubs redolent of slime, and stuck them in. They grew. They multiplied. They bloomed bright pollen yellow. We sank the water lilies too deep for their survival — or so the nursery said. But even with the three young muskrats teething on their stems, they, too, grew florid in one summer. Pickerel weed had purpled already by mid-July and bloomed on through Labor Day. The only loss was the golden club, on which Marty, to whom infant plants are beneath notice, placed a fine, large rock.

The memories a pond holds transcend nostalgia; there lingers a miasma of the past. Lying on the ground and squinting through a stand of scouring rushes, I take myself back 300 million years to their ancestral forest of towering Sphenophytes. The dragonfly looks very large from this perspective — a Meganeuron dragonfly, perhaps, with wings that span a yard. Down at its level, nose to nose, a salamander would seem to be the first amphibian, a lungfish crawled ashore panting air with palpitating throat and necessarily returning to the water to lay its fish roe eggs. Startled by my lurking on the shore, the heron arises with reptilian croak, slowly flapping its feathered dinosaurian wings. My nostrils fill

A good way to plant aquatic tubers: cut ten-inch squares of cheesecloth, place on each a few tubers and a handful of stones or coarse gravel, draw up the corners, and tie into a bag with string. Then drop the bags into the pond at the proper depth. The weight of the stones keeps the tubers down in the mud, where they easily root through the cheesecloth.

with bacterial effusions, the very odor of antiquity. This is our ancient history, this clay, this muck, this algal slime, this rich reek of life's beginning.

The frogs did not return in their former numbers. The cause of their decline was not the illness of the pond. Amphibians are mysteriously diminishing all over the world: the common frog in Denmark, the common toad in England, rice paddy frogs in Japan, Goliath frogs in Cameroon, the Corroboree toadlet down under in Australia. America has its own litany of losses: in Arizona, the Tara Humara frog; in Colorado, the tiger salamander; in Oregon, the Cascades frog, western spotted frog, and red-legged frog; in California, the red-legged frog again and the Yosemite toad, spade-foot toad, and the mountain yellow-legged and foothill yellow-legged frogs as well.

Amphibians are peculiarly vulnerable to modern hazards. Their thin, moist skin, a supplemental respiratory membrane through which oxygen is absorbed, also absorbs lead, mercury, pesticides, and other pollutants from the air and water. So yes, spraying might explain the losses from our pond. So might predation. The storied Calaveras County jumping frog was eaten to vanishing by humans, then to extinction by bullfrogs imported

*Red eft, the juvenile
terrestrial stage of the
common newt*

into California to supplement the vanishing supply. Cattle egrets, arrived here from South America early in this century and multiplying to pest proportions wherever cattle graze, are hunting ponds to froglessness in Texas. Game fish stocked for sport in private lakes and ponds prey heavily on tadpoles. Alas, the largemouth bass in our pond were stocked for children's sport by the previous owner.

But amphibians may suffer most of all from drainage. Rice paddy frogs are diminishing as paddies are drained for golf greens, just as the frog pond of my childhood was drained for lawn, just as such puddles all over this country continue to go underground. Who can guess how many salamanders, on returning to their natal pond to breed, have found a condominium instead?

Details of these amphibian disappearances came to me through a report on a conference held to discuss the problem. The remark of one participant nagged at me particularly. Frogs, he reminded his listeners, lay their fragile jelly eggs all together in a mass that floats at the water's surface close to shore. Ten thousand unhatched tadpoles can therefore be wiped out in a single predatory event. Like two children playing toss the jelly, he suggested.

I think that if I had no pond, shared no lakeshore, abutted on no stream or marsh or river, I would build a little artificial wetland, however much tinkering it took with pipes and pumps and electrical connections. Maybe it wouldn't be as ambitious as Michael's meandering stream. Maybe it would be just puddle size. Maybe it would serve no more than the couple of hop toads whose burrows are underneath the garden wall.

Toads live for thirty years. That should be long enough to sensitize several generations of children to the hoppers, pollywogs, and jelly eggs we must relinquish to their recollections and their care.

11

Smiles of Vanished Woods

THE *Town of Pound Ridge Local Law No. 1 of the Year 1990* reads in part:

> The Town Board finds it has been established that trees stabilize the soil and control water pollution by preventing soil erosion and flooding, reduce air pollution, provide oxygen, yield advantageous micro-climatic effects, temper noise, and provide a natural habitat for the wildlife of the town. . . . Indiscriminate removal of trees causes deprivation of these benefits and disrupts the Town's ecological systems. . . . The Town, furthermore, takes note of the findings of the New York State Environmental Quality Review Act, among them being the obligation of the Town to serve as steward of air, water, land and living resources and the obligation to protect the environment for the use of this and further generations.

The following paragraphs prohibit without a special permit clear-cutting, cutting trees on steep slopes, cutting protected tree species, cutting large trees except to relieve crowding, and cutting trees that grow within twenty-five feet of the boundaries of one's property.

The law is welcome as a measure of preservation, but it doesn't see the forest for the trees.

On the way to the supermarket, we pass a property that has been cleared of every stem and sapling that loppers can bite between their jaws, of all redundancy of four-inch trunks that handsaws can sever with their teeth, of all larger trees that, because they grew too close together to please the owner's eye, were flagged for the chainsaw and chipper. The result is a stand of same-age trees uniformly spaced over clean ground that was once woodland but is no longer. Yet this radical surgery is legal.

Seedlings and saplings cut in such blind operations might have been the upcoming generation that would one day have replaced their aging elders. Many other slender trunks may have been understory trees — maybe dogwood, maybe redbud, maybe our lovely hornbeam (*Carpinus caroliniana*). Some were perhaps the ultimate wave of natives that would have brought the forest to its climax as they succeeded earlier settlements of transient pioneers.

This tree collection — I don't know what else to call it — is displayed on raked ground in a setting of grass and pachysandra from which it rises indecently, naked of the leafy edge that should naturally clothe it. There are no shrub laws to prevent such stripping.

The pachysandra is the Japanese species, *Pachysandra terminalis*, and it will live up to its name in this location by becoming a terminal growth. The plant is propagated by cloning; the rooted cuttings that one buys are genetically identical. Although described as bearing a profusion of flower spikes in the spring followed by white berries in the fall, the clone here throws itself instead into rampant spread by rhizome, covering the ground at a gallop as its selectors intended it to do: in shade, among trees, and so thickly that no fern or wildflower grows through it.

Talk of "deprivation of benefits"! Ecosystem services are so compromised by this type of clearing that the very trees are endangered. The controls that woodland species exert over their environment are not possible in this roadside ribbon that is skinned bare of brush at its edges and that has no innards. It is battered by drying winds, exposed to too much heat and light, open to incursions of destructive weedy species. That poor glade needs a protective zone of smaller trees and shrubs to cut wind, hold moisture, moderate temperature, provide shade, enrich soil, and in all these ways seal its severed edge from the injurious and infectious outer world. As far as providing a "natural habitat" for the wildlife communities our town wishes to protect, this entire assemblage might as well be plastic.

The woodland our town is so ardently attempting to preserve is like the Cheshire Cat — the mere smile of an ecosystem that vanished long ago and that can't be reembodied by legislation. The law defines a tree as "a living woody plant with an erect perennial trunk six (6) inches in diameter or more d.b.h. [diameter breast height] with a definitely formed crown of foliage," thus leaving unprotected exactly those smaller woody plants that provide refuge to so many and that have been hit hardest by the loss of diversity. By definition, one is not allowed to cut a Norway maple, even though the black shade of that imported species prevents the germination of no fewer than forty native woody species, according to the ecologists restoring the woodland wounded by those maples in New York City parks.

I worry that as environmental concerns are translated into legislation, they will contribute more to complacency than to action. I'm afraid citizens will infer from regulations concerning woodland or wetland that these ecosystems are healthy, their continuance assured. Municipalities are responsible for the preservation of the ecosystem in an abstract and ultimately impotent sense. They can't legislate woodland complexity or impose species diversity. They can't inventory what grows on my land or on yours or, more important, what is missing from it. Not towns but only individuals can approach their land with intimate concern and understanding, not only to preserve but to restore, to cut as well as plant, to replace red maples with Atlantic white cedars (*Chamaecyparis thyoides*) — listed in the ordinance as a rare and protected species.

We had a run-in with the tree law when a neighbor called the building inspector to report our cutting down the crack willows in the woods behind our pond. We had broken laws of both size and location: the trunk of the largest of the dozen trees was five feet in diameter; all but two of them were in the inviolate twenty-five-foot zone along our boundary. We had, in addition, transgressed the wetland regulations. Luckily, all the willows had terminal rot, and all were prone to dropping tonnages of deadwood unexpectedly. One is allowed to cut diseased trees and those that are a danger to life, limb, or property. The building inspector came and went without noting the quite extraordinary size of the woodpile where the black snake lives.

The woodpile records an archaeology of clearing: at the bottom, fallen pioneers — poplar, sassafras, birch — long retired from succession and sawed up after death; in the middle, cherry and ailanthus, selected for removal here and there because we didn't like them; on top, green ash and red maple, thinned from the woods behind the pond.

This woodpile shames me. It doesn't reflect our need for firewood (if it did, it wouldn't have grown high enough to record a decade's cutting). The deadwood on the bottom should not have been removed from the woods. It was the next century's nutrition. It supported more forest life — fungi and minute animals similar to the myriads that digest dead leaves — than is supported by living trees. Some deadwood had been what our tree company disparagingly called woodpecker snags — upright, branchless trunks riddled with holes that woodpeckers drill to reach grubs chewing beneath the bark. Snags are woodpeckers' courtship drumming stations and may hold their nests as well. Nest holes excavated by woodpeckers provide homes in later years to animals that can't excavate for themselves: chickadees, tree swallows, bluebirds, bats, flying squirrels.

I remember one apple tree in particular that we cut down, a

relic from the time that the woods had been field. It was not yet dead, but it was hollow, rotted to the core. Possums, skunks, raccoons, and squirrels depend on such cavities; honeybees build their hives in hollow trees.

The sawed-down, cut-up black cherries now fill me with regret. A horticultural encyclopedia, which lists *Prunus serotina* under "Trees to Avoid," briefly describes this native as having messy fruit and tentworms, to which I'll add that it grows crookedly, branches sparsely, gets heartrot, and soon dies. Yet not just tent caterpillars, but the larvae of coral hairstreaks, red-spotted purple butterflies, and a batch of lovely others eat black cherry leaves; those punctuation butterflies called question marks and commas enjoy the cherry's messy, rotting fruits. Sapsuckers drill holes in the bark to release the sweet sap, a service on which other birds rely for carbohydrates. A bird-watcher friend has noted black-billed cuckoos feasting on her wild cherries' pests. Audubon's guide says of cuckoos that they "are extremely beneficial to farmers and horticulturists, consuming enormous quantities of destructive hairy caterpillars, especially tent caterpillars and gypsy moth larvae."

These cuttings and removals were serious mistakes, though they are standard horticultural practice. Tree companies and landscape contractors would approach woodland "restoration" in just such a way: deadwood first, then senescent trees, then pioneers whose primacy is over, then undesirables.

On my way down to the mailbox, in a circle twelve feet in circumference planted by nature, not us, grow an elm, an oak, a hickory, and a birch, all "large" trees as defined by our town's tree law. The ordinance spells out a formula too cumbersome to repeat for thinning out such clumps. Landscaping books traditionally recommend such thinning; a tree company certainly would say, as mine has often said, that some selection should be made among these crowded trees so that only one would be master. Their first suggestion is that the American elm should go, since it will inevitably succumb to Dutch elm disease. Also, the sweet birch, one of whose three trunks is already dead, its tombstone inscribed by a splotch of white fungus. Also, the shagbark hickory, by reason of its winter littering. That would leave the scarlet oak.

But why? And at what cost? No one knows which elm will prove resistant to the fungus that for some half century now has fatally been carried tree to tree by imported beetles. Our elms stand so far unafflicted. In the passage quoted from Ehrlich's and Wilson's article on ecosystem services, the authors mention the importance not only of species but of genic diversity. By this is meant the genetic individualities within species that make me resistant to intestinal upsets and you to respiratory flu. Maybe that elm is the answer.

The sweet birch is senile, I admit it, but I don't know what its fungus means or who might live off it. I'm sure the hickory does its part, whether by raining down ripe nuts to feed the squirrels or dead sticks to feed the soil. I see no reason to reduce it to a woodpile. I'm glad the money it would have cost to thin that group, and the danger of attempting it ourselves, stayed our hand long enough for us to learn from its continuance that forest trees of different species can live harmoniously in crowds.

The top layer of the woodpile opens a new chapter in our history of clearing, for it records the beginning of our effort to restore the woods behind the pond. Some years had passed since we hacked out the vines and brush where once the vicious multi-flora roses forced me to the wall. Those were years of research and transformation. What had started as an idle pastime to discover what was missing had grown into a passion to bring back to the land the diversity of species and variety of habitat that it had lost. We started there, in the vanished woods, with visions of sweet gums and sycamores.

Sweet gum, *Liquidamber styraciflua*, is a tree of mature forests, not a pioneer. It doesn't need much space to get started; it's accustomed to growing thriftily in others' shade, shooting quickly upward toward the canopy through any hole it finds, not spreading its branches until it reaches sun. We used the green ash grove in the corner to protect these young trees, cutting out only one here, one there, to create encouraging hints of light for them to reach. Green ash is a good nurse tree for permanent forest types; its shade is more dappled than dense; its taproot minds its business underneath the tree. American sycamore, though, *Platanus occidentalis*, enters what will become woodland as a pioneer tree (although one that lives for centuries). It wants more sun for growth. To accommodate this need, we cut back the stand of red maple from its edges to confine it to a smaller area along the shore; the sycamores would grow in sunlight beyond the reach of the maples' widespread and greedy surface roots.

We felt we had exercised intelligence and finesse in these preliminaries.

There was no way to finesse the willows. Crack willows are ugly, alien, pulpy, tumorous things that grow to humungous size, get their roots into everything, and, on our land, had dammed the flow of water both into and out of the pond. They are weeds; they had to go. But they didn't want to. The trunk of the largest one, over by the outlet, took a tough sawyer an hour and a half to get through with his oversize chainsaw. And within a month after every willow had been cut to pieces, the severed stumps came up like willow forests. Sticks sprouted fore and aft; logs grew root and branch. A dozen trees cut down threatened the reprisal of a thousand.

This is extreme even for a weed tree, but I should mention that only conifers, which store little nourishment in their roots, usually die when they're cut down. Broadleaf woody species use their stored nourishment to resprout from their stumps, and some deciduous trees — ash and red maple notoriously among them — regrow with appalling vigor. A small amount of 2,4-D herbicide brushed onto the cut surface of a sapling stub or sprayed around the cut periphery of a larger stump prevents that from happening.

Spraying wasn't feasible for such quantities of immortal willow. We shredded the budding sticks. We stacked the logs to air dry them to death. We tried to dispose of their corpses in a bonfire, but they resisted still. Finally, we fed them to the skunk cabbage swamp.

The age of the willows and their even spacing around the shore suggested to us that the suburbanite who had dug the pond earlier in this century had planted them on purpose. The species, native to both Asia and Europe, was imported in colonial times for the charcoal made from its slow-burning wood and the shade provided by its fast-growing crown. In the spring, when the willows' narrow leaves and yellow catkins hung like shrouds over the water, they were even pretty. One encyclopedia mentions that *Salix fragilis* occasionally escapes from cultivation in the East, which means to me that somebody must still plant it.

I'm not surprised. Species that we eradicate because they battle restoration and sabotage succession are frequently attractive in their way. The multiflora rose (from Japan) and Oriental bittersweet (from Japan and China) that we extirpated from our young woods here are both commonly sold as ornamentals.* A gardening friend planted weed bittersweet to screen a boundary fence; quite a few homes here display the wicked rose proudly in their yard. The tree whose arduous planting was described in one of the gardening books I read was a handsome Norway maple chosen for its vigor, rapid growth, and extraordinarily dense shade — exactly the characteristics that have allowed this imported species to preempt the native woodland wherever it has escaped into the wild. It's unfortunate that weed species don't reliably match their bad behavior with equivalent ugliness, but yards are likely to harbor deceitful ornamentals that should be red-flagged for removal as we, regretfully but rightly, marked our buckthorn hedge for execution.

---

* Our native bittersweet, *Celastrus scandens*, a desirable and well-behaved species, is becoming rare as Oriental bittersweet, *C. orbiculatus*, invades and takes over its habitat. They can be distinguished by their leaves and fruit. The weed vine has broadly oval leaves with scalloped edges, and its fruits hang in clusters along the branches; the native has narrower, toothed leaves, and fruits hang in clusters from the ends of the branches.

*In the semiphore of
arborists, blue or green
tape tied or tacked to a
tree or shrub means
that it needs attention,
such as limbing up or
pruning. Red, orange,
or day-glo pink means
to cut it down.*

Wyman's Gardening Encyclopedia lists seven buckthorn species, three of which are native Americans — *Rhamnus californica*, *R. purshiana*, and *R. caroliniana*. Of the imported ornamentals, two — *R. cathartica* and *R. frangula* — have escaped cultivation. The former is the species that in the Midwest must be burned away to reestablish prairie; the latter is the alder buckthorn that invaded our woods and that we, not realizing that a variety called 'Tall hedge' was the same bush in fastigiate disguise, planted to screen a parking area. The flowers of both exotics appeal to bees; the fruits of both feed birds (the leaves of our Tallhedge hedge were popular with Japanese beetles, for whatever that relationship between weed and weed is worth). Also, our eastern immigrant is pretty: it has glossy foliage, shining blue-black berries, and a gracefully arching crown when grown out in the open. And it's healthy. And unfussy about soil. And drought-tolerant. And flood-tolerant. And sun-tolerant. And shade-tolerant.

But prolific.

The seeds of this plant must enjoy one-hundred-percent germination. I pull out thousands of seedlings every year. They grow as well along edges as in the woods and have a particularly annoying habit of sneaking up through bushes, where they grow unobserved until they are too deeply rooted to be yanked out. If ignored, the saplings expand rapidly into thickets through which nothing else can grow, not even the bush through which they made their entry. Yet for years I didn't recognize that the weed I was killing was the same as the hedge I was cultivating and from whose seed the land was being continually resupplied.

I did know it was *a* buckthorn. That's not enough. How, without getting down to genus *and* species, could I tell my warty-barked *R. frangula* from wartless *R. caroliniana*, the native Indian cherry that I'd treasure if I found it?

For each geographic area, there are other woody weed species that restorers ought to enter on their hit list: on the dry central plains, not alder buckthorn, *Rhamnus frangula*, so much as European buckthorn, *R. cathartica;* in wet soils in the far north, not alder buckthorn but an actual alder, *Alnus rugosa*, known as tag or speckled alder. Russian olive, *Eleagnus angustifolia*, is widely planted here to feed the birds but is a serious pest in the Midwest. English ivy infests forests in Washington and Oregon (one of our native rhododendrons is a noxious woodland weed in England!).

All these weed species are able to move quickly into a disturbed area and take it over. But they are not all aliens like our prolific buckthorn; native species, too, have become weeds in ravaged landscapes. The alder that is such a nuisance north of here is a native that thrives in the stagnant water of sumps and ditches; its success is due to altered drainage patterns. Fox grape (*Vitis labrusca*), our northeastern native and a parent of the hybrid Concord grape cultivated for jelly, juice, and wine, invades woodland edges ripped open by road cuts and subdivisions. Smooth sumac (*Rhus glabra*), an attractive plant whose berries are an important winter food for birds, spreads rapidly by root sprouts through scraped, eroded, compacted, or sterile soil too poor for other trees — a description that fits many yards and our meadow, too. As is true of animal pests, overpopulation by these plants is not intrinsic to them but to the circumstances that have freed them from restraint. Reestablishing control over their numbers is necessary if we are to restore diversity and balance.

If one can identify them. If one can tell native from exotic, weed from rarity, one buckthorn from another.

·   ·   ·

Among the memorabilia that Marty's mother kept to remind her of her little boy is a piece of plywood mounted with two-inch sections of branch from various woodland trees, each neatly labeled with its species. Thus did the Boy Scouts of America attempt to teach this city child his trees. The lesson was lost on him, but never mind; the few species that fit onto the board were insufficient to the task of inventorying even an impoverished lot. The samples were from canopy trees — elm, ash, beech, birch, hickory, cherry, maple, and oak (conifers were a separate lesson, not included in that deciduous display). The board lacked twigs from the tiers of understory trees and shrubs and from those thickets that crowd the sunny edges. These, unhappily, are the most difficult to identify.

Take winterberry (*Ilex verticillata*), a native deciduous holly that appeared on its own some years after our dismaying clearing of the woods behind the pond. This tall shrub of edge and hedgerow, shapely and loaded with bright berries all through the winter, is certainly not a species one would want to cut in error. I happened to recognize it because it is often sold in nurseries, but it is an example of the frustrations one may go through in identifying even the commonest species.

My field guide to trees doesn't list winterberry because there is some mysterious cut-off point below which a woody plant — mountain laurel as well as winterberry — is too short to be a tree. Mountain laurel made it into my guide to wildflowers because of its showy blossoms, but hollies, with their inconspicuous flowers, didn't. There is no field guide to shrubs. There are, though, *garden* shrub guides. Mine illustrates both winterberry and mountain laurel, but another northeastern beauty, lowbush blueberry (*Vaccinium angustifolium*) isn't described because it's considered a wild, not a garden, plant. So, supposing that I've found some plant resembling a blueberry, I might turn to *Hortus Third*, a weighty reference for some thirty thousand plants grown in North America, but it is strictly alphabetical, tersely botanical, and sparsely illustrated. There, sure enough, lowbush blueberry is described at the head of a list of forty other Vacciniums.

But what if I hadn't guessed it was a blueberry?

A last resort, but one that I have often turned to, is to send a sample of the unknown plant, in a plastic bag and preferably in bloom or seed, to the Cooperative Extension (informally known as the county agent) listed in the Blue Pages of the Yellow Pages under Name of County.

Maybe.

In a neighboring Connecticut telephone directory, the county agent is listed under Name of State (not County), Higher Education Board Of. Why would anyone think of looking under Higher Education to identify a bush?

Anyone wishing to restore a lot must go through this puttering through the literature, this wandering about, this bafflement and bright surprise as when I found a nannyberry (*Viburnum lentago*) where I had least expected it: under my nose, right beside the driveway, passed daily for fifteen years without my recognition.

Nothing in ordinary gardening is so exciting.

I've failed, however, to earn an E for excellence in earnestness. Why haven't I joined a native plant society or searched the literature that I'm certain must exist for native bog plants of southern New York State?

I'm afraid of losing my sense of humor. I'm shy of ideologies that, like gardening itself, may by their intensity and expertise narrow the gate that amateurs can enter. I did go to a natural landscapes workshop. I met a man there who was involved in the restoration of some thirty habitats on acreage that included everything from hemlock ledge to sundew swamp, and his purity scared me. Restoration purists insist on removing all exotic species whether they are weeds or not. I haven't the personality for ethnic cleansing. Much as I take pride in being botanically patriotic, I stop short of that degree of xenophobia.

The all-American issue hinges on what constitutes biodiversity. In one sense, any of the thousands of aliens that have settled into gardens or naturalized beyond them could be said to have enriched the biodiversity of the land. But this is not what ecologists have in mind. Exotics that don't naturalize fail to spread beyond the confines of the garden because they can't make the necessary ecosystem connections that enriched biodiversity in their original habitats. Those that spread aggressively beyond the garden can do so because they are relieved of the checks and balances that controlled reproduction in their native ecosystems. To put it succinctly, tea roses have nowhere to go, multiflora roses have nothing to stop them, and our dozens of native roses are losing ground to both pampered ornamentals and unchecked exotics.

This is the purist's argument.

My pluralist argument respects exotics that have naturalized as responsible citizens. An example is the dogwood, *Cornus mas*, called cornelian cherry for its plump red fruit, that is native to Eurasia and that we planted on the island. Cornelian cherry has joined the edge and understory community without either aggression toward natives or dependence on gardeners; I see no reason to be prejudiced against it on the basis of origin alone. I feel the same way about Alpine currant (*Ribes alpinum*) and beaked hazelnut (*Corylus cornuta*), confusingly listed as native or naturalized depending on one's source. I think of redvein enkianthus (*Enkianthus campanulatus*) as an adopted child. With which color shall I flag wild pears and apples that accompanied the early colonists from Europe? How mark the exotic burning bush, *Euonymous alata*? Shall we have an annual national daylily dig to root out that foreign species along our roadsides?

Or, to put such questions in the democratic tradition, When does an immigrant become American? It is a matter of time.

When, though, and from where, and by what chancy route will the American hornbeam return? Here is where I begin to think in restrictive terms, for if I could buy only one tree, I'd have to favor a rarer native over a commoner exotic. There's no other way to repopulate the land. The trees must come from us, our gift. From planters. From reserves created by ordinary peo-

: who, noting the missing, plant them so that other woods and thickets might be reseeded by birds and breezes with the species they have lost.

The original inventory of trees and shrubs that arrived here since this land was pasture a half century ago amounted to thirty-three species, of which eight — a full quarter — were aliens. Since we cleared that vanished woods, we have planted there and elsewhere fifty-one native tree and shrub species, a total of three times the number that had, or possibly ever could have, arrived here on their own. Of course, this has been ambitious. But what if fifty-one people each planted one species?

More tedious than identifying plants to be cut or saved — but more educational, involving as it does a heap of books and catalogs to answer questions of height, habit, habitat, culture, and national origin — is to identify the missing and decide which among them might be worked into the landscape. At a minimum one needs a good horticultural encyclopedia, tree and wildflower field guides, lists published by native plant societies,* and — because local nurseries seldom offer much in the way of indigenes — catalogs from mail-order nurseries that specialize in native species.

And a notebook, too, of course. Mine is kind of messy: "SHADE!!!" it says of *Vaccinium vitis idaea minus*, a bog plant known as mountain cranberry; "CREEPS!" it adds regarding *Vaccinium crassifolium* and, following the vital statistics for this unfamiliar but coveted blueberry species, the plaintive note: "But where?" Then, on a later page written in a firmer hand under the underlined title *Groundcover Groupings*, "With bayberries: *Aster spectabilis* and *Thelypteris novoboracensis* (NY fern) plus a short aster — let them fight it out. Forget creeping blueberry."

---

* Membership in the National Wildflower Research Center gives access to their clearinghouse service, which provides native plant lists by region, nursery sources for native plants and seeds, and bibliographies on such subjects as butterfly gardening and attracting birds. Write to NWRC at 2600 FM 973 North, Austin, Texas 78725, or telephone (512) 929-3600.

COMPONENTS OF A
POCKET WOODS:

edge and understory species to protect the interior, provide spring bloom, and possibly offer nuts and berries; ground-covering ferns and wildflowers, edible as well as ornamental; canopy trees in every stage from sprouting seeds and saplings, from which the woods regenerates itself, to fallen trunks, whose slow decay recycles woodland nutrients

Carolina silverbell,
an understory species

Bunchberry,
a wildflower
ground cover

Scarlet
oak acorn

Shagbark
hickory log

Last summer I found *Aronia arbutifolia* 'Brilliantissima' listed in a nursery catalog from Oregon; it was described as a thicketing shrub with bright red fruit in large numbers remaining on the bush until late winter. The nursery didn't mention whether the plant is native. For that, I turned to a horticultural encyclopedia: the common name is red chokeberry (I knew choke*cherry*, had never heard of choke*berry*); it grows to nine feet in almost any soil, is widely native in the East, and has no apparent faults. But what does it look like? Turn to the field guides: not there. Try the garden shrub guide: aha!

This hunt-and-peck method, frustrating as it is, does eventually work. I first discovered there were such things as native filberts in a gardening encyclopedia. Neither of the two species mentioned, beaked hazelnut (*Corylus cornuta*) and American hazelnut (*C. americana*), were depicted in my field guide, but I hankered after them enough to be willing to buy them sight unseen. I riffled through several nut tree catalogs. Not there. A final glitch awaited when at last I found a nursery that carried *C. cornuta:* not native. Encyclopedias aren't always right; neither are nurseries. *Hortus Third* says the nut is native, and I believe it.

The catalog didn't list the larger, coarser, but uncontested indigene, *C. americana*. Then, visiting a specialist nursery in Georgetown, Maine, I ran into an American filbert growing wild in the woods. Not that I would have recognized it. I had asked Mark Stavish, the owner of Eastern Plant Specialties, if he knew where I might find a hazelnut, and he pointed out that I was stepping on it.

It's odd how one can spend fifty years tooting around the countryside seeing the texture of the landscape change from mile to mile in a picture-postcard blur of scenery unsharpened by a perception of what accounts for this or that particularity of form, shade, texture, or color. With my continuing education came a new sharpness. I remember one day seeing through the car window as though through a zoom lens the oddly pale leafiness below a steep embankment clarify into a grove of baby sycamores. I had previously known only vaguely that there was such a thing as an

American sycamore — it is one parent of the hybrid London plane, a popular street tree for its ability to withstand the city's soot and fumes — but suddenly, once I could identify the species, the chalk-white, gesticulating branches of mature trees fairly grabbed my eyes from the gullies and bottomlands where I had failed to notice them before. What once had been just brushy wetland resolved into summersweet and pinxterbloom. I had certainly noticed how the woodland in the neighborhood of the tree collection blushed nearly shocking pink in fall. Not until I identified the understory shrub as *Euonymous alata* did I also notice how in winter its arched branches form a filigree against the snow.

Not only individual species became clear against the background, and therefore movable elements in my imagination, but the background itself came into focus. In my mental album, American holly (*Ilex opaca*), mountain laurel, and our rosebay rhododendron pose against a rocky hill under a canopy of oaks. Or, in another snapshot, the rhododendrons stand darkly heaped below the white tracery of a grove of sycamores silhouetted by ranks of hemlocks climbing a rise behind. In an August shot, summersweet in spikey bloom rises in thickets against trunks of red maple from carpets of lowbush blueberry. In one taken in October, highbush blueberry (*Vaccinium corymbosum*) flames scarlet in a grove of quaking aspen (*Populus tremuloides*) afire with gold in the lowering sun. And, again — this time it's spring — blueberries loaded with white bells on ruddy twigs are caught among fringed skirts of deep green, fragrant sweetfern (*Comptonia peregrina*).

This growing collection of mental images, snapped sometimes in passing along the roadside and sometimes during walks in wilder places, becomes an album that to anyone interested in restoration must serve in place of the graven images in gardening books. If I wanted to find a dozen ways to enhance my garden with irises, there's no problem: I could find in an armful of books at least a hundred photographs. But if I want to enhance the land with blueberries, there is no place to look except the album of my ṅind. There, without reference to the experts, I can move the bushes within the habitats in which I've seen them growing: place them with birches, plant them with wild roses and red cedars, mingle them with bracken, clump them by the pond. The particular species of aster, goldenrod, and fern entered in my notebook as potential underpinnings for bayberries aren't the same species as those I've seen with bayberries elsewhere, but I can almost smell their heady mix of odors under the hot September sun.

Taking this snapshot approach to restoration has made the job of planting the woods behind the pond less daunting. We haven't needed to do a great deal all at once. Part of each picture already was there: a soggy area where skunk cabbage grew needed only ferns and bugbane to complete it. In the next snapshot over, some arrowwood remained, edging the shore where originally there had been mostly buckthorn thicket. We filled the brightened clearing with the shorter and less coarse viburnum nicknamed hobblebush (*V. alnifolium*), another wetland shrub called buttonbush (*Cephalanthus occidentalis*), and a group of summersweet. Across a path, still in sog, went swamp azalea (*Rhododendron viscosum*). In the several years since clearing had allowed the sun to reach this enclave, a rich crop of soft rush and jewelweed had arisen: an unexpected touch not in my mental snapshot of swamp thicket, but natural and pleasing. Three American holly trees fell into place on higher ground, facing the imposing rock that rises like a dromedary's hump about halfway through the woods. Still missing from that snapshot is mountain laurel planted in the cleft, but we'll get to it. Meanwhile, a fern glade spreads and thickens around a rotting willow stump, the sweet gums are growing fast, the American hornbeams seem to be adjusting to their red maple neighbors, common witch hazels (*Hamamelis virginiana*) are coalescing into a November-blooming thicket, and the group of American sycamores underplanted with rosebay rhododendron is experiencing its first peeling toward eventual whiteness. These things take time; the woods behind the pond is not yet ready to have its professional portrait taken.

By the time it is ready, the woods will, in a way, have vanished again. Already, the edge along the shore is nearly sealed in foliage. On one side, the margin is becoming obscured by blueberries, on the other side by rhododendrons. Tree trunks are becoming veiled in shadblow and azaleas. The brown ground is disappearing under creepers, wildflowers, and ferns. Woods are not tree collections; one shouldn't be able to count the trunks, to detect one master in the crowd, to see the trees for the forest.

We have a preview of the future in the older strip of woods where we cut down the cherry trees in our former lives. There, a tulip tree (*Liriodendron tulipifera*) and an American beech (*Fagus grandifolia*) have come up, the first of these fine species to enter on their own. Arrivals of this sort signal a change in character. The shade is deepening, the soil is improving, moisture is held better now in that scrap of land. In the "further generations" for which preservation is intended, beech and tulip tree will have replaced oak and hickory, bringing the woods to a climax of leafy maturity. The woods behind the pond will similarly change as the sycamores grow to lowland giants, as the ash retires, as the orchid that appeared under a witch hazel this year (a mystery, a dream come true) spreads its dusty seed.

During that same period, what will happen to the tree collection on our way to the market? Its tops will grow taller; its trunks will grow thicker. Sooner or later it will topple onto its bed of pachysandra.

My notebooks fill up, pile up. Under bog plants to try in a peaty dip where water seeps all summer: leatherleaf (*Chamaedaphne calyculata*), bog rosemary (*Andromeda polifolia*), sweetbells (*Leucothoe racemosa*), sheep laurel (*Kalmia polifolia*), Labrador tea (*Ledum groenlandicum*). Under ground covers already tried and proved to be successful: crested iris (*Iris cristata*); paxistema (*Paxistema canbyii*); beetleweed (*Galax rotundifolia*), bloodroot (*Sanguinaria canadensis*), squirrel corn (*Dicentra canadensis*), foamflower (*Tiarella cordifolia*), maidenhair fern (*Adiantum pedatum*), a club-moss (*Lycopodium* spp), and three species of woodland sedge (*Carex muskigumensis, C. flacca, C. nigra*). None of these bog shrubs or herbaceous woodland natives could have grown through buck-thorn thickets, none grow wild anywhere that I have found in this deeply disturbed vicinity, and none, I'm sure, would have alighted here but through the efforts of an obsessed ex-gardener.

Or am I really still a gardener altering the land to suit my image of it? How authentic is it to cram onto a sliver of land so many more species than arrived there on their own?

I'm really not sure. The examples of the wetland thicket that we planted were growing in extensive marshes on a preservation along the Hudson Valley an hour's drive from here. The nearest site where I've seen rosebay rhododendron growing wild is even farther, across the Hudson, along the steeps of Bear Mountain Park. The mountain laurel with which it intermingles there clothes the rocky oak woods on the other side of town but is inexplicably absent here. A magnificent forest of sweet gum and tulip tree backs the New Jersey development where my niece lives. Tulip trees are fairly common here, but I have yet to find a wild sweet gum. Mark Stavish told me of a day he spent trekking the coastal woods of southern Maine in a vain search for the indigenous black tupelo, only to spot it at last through the rim of a beer mug across the street from the local bar. It's hard to visualize the fulsome body of a natural world that has left only such teasing grins behind.

Nevertheless, by planting in snapshots, we know at least that each of those species we chose is found in association with at least some of the others in a similar habitat. Whether these associations are critical, whether they will become reestablished here, or whether they will be self-replicating beyond the original planting remain unknown. We are merely stocking. Any spread from this artificial center of biodiversity over a larger area is in the hands of winds, pollinators, seed dispersers, and other wild contingencies beyond our control.

But. Our neighbor Bob DeFranco has discovered some dozen seedlings of American holly sprouting in his woods, and he is delighted.

Hey, we planted the mothers.

12

Revisitations

THIS SUMMER my old aunt, the last remaining kin of my parents' generation, died on her sofa at the age of ninety-five. She hadn't been a gardener. She hadn't cared much for children or other animals. Yet until six years ago, when she moved from her home to an apartment building a few doors down the block, she had presided over a child-delighting enclave of fireflies in Elizabeth, New Jersey. She didn't realize her accomplishment (she wouldn't want to be known for it): her urban backyard refuge was the result of a certain snobbery that runs strong in our family on my mother's side and that is expressed in a degree of eccentricity. Thus, when others on her block cut down their cherries, she let hers be; when others displayed trees on showcase lawns, she hid hers in woods; when others felt obliged to maintain vistas through chain-link fences, she impolitely buried her boundaries in shrubs. So, unwittingly, she supported the fireflies, which mistook brush and border for their natural habitat of edge and meadow.

On the day of the funeral, in August when the present owners of my aunt's house were on vacation, I trespassed on the familiar

Pennsylvania fireflies,
sometimes called
lightning bugs

paths, now almost obliterated by disuse. (Are there no children in these people's lives? Do they never take a stroll?) Our oldest son was with me. This back yard is where he and his brothers and cousins played hide-and-seek and waited in ambush to pelt one another with horse chestnuts. This is where they established the ritual of a firefly hunt on Independence Day, the date of the annual family picnic. To either side, others' yards had been reduced to a glance by their plain-mowed rectilinearity; my aunt's yard grew bigger the more that grew in it, and not only in the perceptions of the fireflies, but in the human experience of meandering, observing, delighting, comprehending. I think a child adventuring in my aunt's back yard would grow up a bigger person than a child cramped by lawns and swing sets.

   In no hurry to leave this urban enclave, and with the realization that my inheritance from my aunt is to have become, with her death, the oldest generation, I poked about awhile to see what messages she might have left for me to carry forth from her back yard. Except for the cherry trees, her choice of plants had been conventional: yews, dogwoods, rhododendrons, daylilies, roses, ivy. She had gotten the structure right, though. The woodland, placed toward the rear of the lot and taking up about a third of it, was tiered within, aproned in shrubbery without, and descended to flower beds embracing a small crescent lawn centered on a birdbath. Along the fence to one side was a tool shed and, beside the kitchen door, a barbecue. How many had attended that yearly picnic? I counted twenty-four, distributed for lunch at tables on the flagstone terrace, with room for Simple Simon and Red Rover on the lawn between the terrace and the birdbath and for adult-evading escapades on the looping woodland paths beyond.

I had been irritated during the eulogy to hear my aunt extolled for her cleverness and taste in home decorating, as though making her husband comfortable and entertaining guests were sufficient to that sharp mind, but I saw that the back yard was, in fact, an extension of the living room. The birdbath was an ornament; the shrubs a screen against the neighbors; the woods a touch of creativity and spunk intended to be remarked on by visitors. The message that my old aunt left for me was as unintended as the fireflies she harbored: with good taste, in a small space, and even in Elizabeth, New Jersey, back yards are big enough to share.

We had just arrived on the Maine island where we vacation when the call came that my aunt had died. I had saved this chapter to write then because I needed distance from our projects and a reduction in scale. The island is small; the house where we stay is on a lot at the end of a street in a village where houses are separated by little more than the length of a clothesline. The quarter acre is all tough grass; a ten-foot band around the house is kept mowed.

Within the band two peony bushes survive from long ago. I'd always thought they ought to be mowed down. This isn't something an islander can do. Things aren't wasted there; nothing is discarded. Everywhere that any flower grows — at the doorstep, in a corner, along a walk, beside a curb, in the middle of a lawn — it is carefully preserved. These patches aren't flower beds, although they may be remnants of them or may harbor strays from former gardens. They aren't shaped or weeded; they don't need to be. The flowers grow embedded among clumps of grass, like wild bouquets, their edges defined simply by the mower. Here a tuft holds honesty, there one carries mallows. Some are merely goldenrod and Queen Anne's lace, or ferns with daisies.

One startling bouquet dropped beside a ditch holds cherry-red daylilies and yellow tansies laced with panic grass. My favorites are nosegays of blue harebells softened by purple love grass growing between granite curbstones near the library.

During the days spent traveling to and from New Jersey for the funeral, these untended but respected scraps of bloom continually came to mind. Where, elsewhere, have all the flowers gone? Everything was green, the color of mourning to my eyes during that trip. The island is where monarch butterflies spangle the meadows in September, where the grasshoppers of my childhood still leap and fly. In an angle of the porch near the kitchen door lives a black and yellow argiope, the spider I came to know beside the frog pond long ago. I find snails below the porch and in the woodpile. (Suddenly, I remember: I haven't seen a snail for years and years at home.)

Berries are preserved in the same way flowers are. Hardly any boundary between lots isn't marked by canes of raspberries or blackberries, chokecherry bushes, a remnant stand of gooseberries or currants — all growing, like the flowers, through tall grass. It's like going back in time to come here, an ecological revisitation, as it were. Couldn't insouciant plantings of this sort — modest in scale but combed out a bit to look less wild and careless, with chosen grasses and studied composition — inaugurate elsewhere the tradition of preservation that gardening has heedlessly discarded? It seems to me a small step from using exotic grasses as ornamental accents to using native ones as matrices, from my aunt's cultivated tea rose bed to one of wild roses bedded down in ferns, from her conventional yews to berried hedgerows. Any of these steps, however small, are steps in the right direction.

The harebells that I so particularly admire among the curbstones near the library are *Campanula rotundifolia*, a naturalized immigrant that has the virtues of blue color, late summer bloom, and neat habit, plus the practical bonus of vigor and independence even when grown with grass, without a gardener's care.

My aunt, I believe, would not have minded a patch of love grass and harebells to set off her barbecue.

(I make a note of this new snapshot to add to my collection. I won't again complain about the mower, preserver of old peonies.)

My mother, who somewhat resembled my aunt in looks and temperament, had a certain way with people at a party. I used to watch her moving among awkward guests, hooking their elbows, maneuvering them gently in and out of conversations, introducing them to congenialities they could not have achieved without her wise transitions. She could blend disparate individuals and dismissive cliques into a happy mingling.

We, similarly, are hosts in our gardens and face similar challenges. How to connect an isolated shade tree to the line of woods behind it? How to bring a row of maples forward to a path? How to encourage a cultivated island bed to spill into a meadow? How to make a formal boxwood at ease among the berries? How to get the conversation flowing?

My mother at least could choose her guests, whereas we may be forced for lack of other company to entertain Mother Nature's cherry trees or some former owner's privet. Or, as is true of the empty yards to either side of my aunt's house — and was true of our place after we'd overcleared it — one may face a large room with too few guests to form a party. Where to start? Whom to invite? Everyone must have some person — some plant — with whom to feel most comfortable. I'm most comfortable with blueberries, and blueberries are where I frequently begin.*

Blueberries suit me through the year. In the spring, they're covered with white bells set among the pale tints of their unfurling leaves. Their summer foliage is neat, rich green, and glossy;

---

* The highbush species, *Vaccinium corymbosum*, is available in many cultivated varieties that have larger berries and vary in ripening time. For landscape purposes, the wild form is superior and just as delectable to birds. Other species are suitable to other areas, but all Vacciniums must have acid soil.

their ripening berries are lightly frosted over a purplish blush deepening to a rich blue. The fall foliage is a spectacular neon pink and scarlet that, caught in the sun, holds every eye. But I love blueberries most in the winter, when their shredding bark, intricate branching, and bold crown haloed with red twigs make merry of the gloom.

I could say of something rare — a dwarf holly, a cutleaf maple — that it would equally ornament my table at all seasons, but of blueberries I can say much more. They are natural raconteurs, amusing birds with their witty ripening and keeping them in a flutter of attention for weeks during the summer. They have the common touch. They're chummy with evergreens, comfy among flowers, at ease in tall grass, as much at home in a foundation planting as in a hedgerow. No one could ask for a less demanding friend. Blueberries are happy in full sun, relaxed in dappled shade, uncomplaining of drought, but just as pleased to grow in damp. No blueberry pal of mine has ever asked for pruning, wanted my protection from pests or weather, or even expressed the slightest appetite for food. They are companions whose kin are also welcome: their lowbush cousins, their huckleberry relatives, their dwarfs and creeping species. And this tribe has what has become for me the authenticity I seek: they are American natives.

I've started not once, but over and over again with blueberries: as a hedge to face the drive, as an edge to meet the woodland, as a base beneath a grove, as specimens to spike a rise, as groups to blur a boundary. Plant old friends first, I say, then let them help you entertain the strangers.

Over the years, we have expanded the guest list and, after each new invitation, noted how things were going before introducing other old friends or new acquaintances. Where an oak was left stranded some thirty feet from woodland, we reconnected it by letting the grass in between grow long and planting directly in the turf without benefit of mulch a grove of birches. This is a successional approach: the fast-growing birch grove soon began to shade out the grass and prepare the ground for planting a permanent link of woodland species. As the grass declined, we dumped lawnloads of fallen leaves on the woodsy side to urge the early death of grass and add a top dressing of humus. Later, we planted cornelian cherry and enkianthus (a not-too-distant relative of blueberries, as it happens) to begin the understory. Squirrels and chipmunks probably can be relied on to plant the acorns and hickory nuts that eventually will dignify the connection. (I noticed in my aunt's woods several young oaks arising to challenge the aging cherries.)

Where there was a stiff row of red maples along a boundary wall, we brought the woods forward to a mowed path by interspersing an arc of flowering dogwoods. The dogwoods are planted only six to eight feet apart — a mingling distance. Because they are in the maples' shade, they are growing thriftily, not full in branch and foliage as a specimen in the sun would do. Anchoring the dogwoods is an underplanting of evergreen inkberry (standard size and dwarfs), skirted with — of course! — lowbush blueberries to billow down nearly to the level of the path. Right next to that group, though, a thicket of four-foot *Amelanchier stolonifera* — the running serviceberry or shadblow I discovered in my bookish wanderings — grows right up to the path and is mirrored on the opposite side by a planting of the same species. The path therefore appears to cut through a wash of thicket at that point, honoring continuity while avoiding the too-carefully graded shrub plantings that stiffen suburbia.

Paths that cut *through* are exciting. They suggest the plants' spontaneous growth, the human's willful forging. The path that leads into the woods runs through a blueberry thicket. The most effective grassland paths are those that cut through rather than skirt the meadow. Even low growth is effective if it reverberates from side to side across a path. On a steep, shaded slope where we had plunked mountain laurels like bumps on a bed of wood chips, we interwove the young shrubs with Christmas fern (the evergreen fronds trap blowing leaves in autumn, obviating the need to keep on mulching), then swept the ferns along to the other side of a path that runs below the rise. Among the laurels, a

*The path through the
meadow past the
bluebird house*

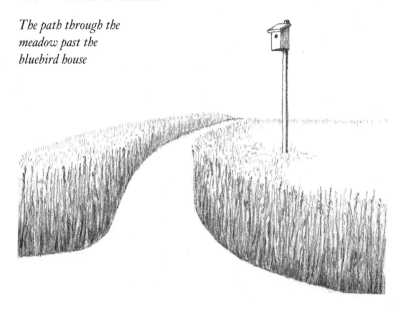

drift of native deciduous azaleas starts thinly at the top of the slope, becomes thicker as it approaches the bottom, then hops the path to a blooming crescendo. Or at least that's how we imagine it; the planting needs to grow some: the laurels are knee high now; the azaleas maybe half that. Yet the ferns in the meantime hold it all together.

Sometimes a stranger takes the conversation on a new tack altogether. I ran across a list of woodland sedges in a native plant catalog and ordered several species just to see what they would say. One, a pale gray, fine-leafed, mat-forming sedge called *Carex flacca* that grows about ten inches high, suggested an interplanting with leucothoe and andromeda beneath a curve of crabapples. As the sedge fills in, the shrubs come up through their blending matrix as naturally as bayberry comes up through meadow or seedling spruce through moss. One side of the bed is bordered by a path, so by extending the sedge to the opposite "shore," the design will again cut through a continuity. (In the past, that bit of path gave us no end of trouble: it kept going to moss instead of grass. Now, graciously, we let it.)

Knowing my aunt, I suppose that her backyard landscape arrived in a truck and was professionally installed, an approach as conventional — as lacking in gardening conviviality and wit — as most of the plants she chose. I'd rather the sort of party that goes on into the wee hours of the future, slow-paced and home-cooked like my mother's parties. Not having known my mother during her formative years, I can't guess how she came by her social talent, but surely some inner fluidity is needed, some willingness to regroup not only objects — people or plants — but one's perceptions of them and one's ideas about their place. Plants take time to reveal their character as species, as individuals, and as members of a group; they make their needs known over years, not months. As I think back, I realize that what we are involved with here is not so much a landscaping project, to be planted and done with, as a sort of friendship with the land. "It wants," I find myself saying of a rocky corner overlooking the pond, "some silvery bushiness," as one might say of a friend that she wants a good chat or a strong drink.

This growing intimacy puts me at ease, gives me the inner mobility to reroute paths, change the shapes of beds, move and remove plants without embarrassment, and invite new species to participate. Since the flow of a natural landscape is over time as well as space, its design admits changes of mind along the way — the equivalent of moving a guest from one group to another or, as is sometimes necessary, showing an uncongenial one the door.

We booted German irises from the peony garden this year. Who wants guests with borers? Who wants to interrupt the fun with fungicide? Instead, we planted groups of sideoats grama and New England aster. Based on chats with the peonies on the island that grow through rougher crowds by far, I'm pretty sure these foreigners can sit comfortably among the native company. The grass and asters will echo the outlying meadow and will grow tall enough each season to embed the peonies only well after their blooming time. Both are well-behaved clumping plants that stay where they are planted.

The peony garden started out as a perfect rectangle, and it still is — inside. Outside, we reshaped it into a pleasing sinuosity that reaches out to connect that garden with other, originally isolated plantings: the crabapple border, a stand of red cedars, a rock garden, a bank of daylilies under the old white oak. We kept extending these curves from one place to another — joining outcrops, bridging lawn, embracing trees, encompassing the vegetable garden — until what had been an archipelago of features has become a continuous, meandering growth of copse and thicket punctuated by taller trees and lower bursts of flowers. Now, coming upon the rectangular opening is quite a surprise — as, in nature, it certainly would be.

I like surprises in a garden. It's all very well to sit on a lawn and enjoy a vista up the meadow or over the pond, but it's more exciting if the view suggests, by dark openings and glinting curves of paths, that secrets lie hidden out of sight. When every-

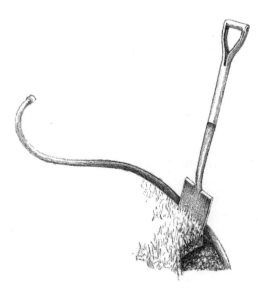

The easiest way to redesign the shape of a bed is to lay out the curve with a hose, warmed in the sun so it handles easily. Leave the hose in place while cutting the new line with a shovel.

thing was cleared, people used to bunch beside the house, cur-
dled to solidity by so much open space. Now, paths move them.
It's hardly possible to eye the path winding up the meadow and
dipping into shadow behind the rocky crest without one's feet
moving to see what's down there in the hollow — a mossy clearing (a compost heap), the path continuing, arriving at the pond,
splitting, tempting adventure in either direction: over a bridge
and into the woods or to the rowboat resting in a bed of pickerel
weeds. We split a path around a grouping of shadblow and azaleas
and rejoined it on the other side. The right arm takes one through
a sunny glade of hay-scented fern, the left through shaded rhododendrons. The distance is the same — no more than twenty
paces either way — but the experiences are surprisingly different.

Surprising, too, are the groupings one comes upon in wandering. The more conventional and alien one's previous guest list has
been, the more opportunity there is to enliven the party with
Americans whose casual ways loosen up the others. Creeping
junipers now thread their way through Siberian irises, shadblow
shoulders against Korean lilacs, the native clematis called virgin's
bower insinuates itself among foreign rhododendrons that would
otherwise perhaps never have met it. One memorable social
triumph was moving a pair of portly and pretentious Japanese
hollies (*Ilex crenata*) from their station at the front walk into a
group of wild blueberries with whom they now chat amiably.

Blueberries and blueberries and blueberries. They are our
background music, our theme and our refrain. Others might
entertain with roses or with ferns; our garden reverberates with
blueberries. Five tall and stately elders are especially dear to us
because we rescued them from where they were sullenly awaiting
death, in woodland that had overshadowed them, and transplanted them to a sunny bank along a boundary wall. Straight
walls, whether of romantic tumbled stone or practical chain-link
fence, diminish the apparent size of gardens by displaying too
clearly where they end. We blurred this one with an undulating
hedgerow: first, a spine of the six-foot blueberries, somewhat

COMPONENTS OF A HEDGEROW:
*a variety of fruiting shrubs chosen for their value
to wildlife over an extended period of ripening;
interplantings of herbaceous perennial
wildflowers and grasses to maximize habitat and
minimize weeding; accents such as broadleaf
evergreens, small conifers, or boldly textured
species to give shape and contrast.*

*Blueberry,
a summer fruit*

*Goldenrod,
a fall flower*

*Oakleaf hydrangea,
a bold accent*

staggered. The blueberries, alone for their first year, wanted bayberries the next, then these new knots of small talk wanted to drift off into other groups — dwarf fothergilla (*Fothergilla gardenii*), zenobia (*Zenobia pulverulenta*), New Jersey tea — and then, bored with politeness, unexpectedly requested the coarseness of oakleaf hydrangeas. Now the hedgerow has reached one of those social lulls from which, if I hear it right, it wishes to be lifted on that particular chorus of New York fern and showy aster, which I had jotted down as possible company for bayberries someday, and a lovely goldenrod with the unfortunate name of *Solidago uliginosa*.

I'm particularly fond of this berried, blooming, and richly textured hedgerow. I'm particularly eager for you to try something like it in lieu of yews and privet. I urge you to imagine the interlaced abundance if, throughout suburbia, every stockade fence, every chain-linked boundary, were to be buried in varied greenery and each of them and every hedge transformed into a hedgerow!

I ask you, at least, to open the door to some first guest that your party might begin.

A gift sent to me by a friend opened wide for me a door that let in more plants than I had known the names of or that I could previously have afforded to entertain: a paperback called *Gardening by Mail, A Source Book*.

This book, written and regularly updated by the librarian and gardener Barbara J. Barton, lists plant societies, horticultural libraries, books, periodicals, sources for gardening necessaries and accessories, and more than a thousand nurseries that sell plants and seeds by mail. *Gardening by Mail* lists, along with the L. L. Beans of the mail-order nursery world, a grower who offers thirty-four varieties of persimmons, a plantsman who has taken on the task of propagating every threatened wildflower from here to Siberia, and raspberry specialists, purveyors of eastern U.S. ericacious shrubs, suppliers of Rocky Mountain grasses, propagators of West Coast native bulbs, people who sell moss. Who

would have known that there are cacti native to the Northeast?
Who would have guessed that sedges are commercially available?

To request from one's roadside nursery the fall-blooming native Alleghany pachysandra or even an American sycamore is
futile. Local outlets sell what sells best: the same exotics that
already ornament one's neighbors' yards. To request a young
whip of a tree instead of weighty (and costly) balled and bur-
lapped stock also is useless. The nursery trade is designed so that
the cost of a plant grows faster than its size, and garden centers
profit at top dollar. The trick is to intercept plants before they
have reached that point, when they are younger and cheaper, and
to buy from growers who are less interested in corporate profits
than in supporting a dedication to their singular passion. Most
retail mail-order nurseries offer discounts on plants bought in
quantity — three or ten of each, for example; some sell at wholesale. Through the door that the gift book opened came a blizzard
of catalogs, followed by a rising flood of the plants I soon ordered.

Fortunately, this acute buying spree was brief. My records
show febrile excess only in that first season's orders; I'd describe
my condition now as chronic low-grade fever from February,
when the catalogs arrive, to the end of the spring shipping season
and subclinical the remainder of the year except for a minor
relapse in the fall. In fact, these repeated flushes of excitement
have become central to my gardening pleasure. Catalogs introduce me to those plant strangers whose new ideas inspire me and
to the growers whose culturing of native plants is critical to their
preservation. (One nursery propagates the endangered yew *Taxus
floridana*, the rarest of American conifers, but out of my zone,
unhappily.) Through the mail, I've met dwarf birch (*Betula nana*),
a bronze-stemmed, glossy-leaved shrub that grows to only four
feet; *Zenobia pulverulenta*, the blue-green beauties that now attend
the stately blueberries; and *Gaylussacia brachycera*, the tiny and
slowly spreading box huckleberry, a remnant stand of which is
thought to be the oldest plant alive, already carpeting its sandy
habitat twelve thousand years ago.

Try finding these in your garden center!

(Try resisting the temptation to order one of each.)

Gardening books warn not to buy a plant until one has found a place for it. The result could be a one-of-a-kind garden, a hodge-podge of mismatches. But until the stranger is welcomed, one can't guess what company will suit it. And if one is buying ordinary plants in quantity — for a hedgerow, for example — there may not be time that season to seat them properly. Our solution has been a small nursery, the strip where we heeled in berry plants that plastic-pumpkined fall.

There, in about the space of a front walk, we plant infant trees and shrubs — in the sizes catalogs describe as whips, liners, or transplants — and grow them. This saves a lot of money. One can figure that each year the monetary value of one's stock increases by roughly 50 percent. That's at wholesale. At retail, and after three summers' growing in a nursery bed, a shrub bought for $3 is the size of those sold at garden centers for $25. More demanding plants or rarer species might easily leap to $60. My aunt, who turned gooseberry eyes on our other gardening goings-on, approved of the nursery.

As the first crop of young shrubs emerged from their bed heavy with flower buds, as well-branched and full-foliaged as the fine specimens at the nursery down the road, a glowing pride stole upon me. No doubt a tomato is a prideful item, too, but its display is brief. Years and years from now, people strolling along these paths will beam upon that first year's babies grown up thick and strong, rooted more permanently here than we who grew them.

How came to be the famous cherry trees of Washington, D.C., the great garden magnolias of the South, the giant sycamores and sugar maples that shade New England towns, the dogwoods that line our parkways, the orchards that grid our hills? All from the grower's hands, all through the grower's work, all in the grower's beds! I felt I had, in a backyard sort of way, joined the grander company of plantsmen whose efforts now are providing stock for well into the century to come.

I've come to know some of these people — not the big-business ones, the Cadillac growers with full-color catalogs and customer service, but small growers who are more likely to carry the plants that interest me. A call to one such grower roused the missus, busy in the kitchen getting supper while she took my message over the company's only phone. Her husband called me back when he came in from the fields, answered in detail my question of how to deal with quackgrass, discoursed on the difficulties of getting high school help, the use of ice trays for sorting anthers for pollination, and the flora of Hawaii.

This blend of earthiness and expertise, this eagerness to talk shop with even a novice, is typical of small growers. You can get past customer service at the famous mail-order growers to seek advice from the resident horticulturist, but you can't chat with him as, boots shucked on the porch outside, beans baking in the oven, he takes his well-earned ease at the kitchen table. The horticulturist will answer what you ask. The individual grower will anticipate questions you'd never thought to ask.

Thus I called Mark Stavish, at whose Eastern Plant Specialties nursery I eventually bumped into our native hazelnut, about his home-bred zenobia 'Misty Blue' and got a rundown on hobble-bush, staggerbush, paxistema, and sweet-fern — as well as an earful of abuse for *pendulas*, *contortas*, and *compactas* of all sorts. Plantsmen are nothing if not opinionated. They want you to think their way, grow what they love, cover the hills with erica-cious shrubs, bank ponds with duck potatoes, restore the natives to their rightful place.

Mark, who was raised in New Jersey and ran a landscaping business there, moved to Maine to escape customer resistance to his passion for natural plantings — leaving behind, as he put it, "a trail of blueberries." Had he joined my club? Have I joined his?

The catalogs have made me realize that the price of entering the community of growers is no more than a box of bushes.

People ask me questions, too. Do we have ticks? What about slugs? How do we deal with creatures that eat our vegetables?

Behind such specific questions I believe I hear a general query: Is living and working in a natural garden like being stranded in the bush?

I'll tackle the specifics first.

Yes, we have ticks. We have dog ticks and cat ticks. We have about the same number as we used to have in our mowing heyday because we, the dogs, and William, too (now that he has gone back into retirement after his brief rabbit revival), stick to the paths. We have hardly any deer ticks, though; deer hardly ever get through the fence. (I just read that the first extensive field trial of a deer contraceptive delivered by dart is about to be launched in a Washington suburb; the fence may soon become obsolete.)

I don't deal with creatures that eat my vegetables. My father, who grew up with guns and horses, enjoyed popping off a wood-chuck now and then; I'd rather see a woodchuck than watch a salad grow. They haven't come back yet anyway. Raccoons ate the early corn last year. The only way to deal with them would be to cage the garden — all around and overhead as well. They let us have the late crop, 'Silver Queen'; I highly recommend it.

A birdhouse in the vegetable garden seems to have done won-ders for the cabbage worms, unless the family of wrens and the paucity of loopers this season is merely a coincidence. Or the reason could be the meadow. Cabbage white butterflies seem to be so distracted by what grows there that they have no time for cabbages. Potato beetles are still a nuisance on the eggplants. The predatory insects due to arrive by mail won't come 'til next spring and may require several infusions for their eventual establish-ment.

But I'm glad people ask me about slugs.

Recall the slug question posed to Elsie Cox and her answering options of grit, beer, copper, poison, or bare-handed combat: I herewith add fireflies to Elsie's elegant list.

At the time I read that column, when we still controlled slugs with poisoned bait, our firefly display resembled Tinkerbell's near brush with death. I can't speak for professional ecologists, but from my own observations over decades, my opinion is that this common beetle is an indicator of habitat destruction: one can't mow the yard and breed fireflies too. Those who haven't seen fireflies' normal evening sparkle may not realize that the fireworks have gradually petered out. The loss has been insidious, one yard at a time, like lights blinking out unnoticed over the nation as night comes on.

The disarray of my aunt's garden suggested to me that the present owners don't know what to make of that eccentric planting, don't know how to care for it, and might, in a single predatory episode, do away with it. It's that easy to put out the lights. In the middle of a city, where there are few refuges left to resupply the population, it might take years to turn them on again, but here the rekindling of summer nights has been rapid and dramatic. This July, fireflies emerged like sparks from a kicked log over the meadowed hillside and along the brushy woodland edge. My sister and her family were visiting from abroad; together we held a family picnic on the Fourth — my aunt's last, but the first for her youngest grandnephew, who has grown to puberty without fireflies in Morocco. In a reinvention of a ritual he knew nothing of, he begged a jar and sallied forth to swipe them from the sky. (We bade him let them go again, of course.) I suppose young Omar would have enjoyed a slug hunt by flashlight, too, but their rarity this year would have spoiled his sport. Fireflies had gotten to them first.

With the general increase of insects, especially in the meadow and along the shore, has come an equivalent increase in the bird population. In the hope that birds would obviate the use of pesticides, we stopped all routine tree spraying and injection. So far, the caterpillar damage has been minimal, well within our tolerance for nibbled holes and edges and certainly within the tolerance of native trees. However, three unidentified — but probably European — birches that had been mislabeled and included by error in our river birch grove succumbed almost immediately to the leaf miners and trunk borers against which they had been inoculated in previous years. We didn't shed a tear. They were, in our new mind-set, gone geese.

Learning to let plants and animals go without grief is not easy. When the Gone Goose was first injured, I had called our Audubon Society for advice or consolation. Bear it, I was told; do nothing. A goose hits a wire and breaks its wings; one gosling is taken by a snapping turtle, another by a hawk. Geese as a group go on. Let European birches go on where they belong, which isn't here. It's the flock, the grove, that matters. Our responsibility is to species, not to specimens, to communities, not to individuals. (Conversion hasn't convinced me to let the oak at the bottom of the peony garden succumb to fungus. That susceptible individual has its limits, and so do I.)

I find this new mind-set wonderfully relaxing. It lets me bid good-bye to German irises without regret, to admit that sycamores have recovered from anthracnose for longer than gardeners have been around, to leave the hose lie and the slug bait box closed, to get off the hook.

The peony and iris gardens are all that remain now of the perennial beds where we used to labor. When they, in mimicry of the island's flower patches, fill in with weed-discouraging grasses, they won't want much of me. I don't intend to divide irises again. On the island, wild iris rhizomes grow outward among clumps of grass as grass reoccupies their dying centers. They simply move. If cultivated irises won't do the same, I'll invite grass-accustomed natives in their place.

Only the vegetable garden will continue to require what crops asked of Adam: the same tilling, feeding, hoeing, staking, weeding, watering, picking, pulling, and composting in dull circularity that winds around inevitably to tilling it again. This is maintenance — housekeeping duties, janitorial chores.

It's a humbling lesson one learns by trying to be the king of cabbages, dictator of the beds. The more one tries to rule the garden according to one's arrogant designs, the more the citizens require special support or undue suppression. One ends up less the tsar of a suburban Sissinghurst than a harassed civil servant perennially behind on the work required to maintain order in the yard. We've come down off this false throne held through numbing drudgery and have assumed instead a middle-management position. We exercise tact, we explore diplomacy, we negotiate with Nature to see on which plants all of us can agree.

Novel solutions have arisen from these negotiations. A rebellious scouring rush had staged a coup on the slope beside the vegetable garden; a spiteful spurge had been in uprise there for as long as we had fought to keep it down. There's a nice cultivated euphorbia, *Euphorbia epithymoides*, that resembles the wild spurge in foliage and flower but forms dense clumps instead of spreading. We planted it in the weed spurge's territory, where it keeps the wild one in check and blends it to invisibility. It took a mental effort to perceive scouring rushes as ornamentals (although they are sometimes suggested as potted decor for artificial pools), but once that hurdle was overcome, we had only to imagine what might accompany them. We settled on native *Coreopsis major*, whose blur of ferny foliage masks the scouring rushes in their leafy stage of growth and contrasts nicely with them in their reedlike sporulating stage. The coreopsis blooms so brightly through the summer, flowers so profusely, and bushes out so quickly that only the most discerning eye could make out any weed at all on that gleaming golden slope. (We threw in the cream-white goldenrod called silverado, *Solidago bicolor*, for a cooler look in the fall.)

We remain unbending about buckthorn and bittersweet (islanders are making a serious mistake by preserving with undue respect gigantically invasive Japanese knotweed, *Polygonum cuspidatum*, also called bamboo), but our negotiations regarding Virginia creeper are typified by a give-and-take that changes with circumstances and from year to year. This fine native vine, prized by British gardeners who have imported it for its red banners fluttering from treetops in the fall, can be a pest similar in reach and spread to the English ivy that we imported from them and that at present gives my aunt's garden its air of sad abandonment. But Virginia creeper has its place. It climbs the oak tree at the bottom of the peony garden, and I say, Okay, climb. What harm can it do? This is not a vine that strangles in its coils as bittersweet can do; it clings to rock and bark by pads, that's all. It reaches for the sun like any vine — and won't bloom and fruit until it gets there — but it tends to drip from limbs in graceful streamers rather than smother the crown, as fox grapes do.

The ivy in my aunt's woodland was meant as a ground cover, not a tree drape. Virginia creeper can be used that way, too, with management. Where we reconnected the stranded oak to the woodland with a bridge of birches, the ground has become attractively foliaged with Virginia creeper acting in its youthful capacity as ground cover. That won't last. Soon it will begin to climb small shrubs that won't get along with it as well as great oaks do. We'll pull it off and snip the tendrils back to the ground. We reached a horticultural agreement regarding the Virginia creeper that the birds plant annually below the crabapples outside my attic window. That garden is too small for forest vines. We agreed, Mother N. and I, that a dwarf relative, the foreign but pleasing *Parthenocissus tridentata*, which fruits abundantly atop the garden's waist-high wall, would be fair trade. I take these agreements seriously. I don't think one ought to take out fruiting plants without replacing them with others.

Each year, we have many shrubs and trees to choose from. I say no to hickories in the herb garden, yes to hickories among the mountain laurels. A pagoda dogwood (*Cornus alternifolia*) there? Yes; I take it as a bonus awarded to me in my new management position, a stock option on the future. I accepted the seedling four years ago; the young tree came into fruit this summer.

These negotiations aren't like global crises, when hesitation can launch missiles and lose nations. If I don't hit the vegetable garden hard and fast when mildew strikes, good-bye tomatoes, but if it takes a year to decide whether things have gotten to the burning point in meadows, that's time enough. I go on a herbicidal hunt for aliens in the woodland about once a year — at any time of year, for the management of natural landscapes is seldom dictated by anything more pressing than inclination.

What surprises me is the effect this landscape has on others. Marty's mother, who never actually saw us working, was convinced that everything outside the peony garden had grown up on its own. The members of a visiting gardening group this summer didn't want to leave. They said it was a garden where they could relax because, it seemed to them, anyone could plant it, and no one had to work.

But, the curious and dubious may insist, what does this landscape look like?

By the time of the garden tour, most of this book had been completed. I realized that it may create a wrong impression, for I plan faster than I can plant. I write faster than gardens grow. Much as my visitors enjoyed the garden, I fear that if they had read about it first, they might have been disappointed.

The blueberry hedgerow is mostly mulch. What I see as solid mounds of New Jersey tea, others with minds less colored by the future see as the small and separate baby bushes that they are. The elder blueberries have the gaunt look of wild shrubs not yet recovered from transplanting. The oakleaf hydrangeas, on which the hedgerow will depend for boldness, seem frightened that so much is expected of them. The ferns, goldenrod, and aster are still growing in a nursery in the foothills of the Blue Ridge Mountains.

Moreover, this young bed is nearly as demanding as our perennial borders were. Newly transplanted stock wants watering for the first year at least, even species like bayberry that are adapted to dry terrain. Although we've learned by handling so many plants to get them into the ground without much fuss and don't amend the soil for forbs and grasses, we daren't transplant shrubs without mixing into the soil the usual dose of peat and organic fertilizer. The bed has been tedious to keep clean. Its soil held a hidden stash of tubers from that Medusa of the weed world, yellow nutsedge. So while insecticide and fungicide aren't needed, herbicide is, and not according to inclination but on a crisis schedule lest nutsedge crash the party planned for ferns and flowers.

I didn't take my visitors along that path. It was bad enough explaining that the ten sticks in the woods were a hazelnut thicket. They didn't ask for, and I didn't offer, an explanation regarding the portion of our land that neighbors, visitors, and Sunday drivers see as they pass by: the weed patch along the road where we tried and failed to make a meadow, the wild original that is a bonanza to birds, a refugium to insects, and an affront to the neighborhood.

Wait another year! I want to say. The sedges are coming! Wait until you see this alternative lawn, this flowering mead whose canvas of *Carex pensylvanica* will be stitched like the Milles Fleurs tapestry with robin's egg blue birdsfoot violet (*Viola pedata*), pink prairie smoke, bright blue-eyed grass, lavender wild petunia (*Ruellia humilis*), and starry heath aster (*Aster ericoides*) weaving into September among the autumn-fading sedge! Mr. Schnekenburger, prepare to lift your blade!

The sedge lawn, though, will need several years to cover the ground. It takes more years still for a shrub planting to graduate from maintenance to management: three years for small bushes to grow enough that one dares fill in around them with a matrix

TO PLANT SMALL BAREROOT SOCK:

instead of dangling the transplant over the center of a hole and trying to estimate its depth, hold it at the right height against the flat side of the hole with a thumb. Fan the roots out, then fill the hole with the other hand. With one person digging and another planting, a hundred transplants an hour is a reasonable goal.

of herbaceous plants, two or three more for the fill to cover the mulch entirely, and longer still to develop the weed-defying density that time has bestowed on the island's carefree patches. We have no plantings less than five years old that don't embarrass me.

But five years pass, and five again, and another five. Trees we planted as six-foot striplings reach to the rooftop now. Older plantings that once required our full attention leave us be. Hostas feed on oak leaves and their own rotting litter. Mountain laurels rooting among Christmas ferns find their own nourishment and water. Like children, who take work and worry to raise up, a landscape well started comes into its maturity and, as little boys grown to manhood surprisingly welcome their parents for the holidays, gardens invite their former keepers to join them for a stroll and so turn hosts to guests in their own yards.

Sitting here in Maine at this different window watching cormorants hang out their wings to dry, I feel a pull toward home. How are things in the woods? Have new mushrooms fruited? Have this summer's goslings learned to fly? Are the rose hips ripening in the bramble? Have the asters bloomed? I wonder if the mounds of gray dogwood below the hill crest have begun to purple voluptuously on this cloudy, end-of-summer afternoon.

As one grows a garden, each return to it is a revisitation in which the present strikes chords of the past and hums with intimations of the future. Looking through a wildflower guide to identify the harebell, I realized that a blue flower I noticed when I returned home last year is spiked lobelia (*Lobelia spicata*), a member of the same bluebell family, a native, and a possible update to my mental snapshot. I'm in the past: I remember just that shade of blue in an orchard once. I'm in the future: maybe I should plant apple trees and put the snapshot there. Last year when we got home, enormous puffballs had come up just where an orchard might be feasible. We ate them for breakfast fried in butter. I ate puffballs as a schoolchild; I found them once again. Fireflies are new to Omar, recall their great-aunt's garden to my children, and summon up to me full fifty years of diminution and rejuvenation.

I don't know much about hazelnuts, but I know this: someday Marty and I will come home from Maine in the fall and, walking along the path we hacked through the buckthorn years before in the woods behind the pond, we'll check out the bareroot mail-order sticks we planted in that first full flush of catalogs, and there will be nuts.

13

Home Comes the Bluebird

So HOME WE COME by boat and car, with dogs and cat, and mount the drive whose curve we staked through grass and goldenrod with four young sons one bright October day when the land was new to us. And now it's home. We've made it so by building our house, by furnishing it with books that indulge our interests, photographs that relate our history, scraps of the past like the chair my mother used to sit in to do her needlepoint, and hints of the future like the small guide to insects that I found on the way to New Jersey in August and thought might amuse my granddaughter on her birthday. Robins are enjoying their last hurrah among the dogwoods. The goslings are flying with their flock. On the pond, a bunch of flowers mysteriously travels through the water, leaving a V-shaped wake. Its propeller is one of the muskrat family, bringing home a meal.

This is home because I know everything that grows here. I visit the maidenhair ferns we planted and the unknown orchid that came up by itself. I check the berry crop, note the reddening tips of maple boughs, see that the pinxterblooms have set their buds for spring, decide that the witch hazels in the nursery are ready to be planted out this fall. This is home because I know its paths and contours, where the rocks rise, how the soils feel to hand and shovel.

This is home because it looks and smells and sounds the way it ought to in this corner of our country that, in a larger sense, is my home. On the drive from Maine, the texture of the landscape changes gradually over a distance of some four hundred miles from dark spruce and white canoe birch through various permutations of poplar, maple, oak, and pine to this particular mix that begins to settle into the well-known pattern only as one reaches southern New England, the landscape with which my sensibilities are permanently branded.

The scent of home greets us as we open the front door: wax, basement, the wood of the old cupboard, Marty's pipe smoke caught in woolen rugs. We open the windows: the breeze is redolent of home. The island has its own smell of low tide and roses; the autumn aroma here is more subtle, a smoky blend of fungi and fallen leaves with undertones of that miasma that rises over ponds and the sharp spice of goldenrod and aster.

There, gulls cry the morning; here, crows call in the dawn. With clapping bills and urging honks, the geese prepare for flight, presaging the next full turn of the wheel. Months from now, they'll honk in the new year, and around we'll go through the sounds of seasons: chickadees, tree frogs, the mockingbird singing spring's end by moonlight from the roof peak. Crickets carry the season onward to cicadas droning through the dog days until katydids boringly predict with endless repetition the coming of first frost. Katydids are loud on the ear after the foggy quiet of island nights in Maine. The north wind in winter must play a different tune through the island's spruce than through our woods' bare limbs.

So flick my thoughts, unstiffening after the long drive, stretching out. So play the garden themes of place and time, of what is right and fitting on this hill among these granite ridges. I catch a glimpse of azure out the window: one of the bluebird crew. All is well. Yes, I'm here. Now I'm home.

Eastern Bluebird

And now I know what the answer ought to be to the question Mirabel Osler asked in *A Gentle Plea for Chaos:* American gardens ought to be like America is, one way in Maine and another in New York; tall prairie; groves of cottonwood; pine barren; cactus scrub; poppies burnishing the golden hills of California. Our gardens ought to exemplify, ought to participate in, ought to be a distillation of the larger landscape. There ought not to be a simpler answer to her question.

The first bluebird flew in the March after we had let the lawn grow up to meadow. I hadn't seen a bluebird in forty years. We were planting the birch grove, but we left our work to build a nest box and mount it on a post beside the path that curves up through the meadow. We had lunch. We went back to planting. The bluebird moved in within the hour.

What is one to think of seeming magic?

Our granddaughter thinks nothing of it. When I point out to her the bluebirds that have lived here ever since, she's pleased but not surprised. Emma is only three. She quite expects frogs to hop into her hands, bunnies to come to her for carrots, robins to lay their eggs in nests she makes of grass, and all animals, even stuffed ones, to understand plain English. She'll find out, of course, how wrong she is.

And then, I hope, she'll learn in what sense she had been right in the first place. Anthropomorphism isn't popular these days. Children aren't encouraged to consider that the hopes and dreads that haunt our human lives might be shared by others, much less to claim for beasts and creatures thought, judgment, or the conveyance of wisdom from one generation to another. But the bluebirds, non-English speakers that they are, tell me otherwise.

How furious they are at William sunning on the path! Why, when I come to carry him away, don't they fly at me as well? At first I thought it was coincidence that bluebirds perch above us as we garden. Then I saw that they follow us for the insects our activities stir up. I think the bluebird wasn't surprised at the sleight of hand of box and post by which a home suddenly appeared. I think he had hatched in such a box. I think he expected to find one near human habitation. I think that meeting expectations is the very essence of communication, and that yes, Emma, we can talk to the animals.

If we don't reply to others' expectations, we will be terminating a dialog that has continued for centuries between us and those animals that ride the ark of our formerly agricultural landscape. William Cronon, in *Changes in the Land*, traced the cultural evolution by which our race over a period of centuries transformed the northeastern landscape from forest to field; it wasn't within the purview of his book to examine the cultural evolution by which other races accommodated to the change, came to rely on it, learned to profit from it, waxed or waned in population according to how steadily we steered. Over the centuries, the bluebirds' taste in housing has changed with the changing land from isolated snags excavated by woodpeckers in forest clearings, to rotted cavities in fence posts between fields, to nest boxes mounted at the height to which fences accustomed them. They have carried with them from farming days an eye for linearity: young males

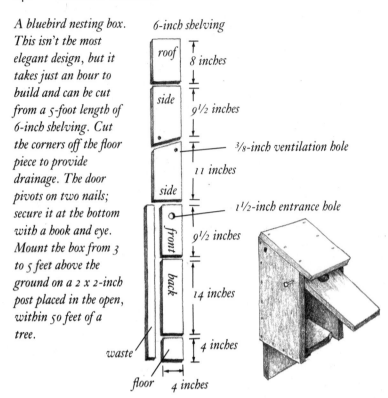

A bluebird nesting box. This isn't the most elegant design, but it takes just an hour to build and can be cut from a 5-foot length of 6-inch shelving. Cut the corners off the floor piece to provide drainage. The door pivots on two nails; secure it at the bottom with a hook and eye. Mount the box from 3 to 5 feet above the ground on a 2 x 2-inch post placed in the open, within 50 feet of a tree.

6-inch shelving

roof — 8 inches

side — 9½ inches

⅜-inch ventilation hole

11 inches

side

1½-inch entrance hole

front — 9½ inches

back — 14 inches

waste — 4 inches

floor — 4 inches

returning to the vicinity of their birth are drawn to row housing, such as nest boxes along a bluebird trail. Had there been a lone snag in the meadow, that first bluebird might not have recognized it as a proper home.

Purple martins certainly would not. In the East, only one colony of purple martins nests in natural cavities, according to ancestral tradition. The rest seek settlement in manmade housing. For thousands of years, the Indians provided gourd homes for purple martins. The custom was picked up by Europeans and carried farther. When I was a girl, an elaborate martin mansion stood on Bedford's village green, one example among many of miniature edifices that were the fashion then. Fashions change. It isn't stylish anymore to build mansions in one's yard.

We prefer our own buildings plain: porchless, eaveless, without overhanging ornament, *sans* open sheds or unused attics, stripped of cupola and belfry, shut tight, cemented solid, devoid of nooks and crannies. How abrupt an end to the dialog by which swallows came to live in barns and owls in silos, chipmunks in rubble walls and toads in stone foundations, bats in attics and phoebes under eaves on window ledges!

Why can't these old companions go back where they once came from — hollow trees, rock shelves under overhanging cliffs? Some can; some do; many can't; most won't. English sparrows have taken over cliff communes where swallows used to nest. The woodland regrown on old farmland is a baby boom population, a peer group of trees only now reaching middle age and not suffering much from heartrot. There is scarcity; there is competition. But there also is tradition, time honored by now and demonstrated to each new generation. Bats don't look for hollow sycamores along the riverbank; they look for buildings. Swallows don't search for rocky ledges; they spot open doors and windows; they seek wood rafters. Purple martins want their houses painted white, prim and proper, and won't move in unless the home is within fifty feet of a human dwelling. They look, you see, for *people*.

We have thus inherited from our forefathers animals less wild than we had thought, bound by tradition to presume on our hospitality and housing. And we therefore face a problem greater than we had imagined, for it is the rule of reproduction that no homeless mother attempts to rear a family.

This year we grew purple martin gourds — just for fun, just to see what it was like to grow giant cucurbits. It was like growing Jack's beanstalk; it was like playing the gardener whom Elsie Cox advised to twitch her figs. But it *was* fun.

The three vines reached thirty feet in length, overgrew the rear wall of the garage, explored the roof, reached into the herb garden, picked up sticks and plucked nasturtiums, and opened a shed door to see what they might finger there. This is not the sort

Calabash gourd. Seeds and dried gourds already cut with entry, drainage, and mounting holes are available from the Purple Martin Conservation Association, Edinboro University of Pennsylvania, Edinboro, Pa. 16444.

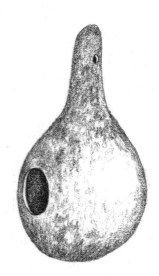

of vine one wants to lean a hoe against lest it be held fast by nightfall.

But the gorgeous white blossoms, of separate sexes and each open only for one night, dropped off fruitlessly each morning. Obviously, the night-flying moth that was supposed to be responsible for this gourd's sex life was either missing or minding its business southward where the vine grows wild. What was I to do but tickle the flowers nightly with a paintbrush? I must have done it wrong, though. By a week into August, I had fertilized all of two gourds.

Then we went to Maine. Now we've returned. Lo! A dozen gourds hang fattening in the late summer sun!

What is one to make of *this* magic?

It was the Indian, of course, resting ghostly on the rock in the oak tree's shade as we came up the drive, smiling to see that someone still grows gourds for purple martins.

Traditions are discarded when they have lost their meaning, and traditions are forged anew when new significance requires their expression. Most likely the Indians housed purple martins to

Purple martin

control flies around encampments (although they can't have failed also to enjoy their sociability and acrobatic flight), and perhaps it is not coincidence that the custom of erecting birdhouses faded out at about the same time that garbage collection became the norm. The ecological sensitivity with which the Indians maintained the land was similarly impelled by their dependence on the land's provisioning. What will be of equal significance to us now? What will impel us toward a new gardening tradition?

Sophisticated ecosystem services — and realizing the critical role our own yards play in supporting the complexity of life by which such services are rendered — are harder to appreciate than killing flies or filling bellies. There will be those of us who experience that twist of view by which perceptions change, and with them the way we garden, but there will be many more who will be reluctant to step off our familiar checkerboard of lawns.

The bluebird had assessed our real estate. He had noted the lay of the land: the availability of water, the potential for insects in the meadow, the protection of surrounding trees. I'm proud that our property rates a bird's approval. But I wish its richness to be valued by humans, too. I want us as a culture to depart from the old tradition of evaluating land according to what can be extracted from it as commodity or abstracted from it as social asset and turn instead toward a new tradition of valuing land by the life it harbors.

Let's imagine a goal: that at some time in the future, the value of a property will be perceived in part according to its value to wildlife. A property hedged with fruiting shrubs will be worth more than one bordered by forsythia. One with dry-stone walls that provide passageways for chipmunks will be valued higher than one whose walls are cemented stone. Buyers will place a premium on lots that provide summer flowers and fall crops of seed. Perhaps there will be formal incentives: tax abatements geared to the number of native species; deductions for lots that require neither sprays nor sprinklers. A nursery colony of bats might be considered a capital improvement. There could be bonuses for birdhouses.

Oh, brave new world!

But we are, we Americans, inheritors of the New World that so astonished the explorers when they came upon it. Perhaps we have forgotten how exotic this land is to others. Fireflies don't light the sky in England; they glow as grubs and flightless females on the ground. Europeans have no skunks, chipmunks, raccoons, or possums. No sugar maples flame on other continents. Our milkweeds are unique. So are the monarch butterflies that milkweeds feed across the kaleidoscopic landscapes of this amazing land of sand shore and rock mountain, grass plain, fir forest, cactus desert. The bluebird lives only in America's back yard.

So there is one appeal: a form of nativism.

Or, for those who don't care one way or another about fireflies or skunks, perhaps we could appeal to a combination of private interest and public conscience by pointing out how garden ecosystems run themselves cheaply and without damage to the environment.

But, if neither intrinsic value nor practical advantage will move suburbia toward a new tradition, then I'll settle for mere fashion.

Put up a bluebird box; grow a patch of grass and wildflowers beneath it; plant nearby a dogwood or a shadblow for bluebirds to pause in before they make their stunning swoop to home. Or hang some gourds.

Surely such ornament could be as catching as garden gnomes and pink flamingos on the lawn.

We were out front the other day making final preparations for the sedge lawn when Mr. Schnekenburger came by, mowing along the roadside. We walked him around the place, showed him the pond, the meadows, the gourds, the gardens. We dare to do that now. We've done a little magic of our own. The place looks neat. We've tricked the eye. We've improved our lot and pleased the beasts and creatures, too.

Magic is a matter of perception. If a meadow is fairly uniform in height, if its edge curves pleasingly and its paths are crisply mowed, a human sees simplicity where there is complexity, sees quietude where there is restless life — and doesn't notice that, yes, the grasshoppers have returned and the meadowlarks to eat them. If shrubs are planted tightly as a hedgerow, visitors see space filled where space actually has been opened up to insects seeking refuge — and to their predators, the ladybugs that had declined and now are on the rise. If stone walls and steps are neatly laid, guests note their solidity, not the holes that provide safe transit for all the many chipmunks whose conduits Marty builds.

Marty has a gift for seeing shapes where I see lumps, for fitting rocks the way I fit words. He transforms what were once no more than stone dumps into ordered walls using the same stones exactly, and no cement. Chipmunks had always dug burrows under the boundary walls some distance from the house, but then came new ones to each rock work Marty built: a stone ditch, the steps down to the pond, a retaining wall that brought them nearly to the house. He sows stones; we reap chipmunks.

Once a garden comes alive ecologically, it displays a humor and richness of meaning that have been missed by the narrow views of horticulture. Significance expands. Meanings multiply.

Each plant or planting becomes much more than what nurseries believe they sell, or gardeners suppose they grow, or visitors would notice.

I've caught a sour gum tree in an act of mild deception. The tree is coloring in a cunning way: a leaf here, a leaf there, spots of shining scarlet against dark green foliage as though it were in berry. And indeed it is — but the actual fruit is dull blue, hung below the leaves, and not very plentiful, either. "Sour gum," says a tree guide dryly, "is one of the earliest trees to show fall color." The author didn't get the joke of this arboreal illusion.

A screen of white pines we planted gives us privacy from neighbors and, in winter, stands as a blue-green accent against the bare, buff land. Screen, accent: those are horticultural words. To the cardinals that overwinter here, a grove of conifers is a lifeboat in the ocean, the focus of their struggle to live through winter storms. The grove is richer for that additional meaning. Add, now, the beetles that kill the trees' succulent young leaders by boring into them to lay their eggs; smile when writers laud the white pine's flat-topped, eccentric "habit": it's the beetles that so picturesquely prune them.

I like the way we laid the brick paving in the herb garden in sand instead of concrete. I like better still the flicker that after summer showers pokes about between the bricks. I like best of all realizing that the flicker comes to eat the ants that use the sand for their own constructions, and that this neat little garden with which I flavor soups and salads serves at every scale.

Yet I don't point out our backyard formicary to visitors, or the dead leaders in the pine grove, or the down on mullein leaves with which hummingbirds weave their tiny egg cups, or the spider webs with which they bind them up, or the strategic opposition of grass blades that spiders are aware of as they weave their necessary silk. I don't suppose the Victorians thought of bird boxes as bird breeders. They may not even have been thinking about flies. Certainly current fashion, not original significance, dictated the ornateness of their designs. That's okay; that's enough. Let visitors get the big view, note the overall design: see richly planted woods, flowers growing through grass, hedges that bear fruit as the latest thing, a new gardening style to emulate, a fresh fashion for the turn of the twenty-first century. It's got to be easier to spread a fashion than to excite in one's neighbors a love of ants.

By the second summer after the pond was dredged, when the low meadow there had begun to bloom and aquatic plants were spreading around the shore, when geese were nesting on the island and green herons, killdeer, and kingfishers had put in what was, to us, their first appearance, I felt the time had come to stock this refurbished habitat with the dear departed: the common newt that never had been here during our ownership, the frog species that had declined or disappeared.

To that end I called the New York State Department of Environmental Conservation, whose job I thought it was to help Jane Q. Citizen conserve the environment.

I was referred to the Bureau of Fisheries (there is no bureau of amphibians), which sent me a packet of information. A note called my attention to a list of regional offices where I might obtain a permit to restock my "fishing pond."

Startled but interested, I read on. Lake trout wouldn't do. They don't reproduce in mud-bottomed farm ponds. Golden shiners were suggested as food for bass, to be replenished as needed every three to five years, depending on how quickly the bass ate them to extinction. The more permanent combination for our circumstances would be largemouth bass and bluegills. That's what lives here already.

The pamphlet suggested that if inferior food species were ruining our sport, we could poison all fish with rotenone before restocking. We were strongly advised to mow the grass around the pond and clear it completely of aquatic plants according to the instructions in another publication, this one devoted to the use of herbicides in wetlands. Still another bulletin was recommended for advice on getting rid of turf-disrupting moles. Traps were suggested for removing muskrats. We would have to tolerate predation by the great blue heron. That species, the pamphlet informed me with regret, is protected under federal law. Fortunately, we wouldn't have to worry about newts and frogs. They don't harm game fish.

I felt I had come full circle to an aquacultural point of view no more related to frog ponds than, horticulturally, topiary is related to hedgerows.

A year later, when a new pheasant was once more strutting on the old pheasant's accustomed display rock up the hill and the meadows seemed ready to feed and shelter other upland game birds — but the grouse had not come back — I again called DEC for advice on restocking. I was referred to the Bureau of Wildlife Management in the person of Randy Stumvoll.

Randy offered no pamphlets. He told me right off that my release scheme wouldn't work. Game birds are raised in captivity for the same reason that game fish are: as meat. Some are supplied to restaurants and specialty butcher shops; most are sold live for hunters to kill. Any that remain after the hunting season fall prey to other predators. He predicted a life span in the wild of no more than a few months for uneducated grouse that, raised in incubators, haven't learned the cautions taught by hawkwise parents.

I was especially keen to release young wild turkeys, but that's against the law in New York State. Captive-bred turkeys infect remnant wild stock with the diseases they carry. They're not the real thing anyway. Turkeys raised on game farms are a semidomesticated breed of similar looks and silly disposition. Easier to shoot, Randy said.

I should have known. I had overstepped a gardener's bounds, gone beyond the gate. For all I know, it could be a mistake to restock ladybugs of unspecified species, stupefied by canning. I'm canceling that order. My job is to restore the real estate, not buy the occupants.

The role is hardly godlike. It isn't even diluvian. Unlike the Neanderthal Noah in the print that decorates what is now our

Eastern box turtle

grandchildren's nursery, we don't stand, staff in hand, to guide the animals two by two to safety. Perhaps the box turtles that I picked up during my childhood to examine their curiously hinged shells still exist; they can live a hundred years. My own children found one here once, before we cleared the land. Surely it would like the wild strawberries that we planted in what ought to be, according to the books, excellent box turtle habitat. But how can I herd a turtle whose whereabouts are unknown? And can it find this place again on its own? The birds of the air — the bats and the butterflies, too — can find islands in the landscape as Noah's dove found Mount Ararat, but those creatures that trot, walk, hop, creep, slither along the ground, need the landscape that Noah could not have fit into the hold of his little ark and that we, his heirs, must roll out across the continent.

But will it really work?

From the very beginning, there had been this question regarding the faunal repopulation of restored suburbia. I hadn't wanted to face it; had hoped to learn, to plant, to write, and to be rewarded with reappearances as rapid and dramatic as disappearances had been. But ecosystems slip into reverse more easily than they are pushed forward. So I asked Randy Stumvoll, Will it work? Will the turtle return, will the fox come by, will I ever see the bobolinks that Mrs. Dana saw?

He said, Yes, if there are corridors.

Words are tricky things. "Corridor" is an ecological term that disarmingly conjures up a stroll along a pathway between, say, Mr. Schneckenburger's land and ours. A turtle might, indeed, stroll from his pond, along his stream, over the road that separates our properties or through the culvert below it and, once safely among the skunk cabbages, meander upstream to arrive after a while at our shore. Paths are important. Pound Ridge, by preserving the wooded strips along boundaries, got that much right. But the ecological meaning of corridors is both figuratively and literally broader.

The movement of animals over longer periods of time than one turtle's amble after a mate in breeding season is similar to those fireworks that, impelled by pressure from the center, burst outward, then burst again from each spreading fragment. For every species — bursting bobolinks or slow-footed tortoises — the center is a refuge, a patch of habitat in which it multiplies, and the impulse to spin out is the centrifugal force of increasing population. A clutch of grouse, a litter of foxes or generation of mantids, spreads in all directions, and each female when she breeds becomes a new center from which, again, her young radiate over the landscape.

The pressure is very real. There is only so much food. Land is shared without argument with other species which, by their differing habits, apportion habitat, but land is not peacefully shared with members of the same species whose competition for the same resources has been the wellspring, even in our supposedly superior race, of bestial goings-on from noisy sibling rivalry to murderous territorial dispute. Among mammals, a female cus-

Opposite: The land, ca. 2000: suburbia regrowing into a continuity of woods, thickets, and meadows linking remnant refuges and reservations

tomarily excludes her mate from her resource center once breeding is accomplished, and, when her young have come of age,
pushes them, too, beyond the periphery of the real estate she
holds. Even species that live in families or tribes for reasons of
mutual defense or cooperative feeding enforce dispersal, as when
young male prairie dogs are impelled by inner restlessness to
leave their natal town and, if that inner urge is insufficient, are
nipped and chased away.

What is meant by corridors, then, is not narrow strips along
which animals might walk from one remote refuge to another, as
our own young these days travel along the highways, but a
continuity of living quarters among which movement is genera-
tional — by dispersal, not migration — from patch to patch
along networks that may well originate in parklands or reservations but that must spread through all of our back yards.

The repopulation of each person's land therefore depends on
neighbors, on whether they stop the flow of breeding — dampen
bursts and snuff out sparks that would ignite new life beyond
their boundaries — or feed the spread by what they plant and
how they plant it. I enjoy my garden's private jokes, but animals
don't perceive my land as private. They don't get this business of
subdivisions. They are, as far as they know, on public ground.
"My" butterflies need your flowers. "My" birds need your grain.
The grouse I hope to welcome back must breed their way here
through your switchgrass and raspberries. Thank you, whoever
you are, for supporting the AWOL owl during our years-long
scarcity of mice.

Last year I asked to join the local garden club. This was, it turned
out, a social gaffe. One doesn't ask to join; one is invited. Nevertheless, permitted to go to one meeting, I immediately understood that even were an invitation forthcoming — which it was
not — I would have been a misfit. The activity was arranging
dried sprigs of this and that in mussel shells to decorate the trays
of hospital patients on Thanksgiving Day. A nice thing to do, of

course, but insufficient to a would-be member afflicted by wild turkeys on the brain.

I wanted to warn them against buckthorn and bittersweet. I wanted to offer to the annual plant sale species more critical than coleus to the ecology at large: infant hornbeams, little hollies, baby shadblow trees grown to transplant size and nicely potted up. I wanted to donate years of finding out and seeing how, regretting losses and celebrating returns. I wanted, I guess, to found a new chapter in the history of garden clubs.

And so, I hope, I have.

Again, Thanksgiving is approaching. The squirrels have nearly finished stocking nuts for winter. My pantry holds our share of fruit in half-pint jelly jars and quart containers. In the herb garden outside the kitchen, sage and rosemary will stay green just long enough to flavor the stuffing for our feast. In schools throughout the nation, teachers are again recounting the tales of pilgrims, pumpkins, corn, and turkeys — the great bird that has become the very symbol of plenty in the harvest season.

America is the homeland of the wild turkey, which once was widespread and abundant from western scrub to eastern forest. Now it survives only in scattered refuges. If Benjamin Franklin had had his way, our national symbol would have been the wild turkey instead of the bald eagle, a scavenger of dead meat. I think about that now. The near demise of eagles due to DDT galvanized the readers of Rachel Carson's *Silent Spring* to take action, and so powerfully that my children's generation, too, reverberates with alarm. Coming home from Maine, stalled in a traffic jam on a bridge above a bay, we saw a male bald eagle, white-crowned on vast wings, lift into the sky where thirty years ago his species was extinct. He held a fish in his talons. He was so big. I don't think our little pond or occasional dead goose could support that national emblem.

But had the turkey stood for America the Beautiful, we might have seen it as our civic duty to assure the gobbler a plentiful supply of nuts, grains, and fruits and of the beetles, spiders, snails, and centipedes that it also likes to eat. The turkey's natural habitat is "open woodlands with scattered natural or manmade clearings." We might, if we had more humbly stuck to our own paths, have kept our wild turkeys with us, sharing the promised land.

Perhaps wild turkeys can return; perhaps they can't. But when each of us, alone and in community, on acreage and in small back yards, for reasons of ecology, economy, or style has done all that can be done to restore the abundance of the land, many other animals surely will rejoin us.

Then it will work. Then there will be plenty. Then we will have reason for thanksgiving.

Wild turkey hen and chicks

APPENDIX

Helpful Books
Plants for Butterflies
Berrying Plants for Hedgerows
Species by Botanic Name
Species by Common Name

INDEX

Helpful Books

These are the books I consult most often for choosing what to plant, where to buy it, and how to improve wildlife habitat.

My basic resources are guides to trees, wildflowers, birds, mammals, insects and spiders, and reptiles and amphibians. There are two popular series: the Audubon Society Nature Guides (Knopf) and the Peterson Field Guides (Houghton Mifflin). I use Audubon to familiarize myself with species I might come upon because the color photographs, taken in nature, often give a helpful context, such as the plant an insect is eating or the tree where a bird is nesting. The Peterson series, though, with its simplified drawings, arrows that indicate distinctive features, and juxtaposition of similar species for comparison, is better for identification. Both series offer ecosystem guides. Audubon's are too broad to give a sense of one's local ecology; the *Audubon Nature Guide to Wetlands*, for example, covers everything from the trees to the mites that are associated with streams, rivers, lakes, swamps, marshes, and floodplains from the Everglades to the Colorado River! *Peterson's Field Guide to Eastern Forests* is, on the other hand, an eminently accessible trove of information organized by, for example, forest type, successional stage, and season. It is the best practical introduction to ecology that I've come across. A western edition is also available.

The standard reference for botanical description and correct nomenclature is *Hortus Third, A Concise Dictionary of Plants Cultivated in the United States and Canada* (Macmillan), a horticultural encyclopedia assembled by the staff of the L. H. Bailey Hortorium at Cornell University. Standard or not, it's pretty dry and doesn't have much to say about how to grow the plants described.

For a modicum of cultural advice, I prefer *Wyman's Gardening Encyclopedia* (Macmillan), by Donald Wyman, even though it doesn't include nearly as many species as *Hortus Third*. Neither volume focuses on native species, and no concise encyclopedia that I know of consistently gives information about a plant's natural habitat. *Native Trees, Shrubs, and Vines for Urban and Rural America* (Van Nostrand Reinhold) does both. This excellent, oversize book by Gary Hightshoe is subtitled *A Planting Design Manual for Environmental Designers*, but don't let that put you off. It's about as helpful a book for amateurs as I've ever seen. Each species is given a full spread that includes a large, black-and-white illustration showing mature size and habit, a detail of leaf, twig, fruit, and flower for identification, and a distribution map. The cultural information is complete, even to the type of soil in which the species normally grows. I find especially useful such data as growth rate, food value to wildlife, and a list of native species with which the plant is associated in its natural habitat. In addition, there are charts of all sorts; one even shows foliage color through the seasons. The 250 species covered are plenty for the average gardener.

To picture color and texture when planning, I use the Taylor's Guides to Gardening (Houghton Mifflin). *Taylor's Guide to Shrubs* and *Taylor's Guide to Trees* complement Gary Hightshoe's manual of woody plants. In these beautifully bound books, each species is given two color plates: the full plant, so one can see shape and habit, and a close-up featuring foliage, fruit, or flower. The cultural instructions are clear, and there are other helpful aids such as silhouettes and summary charts. A new title, *Taylor's Guide to Natural Gardening*, should be of particular interest. It covers native trees, shrubs, wildflowers, ferns, and grasses all in one convenient handbook.

Specific help in choosing plants for birds comes from *The Audubon Society Guide to Attracting Birds* (Scribner's), which has a chapter on landscaping. In addition, a hundred-page section describes the most important food plants, many of which are native. Special lists are provided by area: Northeast, Southeast, Prairies and Plains, Mountains and Deserts, and Pacific Coast. Every other encouragement of birds is also covered, from feeding stations and nest boxes to drinking fountains and baths — all with clear instructions. If you could afford only one book, I'd suggest this one because improvements for birds will automatically improve the land for other wildlife.

Although *Garden Pools & Fountains*, an Ortho paperback available at garden centers, doesn't mention wildlife, its instructions for installing prefabricated pools and building your own wetland are much more complete than those in the Audubon book. The subjects also include landscaping, stocking and planting, and maintaining artificial pools. Suggested species of plants and animals are, however, largely exotics.

The only book-length advice I've found on attracting lepidoptera is *Butterfly Gardening: Creating Summer Magic in Your Garden* (Sierra Club), compiled by the Xerces Society with the Smithsonian Institution. This collection of essays offers lots of gorgeous photographs, but the text is not well organized and information is hard to find. Missing altogether is the comprehensive landscaping approach taken for birds in the Audubon book. Nevertheless, it was my major source for listing nectar and host plants. There is a chapter on night-blooming flowers for moths.

My favorite reference for food plants is *American Wildlife & Plants: A Guide to Wildlife Food Habits* (U.S. Fish and Wildlife Service, 1951; Dover paperback). The book has two main sections; in the first, you can look up an animal to learn what it eats; in the second, you can look up a plant to see which animals eat it. A third section rates plants according to the number of bird and mammal species that depend on them for food, but this information is probably too old to be reliable.

Barbara Barton's *Gardening by Mail, A Source Book* (Houghton Mifflin) is the indispensable reference for mail-order nurseries that sell the plants you wish to grow. Barton has also compiled *Taylor's Guide to Specialty Nurseries* (Houghton Mifflin). This more compact format includes a section devoted entirely to growers of native plants.

An excellent companion volume to these two references is the Andersen Horticultural Library's *Source List of Plants and Seeds*, which lists alphabetically, by species and variety, 40,000 plants available by mail from North American nurseries. A code following each listing indicates which nurseries carry it. The book can be ordered from Andersen Horticultural Library, Minnesota Landscape Arboretum, 3675 Arboretum Drive, Box 39, Chanhassen, Minnesota 55317.

You might also consider joining the National Wildflower Research Center for its clearinghouse service. For example, I've obtained through this service a list of recommended wildflower species for New York, a native plant bibliography for the region, and lists of northeastern native plant associations and nurseries. Write to the NWRC at 2600 FM 973 North, Austin, Texas 78725, or call 512–929–3600.

Finally, for a basic reference on how to grow plants, I've found *The Garden Primer* (Workman), by Barbara Damrosch, to be the most complete, easy to follow, well illustrated, and pleasantly written. The paperback offers more than 600 pages of instruction and explanation covering any question you are likely to have in an exceptionally well organized and attractive format.

Plants for Butterflies

Although butterflies may favor certain nectar plants, most will drink from a variety of species, usually those with deep or tubular flowers that produce copious amounts of nectar. The following is a general list of natives that attract butterflies. They are in alphabetical order by genus; in most cases, any species within the genus will do. Garden annuals popular with butterflies include petunia, zinnia, lantana, and heliotrope. Clovers are favorites, and butterflies enjoy the blossoms of almost all herbs and onions. Don't forget buddleias, butterfly bushes.

Nectar Plants for Adult Butterflies

TREES, SHRUBS, VINES

Aesculus spp   buckeyes
Ceanothus spp   New Jersey tea, snowbrush, buckbrush, wild lilac
Cephalanthus occidentalis   buttonbush
Clethra alnifolia   summersweet
Lonicera spp   honeysuckles
Prunus spp   wild plum, black cherry, chokecherry
Rhododendron spp   rhododendrons and azaleas
Rhus spp   sumacs (and poison ivy!)
Rubus spp   blackberries, raspberries, dewberries
Sambucus spp   elderberries
Symphoricarpos spp   snowberry, coralberry
Tilia americana   American linden, basswood
Vaccinium spp   blueberries

WILDFLOWERS

Achillea millefolium   yarrow
Allium spp   onions
Amorpha canescens   lead plant
Asclepias spp   butterfly weed, milkweeds
Aster spp   asters
Coreopsis spp   coreopsis, tickseeds
Echinacea spp   coneflowers
Eupatorium spp   hardy ageratum, boneset, Joe-Pye weeds, white
  snakeroot
Geranium spp   geranium, cranesbills
Helenium spp   sneezeweeds
Helianthus spp   sunflowers
Houstonia caerulea   bluets
Impatiens capensis   jewelweed
Liatris spp   blazing stars, gayfeathers
Lithospermum canescens   hoary puccoon
Lobelia spp   lobelias
Lupinus spp   lupines
Monarda spp   beebalm, wild bergamot, horsemint
Phlox spp   phlox
Pontederia cordata   pickerelweed
Rudbeckia spp   black-eyed Susans, coneflowers
Ruellia spp   wild petunias
Salvia spp   salvias, sages
Senecio spp   groundsels, ragworts
Solidago spp   goldenrods
Verbena spp   verbenas, vervains
Vernonia spp   ironweeds

What a butterfly eats and what its larvae eat are usually two very different things. Some butterflies lay their eggs exclusively on plants of a single genus, but the caterpillars of others accept several genera or an entire family of host plants. This chart, based on information compiled by the Xerces Society and included in *Butterfly Gardening*, lists popular host plants and seventy common North American species that frequent them. While the list gives a general idea of which kinds of host plants — wild plums and cherries, for example — are used by many species of butterflies, only some of the species may inhabit your area, and the larvae of others may require plants not mentioned here.

Host Plants for Larvae

TREES, SHRUBS, AND VINES	LARVAE
Amelanchier spp (serviceberries, shadblows)	Weidemeyer's admiral western tiger swallowtail
Aristolochia spp (pipevines, Virginia snakeroot)	pipevine swallowtail
Asimina spp (pawpaws)	zebra swallowtail
Betula spp (birches)	banded admiral
Carpinus caroliniana (American hornbeam)	tiger swallowtail
Ceanothus spp (wild lilac, New Jersey tea)	pale swallowtail spring azure
Celtis spp (hackberries)	question mark snout butterfly
Citrus spp (oranges, lemons)	anise swallowtail giant swallowtail
Crataegus spp (hawthorns)	pale swallowtail western tiger swallowtail
Fraxinus spp (ashes)	striped hairstreak tiger swallowtail two-tailed swallowtail
Holodiscus spp (ocean spray, rock spirea)	pale swallowtail Weidemeyer's admiral
Lindera benzoin (spicebush)	spicebush swallowtail tiger swallowtail
Platanus racemosa (western sycamore)	two-tailed swallowtail western tiger swallowtail

Populus spp
(cottonwoods, poplars, aspens)

banded admiral
Lorquin's admiral
mourning cloak
red-spotted purple
viceroy
Weidemeyer's admiral
western tiger swallowtail

Prunus spp
(black cherry, wild plum,
chokecherry)

Lorquin's admiral
pale swallowtail
red-spotted purple
striped hairstreak
tiger swallowtail
two-tailed swallowtail
Weidemeyer's admiral
western tiger swallowtail

Ptelea trifoliata
(hop tree)

giant swallowtail
tiger swallowtail
two-tailed swallowtail

Quercus spp
(oaks)

banded hairstreak
striped hairstreak
red-spotted purple

Rhamnus spp
(buckthorns)

pale swallowtail

Salix spp
(willows)

Lorquin's admiral
mourning cloak
viceroy
Weidemeyer's admiral
western tiger swallowtail

Sassafras albidum
(sassafras)

spicebush swallowtail

Ulmus spp
(elms)

comma
mourning cloak
question mark

Zanthoxylum spp
(prickly ash, Hercules' club)

giant swallowtail

HERBACIOUS PLANTS	LARVAE
Asclepias spp (milkweed, butterflyweed)	queen monarch
Carex spp (sedges)	dun skipper
Passiflora spp (passionflowers)	gulf fritillary zebra
Ruellia spp (wild petunias)	buckeye
Rumex spp (docks, sheep sorrel)	purplish copper small copper
Urtica spp (nettles)	comma Milbert's tortoise shell painted lady red admiral question mark
Viola spp (violets)	Aphrodite fritillary great spangled fritillary meadow fritillary variegated fritillary

Carrot family:
    Dauca carota
        (Queen Anne's lace, wild
        carrot)
    Parsnips, parsley,
        fennel, dill, rue
	black swallowtail
	anise swallowtail

Composite family:
    Aster spp
        (asters)
    Helianthus spp
        (sunflowers)
	painted lady
	Gorgone crescent
	field crescent
	pearl crescent

Grasses:
    Eragrostis spp
        (love grasses)
	common wood nymph
	tawny-edged skipper
	broken dash

Panicum spp   ringlet
  (switchgrass, panic grasses)   golden skipper
Tridens flavus
  (redtop)

Mallow family: checkered skipper
  Hibiscus spp   gray hairstreak
    (rose mallows)
  Malva spp
    (musk mallow, cheeses)
  Rose-of-Sharon,
    hollyhock

Pea family: eastern tailed blue
  Amorpha spp   gray hairstreak
    (leadplant, false indigo)   clouded sulfur
  Astragalus spp   orange sulfur
    (milkvetches)   cloudless sulfur
  Baptisia spp   little yellow
    (wild indigos)   sleepy orange
  Cassia spp   marine blue
    (wild senna, partridge pea,   Melissa blue
    sicklepod)   silver-spotted skipper
  Desmodium spp   hoary edge
    (tick-trefoils)   painted lady
  Lupinus spp   anise swallowtail
    (lupines)   tailed skipper
  Melilitos spp
    (sweet clovers)
  Trifolium spp
    (clovers)

Berrying Plants for Hedgerows

Planting berrying shrubs or trees is the quickest way to increase the value of one's property to wildlife. The natural habitat of the groups suggested here is for the most part open, sunny borders such as along a fence; some could also be used against woodland. These genera have a broad distribution; almost all are represented by at least one species in every part of the country. There are other berrying plants such as Oregon grape (*Mahonia aquilifolium*) on the Pacific coast and bayberry (*Myrica pensylvanica*) on the Atlantic coast whose distribution is too limited to warrant their inclusion, but such species are often very important in their specialized locales.

SUMMER FRUITING

Amelanchier spp (shadblow, serviceberry, Juneberry)
Most serviceberries are woodland understory trees, but they can be grown in full sun in hedgerows, too. *A. stolonifera* is a thicketing species only 4 feet high, with a cloud of delicate white flowers in April, blue fruits in June, and spectacular autumn color that typify members of this genus.

Prunus spp (black cherry, pin cherry, chokecherry)
This enormous genus contains many famous ornamentals and gourmet fruits, but as far as birds are concerned, those that matter most are native pioneers that bloom and fruit best in full sun and typically cope with poor soil. I don't know that I'd buy these bird trees, but I wouldn't cut them down if I could help it.

Vaccinium spp (blueberries, huckleberries, and kin)
Definitely the most versatile summer berriers, ranging from ground covers to 8-footers, with May bell blossoms in white to

pink, dessert-quality berries, and brilliant scarlet fall color. Adaptable as to moisture and light, but all require acid soil.

Rhamnus spp (buckthorns)
Cascara buckthorn (*R. purshiana*), a small hedgerow tree, and coffeeberry (*R. californica*), a more shrublike species, are important wildlife food plants in the West. The eastern counterpart is *R. caroliniana*, Indian cherry. Be careful not to buy European buckthorn (*R. cathartica*) or alder buckthorn (*R. frangula*), both of which are persistent weeds.

Rubus spp (raspberries, blackberries, dewberries, etc.)
Countless species, natural hybrids, and cultivated varieties. For winter shelter for ground birds, grow them as a bramble in unmowed grass the way they grow in the wild, unpruned. They can become unkempt in a hedgerow if not kept in check.

FALL FRUITING

Sorbus spp (mountain ashes)
The eastern species, *S. americana*, grows to 25 feet, but the ferny foliage casts only light shade, so it might be used to good effect in a south-facing hedgerow; green mountain ash, a western species, is a tall shrub. Both are loaded with orange berries from late summer into fall.

Cornus spp (flowering dogwood, gray dogwood, and others, including the exotic but naturalized cornelian cherry, but not *C. kousa*, a monkey berry tree not frequented by birds)
Birds passing through eat first those berries that are most nutritious, and the starchy berries of dogwoods go fast. Flowering dogwood (*C. florida*) is the best known ornamental, but in deep shade try pagoda dogwood (*C. alternifolia*), whose blue berries ripen much earlier. A dwarf form of red osier dogwood, *C. stolonifera*, forms knee-high thickets in moist soil, in sun. The gorgeous gray dogwood (*C. racemosa*) thickets and berries well in either sun or light shade, but it is best planted by itself where mowing will keep it from spreading by root sprouts.

Malus spp (crabapples and apples)
Our native crabapples are seldom offered in the trade, although many ornamentals, commercially grown or naturalized in the

wild, may be hybrids with American species. There's no sense being a purist here. Look for varieties whose fruits are brightly colored and under 1/2 inch in diameter. Even at this size, migrating birds often wait until the fruit has been softened by frost.

Viburnum spp (arrowwood, withe-rod, cranberry bush, blackhaw, and many more)
A great group for foliage, form, flower, and fruit, but beware those species or varieties with the showiest bloom. Fertile flowers, the ones that produce berries, are the inconspicuous ones toward the center of the inflorescence. Large-petaled flowers are usually just for show, to attract pollinators. If the whole cluster is large-petaled, it will look great in bloom but won't bear fruit.

PERSISTING INTO WINTER

Crataegus spp (hawthorns)
Many species, routinely gorgeous in bloom and berry and in both summer and autumn foliage. Most have long, sharp thorns, but a few are thornless. Hawthorns range in habit from small, neatly shaped trees to multistemmed shrubs, and many are notable for picturesque structure that adds winter interest in the hedgerow.

Ilex spp (hollies, evergreen and deciduous)
For a large evergreen, perhaps for one end of a hedgerow, I suggest the magnificent *I. opaca*, a conical red-berried tree strangely neglected in favor of European species. Inkberry (*I. glabra*) is a small-leaved, bushy evergreen shrub with black fruits; the species grows to 6 feet, but a dwarf form is also available. Winterberry (*I. verticillata*) is a tall, deciduous shrub of excellent form that holds its bountiful red berries almost until spring.

Rosa spp (roses)
To give birds an alternative to multiflora roses, hips must be numerous and small. Cultivated roses don't answer the need, nor do naturalized rugosa roses, whose hips are very large. Three native species widely available are swamp rose (*R. palustris*), shining rose (*R. nitida*), and Virginia rose (*R. virginiana*); many others are adapted to various parts of the country.

Species by Botanic Name

Acer platanoides Norway maple
A. rubrum red maple, swamp maple
A. saccharum sugar maple
Achillea millefolium yarrow
Adiantum pedatum maidenhair fern
Aesculus hippocastanum horse chestnut
Ailanthus altissima tree of heaven
Alnus rugosa tag alder, speckled alder
Amelanchier arborea downy serviceberry, shadblow
A. stolonifera running serviceberry
Andromeda polifolia bog rosemary
Andropogon gerardii big bluestem grass
A. scoparius little bluestem grass
Anemone cylindrica thimbleweed
Aquilegia canadensis wild columbine
Arctostaphylos uva-ursi bearberry
Arisaema triphyllum jack-in-the-pulpit
Aristolochia tomentosa pipe vine
Aronia arbutifolia red chokeberry
A. melanocarpa black chokeberry
Artemesia vulgaris mugwort
Asclepius incarnata swamp milkweed, red milkweed
A. syriaca common milkweed
A. tuberosa butterfly weed
Aster ericoides heath aster
A. azureus sky blue aster
A. divaricatus wood aster
A. novae-angliae New England aster
A. spectabilis showy aster

Baptisia tinctoria   wild indigo
Begonia grandis   hardy begonia
Berberis thunbergii   Japanese barberry
Betula alleghaniensis (formerly *lutea*)   yellow birch
B. lenta   sweet birch, black birch
B. nana   dwarf birch
B. nigra   river birch
B. papyrifera   canoe birch, paper birch
B. pendula   European birch
B. populifolia   gray birch
Bouteloua curtipendula   sideoats grama grass
Buchloe dactyloides   buffalo grass
Buddleia davidii   butterfly bush

Calopogon tuberosus   calopogon orchid, grass-pink
Campanula rotundifolium   harebell
Campsis radicans   trumpet creeper, trumpet vine
Caragana arborescens   Siberian pea tree
Carex pensylvanica   Pennsylvania sedge
Carpinus caroliniana   American hornbeam
Carya ovata   shagbark hickory
Ceanothus americanus   New Jersey tea
Celastrus orbiculatus   Oriental bittersweet
C. scandens   American bittersweet
Cephalanthus occidentalis   buttonbush
Cercis canadensis   eastern redbud
Chamaecyparis thyoides   Atlantic white cedar
Chamaedaphne calyculata   leatherleaf
Chelone glabra   turtlehead
Chrysanthemum leucanthemum   oxeye daisy
Cichorium intybus   chicory
Cicuta maculata   water hemlock
Cimicifuga racemosa   bugbane, cohosh
Clematis virginiana   Virgin's bower
Clethra alnifolia   summersweet, sweet pepperbush
Comptonia peregrina   sweetfern
Conium maculatum   poison hemlock
Coreopsis major   greater tickseed
Cornus alternifolia   pagoda dogwood

C. canadensis   bunchberry
C. florida   flowering dogwood
C. kousa   kousa dogwood, Chinese dogwood
C. mas   cornelian cherry
C. racemosa   gray dogwood
C. sericea   red-osier dogwood
Corylus americana   American hazelnut, American filbert
C. cornuta   beaked hazelnut, beaked filbert
Crataegus crus-galli   hog-apple
Cyperus esculentus   yellow nutsedge
Cypripedium parviflorum   small yellow lady's-slipper

Daucus carota   Queen Anne's lace, wild carrot
Dennstaedtia punctilobula   hayscented fern
Dicentra canadensis   squirrel-corn
Diospyros virginiana   persimmon

Echinacea pallida   pale purple coneflower
Eleagnus angustifolia   Russian olive
Enkianthus campanulatus   redvein enkianthus
Equisetum arvense   scouring rush, horsetail
Erigeron annuus   daisy fleabane
Eschscholtzia californica   California poppy
Euonymous alata   burning bush, winged euonymous
Eupatorium maculatum   Joe-Pye weed

Fagus grandifolia   American beech
Festuca spp   fescue grasses
Fothergilla gardenii   dwarf fothergilla
Fragaria virginiana   wild strawberry
Fraxinus pennsylvanica   green ash

Galax rotundifolia   beetleweed
Galium mollugo   wild madder
Gaylussacia brachycera   box huckleberry
Gentiana andrewsii   bottle gentian
G. crinita   fringed gentian
Geum triflorum   prairie smoke

Habenaria leucophaea   prairie white-fringed orchid
Hamamelis virginiana   common witch hazel
Helianthus giganteus   giant sunflower
Hieracium aurantiacum   devil's paintbrush
Hydrangea quercifolia   oakleaf hydrangea

Ilex crenata opaca   Japanese holly
I. glabra   inkberry
I. opaca   American holly
I. verticillata   winterberry
Impatiens capensis   jewelweed
Iris cristata   crested iris
I. versicolor   blue flag

Juncus spp   soft rushes
Juniperus virginiana   eastern red cedar, juniper

Kalmia latifolia   mountain laurel
Kalmia polifolia   sheep laurel, lambkill
Krigia biflora   two-flowered Cynthia

Lathyrus ochroleucus   pale vetchling
Ledum groenlandicum   Labrador tea
Leucothoe fontanesiana   drooping leucothoe
L. racemosa   fetterbush, sweetbells
Liatris pycnostachya   prairie blazing star
Lilium canadense   meadow lily
L. superbum   Turk's-cap lily
Linaria vulgaris   butter-and-eggs
Liquidamber styraciflua   sweet gum
Liriodendron tulipifera   tulip tree, tulip poplar
Lobelia cardinalis   cardinal flower
L. siphilitica   great blue lobelia
L. spicata   spiked lobelia
Lolium spp   ryegrasses
Lonicera japonica   Japanese honeysuckle
Lycopodium obscurum   princess pine
Lycopodium spp   club mosses

Lyonia mariana   staggerbush
Lythrum salicaria   purple loosestrife

Mertensia virginica   Virginia bluebell
Monarda fistulosa   wild bergamot, bee balm
Myrica pensylvanica   bayberry

Nymphaea spp   water lilies
Nyssa sylvatica   sour gum, black tupelo, black gum

Oenothera biennis   evening primrose
Orontium aquaticum   golden club

Pachysandra terminalis   Japanese pachysandra
Panicum virgatum   switchgrass
Parthenocissus quinquefolia   Virginia creeper
P. tricuspidata   dwarf Boston ivy
Paxistema canbyii   paxistema
Peltandra virginica   arrow arum
Penstemon digitalis   smooth penstemon
Phleum pratense   timothy
Pieris floribunda (formerly *Andromeda floribunda*)   mountain pieris
Platanus occidentalis   American sycamore
Poa pratensis   Kentucky bluegrass
Polygonum cuspidatum   Japanese knotweed, bamboo
Pontederia cordata   pickerel weed
Populus tremuloides   quaking aspen
Prunus serotina   black cherry, wild cherry
P. subhirtella   'Autumnalis' autumn cherry
P. virginiana   chokecherry
Polystichum acrostichoides   Christmas fern
Pueraria lobata   kudzu vine

Quercus alba   white oak
Q. coccinea   scarlet oak
Q. macrocarpa   bur oak

Rhamnus californica   coffeeberry
R. caroliniana   Indian cherry

R. cathartica   European buckthorn
R. frangula   alder buckthorn
R. purshiana cascara   buckthorn, bearberry
Rhododendron maximum   rosebay rhododendron
R. nudiflorum   pinxterbloom
R. viscosum   swamp azalea
Rhus glabra   smooth sumac
R. radicans   poison ivy
Ribes alpinum   Alpine currant
Rosa multiflora   multiflora rose
Rudbeckia hirta   black-eyed Susan
R. subtomentosa   sweet black-eyed Susan
Ruellia humilis   wild petunia

Salix discolor   pussy willow
S. fragilis   crack willow, brittle willow
Sagittaria   spp Arrowheads, duck potatoes,
   wapatoes
Sanguinaria canadensis   bloodroot
Sassafras albidum   sassafras
Silphium terebinthinaceum   prairie dock
Sisyrinchium angustifolium   blue-eyed grass
Smilax rotundifolia   catbrier, greenbrier
Solanum carolinense   horsenettle
Solidago bicolor   silverrod
S. canadensis   Canada goldenrod
S. rigida   stiff goldenrod
Sorghastrum nutans   Indiangrass
Sporobolus heterolepsis   prairie dropseed grass
Stellaria media   chickweed
Symphoricarpos alba   snowberry
S. orbiculatus   coralberry
Symplocarpus foetida   skunk cabbage

Thalictrum polygamum   tall meadowrue
Thelypteris noveboracensis   New York fern
Tiarella cordifolia   foamflower
Tsuga canadensis   eastern hemlock
Typha spp   cattails

Ulmus americana   American elm

Vaccinium angustifolium   lowbush blueberry
V. corymbosum   highbush blueberry
V. crassifolium   creeping blueberry
V. vitis idaea minus   mountain cranberry
Vallisneria americana   wild celery
Verbascum thapsis   mullein
Verbena hastata   blue vervain
Vernonia noveboracensis   New York ironweed
Veronicastrum virginicum   Culver's root
Viburnum acerifolium   mapleleaf viburnum
V. alnifolium   hobblebush viburnum
V. cassinoides   withe-rod viburnum
V. dentatum   arrowwood viburnum
V. lentago   nannyberry viburnum
V. nudum   possum haw viburnum
V. prunifolium   blackhaw viburnum
V. trilobum   American cranberry bush viburnum
Viola papileonacea   common violet
V. pedata   bird's-foot violet
Vitis labrusca   fox grape

Zanthoxylum americanum   toothache tree
Zenobia pulverulenta   zenobia

Species by Common Name

andromeda (see bog rosemary or pieris, mountain)
arrowhead   *Sagittaria* spp
arrowwood (see viburnum, arrowwood)
aster
    heath   *Aster ericoides*
    New England   *A. novae-angliae*
    showy   *A. spectabilis*
    sky blue   *A. azureus*
    wood   *A. divaricatus*

bamboo (see Japanese knotweed)
barberry, Japanese   *Berberis thunbergii*
bayberry   *Myrica pensylvanica*
bearberry   *Arctostaphylos uva-ursi*
beebalm   (see bergamot, wild)
beech, American   *Fagus grandifolia*
beetleweed   *Galax rotundifolia*
begonia, hardy   *Begonia grandis*
bergamot, wild   *Monarda fistulosa*
big bluestem grass   *Andropogon gerardi*
birch
    black (see sweet birch)
    canoe   *Betula papyrifera*
    dwarf   *B. nana*
    European   *B. pendula*
    gray   *B. populifolia*
    river   *B. nigra*
    sweet   *B. lenta*
    yellow   *B. alleghaniensis*, formerly *lutea*
bird's-foot violet   *Viola pedata*

bittersweet
  American   *Celastrus scandens*
  Oriental   *C. orbiculatus*
black haw (see Viburnum, blackhaw)
black-eyed Susan   *Rudbeckia hirta*
  sweet   *R. subtomentosa*
black tupelo (see sour gum)
bloodroot   *Sanguinaria canadensis*
blue flag   *Iris versicolor*
blue vervain   *Verbena hastata*
blue-eyed grass   *Sisyrinchium angustifolium*
bluebell, Virginia   *Mertensia virginica*
blueberry
  creeping   *Vaccinium crassifolium*
  highbush   *V. corymbosum*
  lowbush   *V. angustifolium*
bluegrass, Kentucky   *Poa pratensis*
bog rosemary   *Andromeda polifolia*
Boston ivy, dwarf   *Parthenocissus tricuspidata*
box huckleberry   *Gaylussacia brachycera*
buckthorn
  alder   *Rhamnus frangula*
  European   *Rhamnus cathartica*
buffalo grass   *Buchloe dactyloides*
bugbane   *Cimicifuga racemosa*
bunchberry   *Cornus canadensis*
burning bush   *Euonymous alata*
butter-and-eggs   *Linaria vulgaris*
butterfly bush   *Buddleia davidii*
butterfly weed   *Asclepias tuberosa*
buttonbush   *Cephalanthus occidentalis*

catbrier   *Smilax rotundifolia*
cattail   *Typha* spp
California poppy   *Eschscholtzia californica*
calopogon orchid   *Calopogon tuberosus*
cardinal flower   *Lobelia cardinalis*
cherry
  autumn   *P. subhirtella* 'Autumnalis'

black   *Prunus serotina*
chicory   *Cichorium intybus*
chickweed   *Stellaria media*
chokeberry
    black   *Aronia melanocarpa*
    red   *A. arbutifolia*
chokecherry   *Prunus virginiana*
Christmas fern   *Polystichum acrostichoides*
club-moss   *Lycopodium* spp
columbine   *Aquilegia canadensis*
coneflower, pale purple   *Echinacea pallida*
coralberry   *Symphoricarpos orbiculatus*
cornelian cherry   *Cornus mas*
cranberry bush, American (see Viburnum, American cranberry bush)
creeping blueberry   *Vaccinium crassifolium*
crested iris   *Iris cristata*
Culver's root   *Veronicastrum virginicum*
currant, Alpine   *Ribes alpinum*

daisy fleabane   *Erigeron annuus*
devil's paintbrush   *Hieracium aurantiacum*
dogwood
    flowering   *Cornus florida*
    gray   *C. racemosa*
    kousa   *C. kousa*
    pagoda   *C. alternifolia*
    red-osier   *C. sericea*
duck potato (see arrowhead)

elm, American   *Ulmus americana*
enkianthus, redvein   *Enkianthus campanulatus*
evening primrose   *Oenothera biennis*

fescue grass   *Festuca* spp
fetterbush   *Leucothoe racemosa*
filbert (see hazelnut)
foamflower   *Tiarella cordifolia*
fothergilla, dwarf   *Fothergilla gardenii*
fox grape   *Vitis labrusca*

gentian
  bottle   *Gentiana andrewsii*
  fringed   *G. crinita*
golden club   *Orontium aquaticum*
goldenrod
  Canada   *Solidago canadensis*
  stiff   *S. rigida*
grass-pink (see calopagon orchid)
great blue lobelia   *Lobelia siphilitica*
green ash   *Fraxinus pennsylvanica*

harebell   *Campanula rotundifolium*
hazelnut
  American   *Corylus americana*
  beaked   *C. cornuta*
hayscented fern   *Dennstaedtia punctilobula*
hemlock, eastern   *Tsuga canadensis*
hobblebush (see viburnum, hobblebush)
hog-apple   *Crataegus crus-galli*
holly
  American   *Ilex opaca*
  Japanese   *I. crenata*
hornbeam, American   *Carpinus caroliniana*
horse chestnut   *Aesculus hippocastanum*
horse nettle   *Solanum carolinense*

Indian cherry   *Rhamnus caroliniana*
Indiangrass   *Sorghastrum nutans*
inkberry   *Ilex glabra*
ironweed, New York   *Vernonia noveboracensis*

jack-in-the-pulpit   *Arisaema triphyllum*
Japanese honeysuckle   *Lonicera japonica*
Japanese knotweed   *Polygonum cuspidatum*
jewelweed   *Impatiens capensis*
Joe-Pye weed   *Eupatorium maculatum*
juniper, creeping   *Juniperus* spp (also see red cedar)

kudzu vine   *Pueraria lobata*

Labrador tea *Ledum groenlandicum*
leatherleaf *Chamaedaphne calyculata*
leucothoe, drooping *Leucothoe fontanesiana*
little bluestem grass *Andropogon scoparius*

maple
  Norway *Acer platanoides*
  red *A. rubrum*
  sugar *A. saccharum*
maidenhair fern *Adiantum pedatum*
meadow lily *Lilium canadense*
meadowrue, tall *Thalictrum polygamum*
milkweed
  common *Asclepius syriaca*
  swamp *A. incarnata*
mountain cranberry *Vaccinium vitis idaea minus*
mountain laurel *Kalmia latifolia*
mugwort *Artemesia vulgaris*
mullein *Verbascum thapsis*
multiflora rose *Rosa multiflora*

nannyberry (see viburnum, nannyberry)
New Jersey tea *Ceanothus americanus*
New York fern *Thelypteris noveboracensis*

oak
  bur *Quercus macrocarpa*
  scarlet *Q. coccinea*
  white *Q. alba*
oakleaf hydrangea *Hydrangea quercifolia*
oxeye daisy *Chrysanthemum leucanthemum*

pachysandra, Japanese *Pachysandra terminalis*
pagoda dogwood (see dogwood, pagoda)
pale vetchling *Lathyrus ochroleucus*
panic grass (see switchgrass)
paxistema *Paxistema canbyii*
persimmon *Diospyros virginiana*
pickerel weed *Pontederia cordata*

pieris, mountain   *Pieris floribunda* (formerly *Andromeda floribunda*)
pinxterbloom   *Rhododendron nudiflorum*
pipe vine   *Aristolochia tomentosa*
poison hemlock   *Conium maculatum*
poison ivy   *Rhus radicans*
possum haw (see Viburnum, possum haw)
prairie blazing star   *Liatris pycnostachya*
prairie dock   *Silphium terebinthinaceum*
prairie dropseed grass   *Sporobolus heterolepsis*
prairie smoke   *Geum triflorum*
prairie white-fringed orchid   *Habenaria leucophaea*
princess pine   *Lycopodium obscurum*
purple loosestrife   *Lythrum salicaria*

quaking aspen   *Populus tremuloides*
Queen Anne's lace   *Daucus carota*

redbud, eastern   *Cercis canadensis*
red cedar, eastern   *Juniperus virginiana*
rosebay rhododendron   *Rhododendron maximum*
Russian olive   *Eleagnus angustifolia*
ryegrass   *Lolium* spp

sassafras   *Sassafras albidum*
scouring rush   *Equisetum arvense*
sedge, Pennsylvania   *Carex pensylvanica*
serviceberry
    downy   *Amelanchier arborea*
    running   *A. stolonifera*
shadblow (see serviceberry)
shagbark hickory   *Carya ovata*
sheep laurel   *Kalmia polifolia*
Siberian pea tree   *Caragana arborescens*
sideoats grama grass   *Bouteloua curtipendula*
silverado   *Solidago bicolor*
skunk cabbage   *Symplocarpus foetida*
small yellow lady's slipper   *Cypripedium parviflorum*
smooth penstemon   *Penstemon digitalis*
smooth sumac   *Rhus glabra*

snowberry *Symphoricarpos alba*
soft rush *Juncus* spp
sour gum *Nyssa sylvatica*
speckled alder (see tag alder)
spiked lobelia *Lobelia spicata*
squirrel-corn *Dicentra canadensis*
staggerbush *Lyonia mariana*
strawberry, wild *Fragaria virginiana*
summersweet *Clethra alnifolia*
sunflower, giant *Helianthus giganteus*
swamp azalea *Rhododendron viscosum*
swamp maple (see maple, red)
sweet gum *Liquidamber styraciflua*
sweetbells *Leucothoe racemosa*
sweetfern *Comptonia peregrina*
sweet pepperbush (see summersweet)
switchgrass *Panicum virgatum*
sycamore, American *Platanus occidentalis*

tag alder *Alnus rugosa*
thimbleweed *Anemone cylindrica*
timothy *Phleum pratense*
toothache tree *Zanthoxylum americanum*
tree of heaven *Ailanthus altissima*
trumpet creeper *Campsis radicans*
trumpet vine (see trumpet creeper)
tulip tree *Liriodendron tulipifera*
Turk's-cap lily *Lilium superbum*
turtlehead *Chelone glabra*
two-flowered Cynthia *Krigia biflora*

Viburnum
  arrowwood *Viburnum dentatum*
  blackhaw *V. prunifolium*
  cranberry bush, American *V. trilobum*
  hobblebush *V. alnifolium*
  mapleleaf *V. acerifolium*
  nannyberry *V. lentago*
  possum haw *V. nudum*

violet, common   *Viola papileonacea*
Virginia creeper   *Parthenocissus quinquefolia*
Virgin's bower   *Clematis virginiana*

wapato (see arrowhead)
water hemlock   *Cicuta maculata*
water lily   *Nymphaea* spp
white cedar, Atlantic   *Chamaecyparis thyoides*
wild carrot (see Queen Anne's lace)
wild celery   *Vallisneria americana*
wild indigo   *Baptisia tinctoria*
wild madder   *Galium mollugo*
wild petunia   *Ruellia humilis*
willow
    brittle   *Salix fragilis*
    pussy   *S. discolor*
winged euonymous (see burning bush)
winterberry   *Ilex verticillata*
witch hazel, common   *Hamamelis virginiana*
withe-rod   *Viburnum cassinoides*

yarrow   *Achillea millefolium*
yellow nutsedge   *Cyperus esculentus*

zenobia   *Zenobia pulverulenta*

Index

Plants Named

Hellibore- March
Aster - October
strawberry, serviceberries
Rose - hip
blueberries, inkberries
orange crabapples
dogwood (berries)
VA creeper
oaks - acorns
hickory (nuts)
white snowberry
purple coralberry
(blue) viburnum w/ fruits
(not sterile ones)
hazelnuts
bayberry
red/black chokeberry
alpine currant
dogwood
butterfly bush

Jack in the pulpit-
early flies → bluebirds

Siberian Pea tree -
hummingbirds

Trumpet vine ↰
mullein ↱
wild columbine
NJ Tea - flies ↰

Bloodroot - bees - geraniums
+ bluebells
apples
wood aster

Prairie grass -
thimbleweed, Culver's
root, bluestem
Prairie blazing star -
Liatris (p163)
scott's switchgrass
(p. 166) Meadow - penstemon,
wild bergamot, purple
coneflower, Rudbeckia
subtomentosa

THE LAND CA. 1950